An Integrated Approach to Early Literacy

Literature to Language

Susan Mandel Glazer
Rider College

Eileen M. Burke
Trenton State College

Allyn and Bacon
Boston • London • Toronto • Sydney • Tokyo • Singapore

Editor-in-Chief, Education: Nancy Forsyth
Series Editorial Assistant: Christine Nelson
Production Administrator: Ann Greenberger
Editorial-Production Service: Progressive Typographers
Cover Administrator: Suzanne Harbison
Manufacturing Buyer: Louise Richardson
Composition Buyer: Linda Cox

Library of Congress Cataloging-in-Publication Data

Glazer, Susan Mandel.
    An integrated approach to early literacy : literature to language
/ Susan Mandel Glazer, Eileen M. Burke.
        p.   cm.
    Includes bibliographical references (p.   ) and index.
    ISBN 0-205-14192-7
    1. Children—United States—Language. 2. Child development—
United States. 3. Language arts (Preschool)—United States.
4. Literacy—United States. I. Burke, Eileen M. II. Title.
LB1139.L3G513   1994
372.6—dc20   93-17542
                                                                        CIP

Printed in the United States of America

10 9 8 7 6 5 4 3 2 1   98 97 96 95 94

*We dedicate this book to children
who have enriched our lives—our nieces and nephews
Nancy K. Austin
Darren J. Cohen
Brian D. Glazer
Stephanie E. Morrow*

Books are still one of the most important
ways that children extend the range of their
experiences. In the privacy of their reading,
children can test their beliefs and perceptions without having to defend them against
disapproving peers or parents. The writer's
art and the reader's imagination free children to rethink, reassess and refeel their
own attitudes about themselves, about others and about the world in which they live.

Mark Jonathan Harris

Contents

Preface

This text tells a story about growth and development with a focus on literacy. It reflects the body of literature in the areas of human growth that relates to the development of oral language, reading, and writing. The book is arranged much like current literature in the field—as an integrated, holistic account of growth from birth through age seven. We share the development of Ben and Sarah, two children who begin life as illiterates and emerge, as each year progresses, into functional readers and writers. We have chosen to arrange this text developmentally in order to provide you, our audience, with a model for charting growth and exploring expectations for yourselves as nurturers of children and their environments.

Chapters one, two, and three include fundamental research and models necessary for understanding aspects of human growth. It is the foundation upon which the educational activities are designed in the rest of the text. Chapters four through ten are the core of the text. Each chapter focuses on a specific age of development. You will read about Ben, Sarah, and their friends as they grow physically, emotionally, socially, and cognitively. The relationship of these aspects of growth are integrated with a focus on literacy. Environments that facilitate and foster growth in listening, speaking, reading, and writing skills are described for each age. Guides, some in the form of checklists, are included throughout this section of the text. These should provide caregivers, teachers, and parents with tools necessary for collecting and charting data about children's literacy development. Examples of children's performances will define ages and stages of growth.

Each chapter includes annotated booklists for the creation of home and school libraries. The books included in these bibliographies support specific developmental needs at each age and stage of growth. The lists are cumulative from chapter to chapter.

Our final chapter is an epilogue—an attempt to "put it all together." A three-hour time block is used to describe Ms. Turner's primary classroom. Her activities from the beginning of the school day to the end of a language arts period are described. This chapter is written in narrative style. We have selected this format so that you, our audience, can "feel" with the teacher the joys and stresses of creating a successful integrated literature-based language arts program in classrooms.

Acknowledgments

Our combined teaching experiences number seventy years. During those years, we've learned much. We've grown and are still growing because of our interactions with the many good people in our lives. Those who have helped us with this text deserve special recognition. We thank Gail Turner for typing, proofreading, and holding our hands throughout the final stages of this manuscript. Her dedication to educational endeavors and her consistent good nature provided much of the support needed to complete this task; our gratitude is expressed to Katrin-Kaja Roomann for final proofreading; we thank, too, Lucia Taboada, our graduate assistant who organized and typed the reference sections of the text. We express warm thoughts of gratitude to our mentors, students, and colleagues who have guided us to "make a difference in the lives of young people." We appreciate the administration and faculty of our schools, Rider College and Trenton State College, for recognizing our need to "make change." We are grateful to members of our families for their support and encouragement throughout all of our efforts. A special thank you to Milton Austin and Richard Glazer for their photographic efforts which produced some of the pictures in this book. Finally, we thank each other for the healthy and stimulating interactions and morning bagels and muffins that we shared while creating this text.

We thank the following parents and children for permitting us to use photographs and children's graphics throughout this text: Jack Anderson, Catherine Austin, Milton Austin, Britney Carey, Carla Choi, Kevin Chung, Barbara Elsey, Brittanie Ezewrino, Helema Fauzia, Brian Friedeborn, Jennifer Hartman, Morgan Jones, Miriam Kochman, Alicia Lennon, Gary Nucera, Ijeoma Okpava, Keiko Ono, Eloube Orisie, Andrew Parker, Dorielle Parker, Jazzman Plum, Janeria Pullen, Steven Rockoff, Kalev Roomann-Kurrik, Ashlee Rossi, J. Wesley Smith, Cherylynn Spence, Gabriel Tabor, Marcia Tabor, Shana Tabor, Gary Turner, Kelly Turner, Johnny Vines, Kelly Watson, and Nadia Zendaki.

1

The Broad Concepts of Literacy

This chapter serves as an introduction to the broad concepts of literacy. It answers the following questions:

- What does research tell us about literacy learning?
- What are definitions of language and how do they relate to literacy research?
- Which language acquisition theories guide current educational practices for language learning?

It was mid-morning and the doctor's waiting room was packed with people. A three-year-old, called Ben, peered around the room. He focused on several ladies with large straw hats, turning to his mother several times to comment, "They have umbrellas on their heads, Mommy." He moved to a table, selected a magazine, and returned to his chair. Ben sat down, opened the magazine and began to "read." He turned the pages, moving his head from left to right. Ben focused on photographs and drawings, many of them advertisements. He called names of objects, pointing to each with his finger. One page, an automobile advertisement, included a photo of a car and the number $9,542, the cost. Ben looked over the picture and pointing with his index finger under each number said, "Ca-dil-lac, Chev-ro-let." Each of the six figures, including the dollar and comma, represented for Ben one syllable. Ben had learned, at the age of three, that print has a function—it represents sounds that stand for things. He perceived, from prior knowledge, that the page was about cars and that the print named the cars. Naming objects in pictures was probably learned when adults read to him. He also learned that print proceeds from left to right.

Ben has been reaching toward literacy from birth. Ben's world abounds with print and at age three he is aware of its power. It is an assumed part of his life. Language, all of communication, comes to Ben as naturally as eating and sleeping. It is part of his home environment, which has provided Ben with the resources necessary for giving meaning to the graphic symbols on the page. He is beginning to function as a literate human being.

What Does Research Tell Us about Literacy Learning?

Young children possess knowledge of language and print early in life (Goodman and Goodman 1979). The roots of literacy begin as mother and child respond to each other using gestures. The child's natural curiosity spurs the language learning vital to meet emotional, physical, and intellectual needs.

In the past decade, the fascination with language learning has sparked researchers to redefine literacy. Clay (1975) particularly is credited with the term *emergent literacy*. The writings of Goodman (1967), Goodman and Goodman (1979), Holdaway (1979), Piaget (1955), and Vygotsky (1962) served as the foundation for other researchers, such as Butler (1979), Crago (1975), Durkin (1966), Heath (1983), Hiebert (1981), Taylor (1983), and Teale (1986) who have concluded that:

- children brought up in literate societies begin to learn to read and write before formal schooling
- reading and writing are learned simultaneously, reinforcing one another
- oral language serves as a precursor and then as a companion to reading and writing
- literacy develops in real situations, in and out of school, in functional settings
- reading to children is an essential part of their learning to read and write

These conclusions have changed the curriculum used with young children.

Children Begin to Learn to Read and Write before They Go to School

Infants come into the world helpless. Within three years, they communicate by composing language without formal instruction. Most adults take for granted the fact that children will learn to speak in the first three years of life. In an almost effortless manner, infants make lots of sounds as they play with language in response to things they hear, see, smell, touch, and taste in their environments (Menyuk 1963). There is a biological or genetic factor in all human infants that permits them to create and respond to language (Lenneberg 1967). They coo, babble, and cry, often for the pleasure they receive in hearing and feeling the sounds that they create and to receive responses from adults who interact with them. Infants make sounds—more sounds than they need, forming the components of their native language. Children from all countries, e.g., France, Israel, or China, make the same sounds until they are approximately ten months of age. Infants attempt to give meanings to sounds in an active way (Dale 1976). Children have an innate ability and propensity to learn and create language that they have not even heard before. Chomsky (1965) and McNeill (1970) suggest that children acquire language inductively from language in the environment. Chomsky explains this phenomenon by suggesting that humans have a language acquisition device (LAD) that enables them to induce rules for using language based on previous experience. The rules are principles of organization; for example, a child will subconsciously know that when you add "ed" to a word, it usually means past tense. Children test rules as they interact with caregivers; for example, as the baby plays with language, she one day happens to say "da-da." The baby's father hears the meaningless babble and strokes the child with joy, saying "She said da-da, my name." The baby experiments creating "da-da" several times. The response from the father is delight, and the baby learns to repeat "da-da" in order to receive that loving response again and again. The baby learns to repeat other sounds that provide pleasure, but also learns to reject those that have little or no functional meaning. Thus, babies acquire language and develop rules about how it works by participating in an interactive environment. The form of these interactions is illustrated in Figure 1–1.

Children are writers from early years, too. As soon as they hold a writing tool—crayon, chalk, marker—they are writing by scribbling (Sulzby 1986). Babies, at eighteen months or earlier, will scribble spontaneously when given paper and a safe writing tool if demonstrations of how to write are provided (Cattell 1960). Like babbling and cooing, scribbles are spontaneous at first, but with practice scribbles become deliberate, definitive, and differentiated. Toddlers give meaning to print as they learn the distinctive features used in writing (Gibson and Levin 1975). As infants play with sounds for pleasure, toddlers play with writing for pleasure. At approximately two years of age, they scribble for the enjoyment of movement and visual satisfactions provided when the marks, not print, appear (Clay 1975). Between the ages of three and four, most youngsters become aware that people make marks on paper purposefully (Baghban 1984, 20). As Ben did at the beginning of this chapter, they begin to understand relationships between print and objects, letters and sounds, and appropriate uses of these aspects of print (Chomsky 1976; Gentry 1978; Read 1971).

Indeed, from birth, infants test, accept, and reject sounds and written symbols in order to meet needs in their lives. Many societies encourage the development of literacy by exposing children to print early. Studies have confirmed that some children who interact with print early not only begin

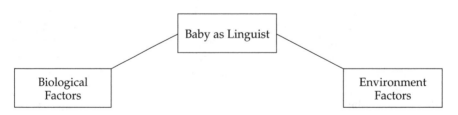

FIGURE 1–1

to learn about reading and writing during the first few years of life, but actually become independent readers even before attending school (Krippner 1963; Reger 1966). The early awareness of print has been confirmed with research carried out by Harste, Burke, and Woodward (1982, 1983) and Hiebert (1981). These scholars point out that print awareness, the root of literacy development, becomes evident among three-year-old children. Naturalistic research conducted by Heath (1983), Taylor (1983), and Teale (1986), who observed children as they learned in their natural environments, affirm and extend conclusions that the awareness of print and concepts about reading and writing occur early in life.

Reading and Writing Are Learned Simultaneously

Some of the current literature in the field of reading and language arts focuses on the concept that when one reads and understands, one is rewriting the text to make meaning for oneself (Tierney and Pearson 1983). If this concept is accepted, then reading and writing are interwoven, inseparable processes. One cannot read without interpreting and paraphrasing the author's language in order to make meaning from text. Adults understand this process when they say to a child after reading a story, "Now tell me the story in your own words." Reading and writing, listening, and speaking are inseparable. These language arts share many characteristics and purposes. For years teachers of young children have demonstrated their understanding of the interrelationship between oral communication and print as they guide children to write stories following talks about their experiences. The children have said the language and teachers have reproduced the children's text by writing it down.

Children, too, demonstrate that they understand relationships between print and talk. As young children draw, they simultaneously tell their stories. When they begin to make lines that look similar to letters and words, they identify the markings, with comments such as, "This is my name" or "See, this says dog." They are talking and beginning to model reading and writing behavior that they have observed. Research has documented the ways in which reading, writing, and oral communication (listening and speaking) reinforce and support each other in the literacy learning process. Read (1975) and Beers (1980) have illustrated that invented spellings (writing words the way they sound) could only occur as a result of children's comprehending that oral language sounds are represented by written symbols, which are produced based on the sounds of language. Marie Clay (1975), a pioneer in the field of early literacy, proposes that a series of principles are learned by children, and evidence of this learning is visible in their drawings and attempts to write. These principles are described in chapter 3.

Oral Language Serves as a Precursor and Then a Companion to Reading and Writing

When caregivers are literate, interrelationships between oral language and reading and writing are modeled routinely. Literacy prevails in functional daily living. Teale (1986), after observing interactions in twenty-two homes, uncovered several types of activities in which oral, written, and reading behaviors occur together. These include religious times when families pray, talk about the activities, read the scriptures and write about them. When members of a family want to communicate, many leave notes, others use tape recordings, and some speak directly.

Storybook reading times clearly illustrate how oral language is a companion to reading and writing. Parents hold the book, talk about the pictures, point to the words, and read them. Oral text, representations of oral text (pictures and print), and the printed text work together during story time to create messages.

Literacy Develops in Real Situations In and Out of School in Functional Settings

Children acquire language in order to function. Brunner and Feldman (1982) confirm this notion:

> *Yes, the one thing that we know with some clarity from the last decade of intensive research on language acquisition is that the child requires some knowledge of the world and how it is arranged socially, and something as well about the human intentions that will be encoded in speech acts, before he is able to use his . . . "innate knowledge" to search for, or invent, linguistic forms. . . . It is impossible to doubt that there is some kind of bioprogram for language that steers the searching and invention. But that program cannot begin to work until the child is inducted into a social world where language has already made a deep impression in shaping and even in constituting the reality to which speech will refer. (p. 36)*

Children learn what works to make things happen in their world. Early vocabulary is selectively made up of nouns (mommy, pet names, and the like) and words describing or demanding actions (bye-bye, up, give, etc.) These permit children to function in order to meet their needs (Nelson 1973). Words learned early in life include those naming food, clothing, animals, toys, and vehicles (Dale 1976, 8). The words learned are those children can act upon easily. Children learn to speak so they can function. Early reading, too, is a functional process. Mason (1977) points out that in early stages, reading is based on content that is familiar. Children will read print on billboards, traffic signs, and food packages first, because these have functional meanings in their lives.

Children learn to read and speak as they use language, and they learn language as they read and speak. Taylor (1983), in her research with families, stresses that parents do not deliberately try to teach their children to read or write. Families share social contexts, stories, and experiences, for it is in language interactions in meaningful social and cultural settings that the desire for, and models for, using the language are found. When language is needed to function, it is learned naturally.

Reading to Children Is an Essential Part of Learning to Read and Write

Research concerned with reading to children has focused on the development of vocabulary (Burroughs 1972; Fodor 1966), the importance of children's intrinsic desire for stories and the relationship of this desire to successful beginning reading experiences (Durkin 1974–1975; Walker and Keurbitz 1979). Findings show that not all children are read to regularly in homes, but those who are find success with reading in school. Wells' (1986) study shows that of several literacy-developing activities, the one most outstanding in its relationship to literacy formation and reading test scores was listening to stories. This powerful finding has strong implications for the role of children's first teachers—parents, older siblings, and grandparents—in literacy learning. When children are read to in natural environments, they create frameworks for stories in their minds. Children learn that stories begin, progress, and end and how this comes about. A sense of story structure is beginning to develop. In addition, children learn:

- how the written language system works
- what print represents
- what are the purposes of books
- what reading is
- that stories can be written down
- that there is some correspondence between sounds and symbols on the pages
- how to predict what stories are about
- how to remember stories and other data from text

Children learn these concepts as they feel the warmth of the humans who love them. They sit on an adult's lap as they listen. The soft touch provides pleasure as the pages provide surprise. Emotional experiences occurring during story times link feelings and reading. This linking fosters the idea that books give pleasure and enjoyment.

Current findings about literacy require a detailed explanation of how literacy develops during the early years (birth through age seven). It seems logical and interesting to begin by examining definitions of language. Examination of widely accepted theories of the development of thought will be shared as well. Although no one questions the relationship between the two, the exact nature of that relationship is disputed.

What Are Definitions of Language and How Do They Relate to Literacy Research?

Definitions of Language

To presume that one can define language easily is nonsense. Linguists and psychologists have tried for centuries. The following are a few of the ways in which language has been defined in our sources.

> *Language is a system of arbitrary vocal symbols used for human communication. (Wardhaugh 1972, 3)*

> *Language is any set or system of linguistic symbols as used in a more or less uniform fashion by a number of people who are thus enabled to communicate intelligibly with one another.* (Random House Dictionary of English Language *1966, 806)*

> *Language is a system of communication by sound, operating through the organs of speech and hearing, among members of a given community, and using vocal symbols possessing arbitrary conventional meanings. (Pei 1966, 141)*

> *Language is a system of arbitrary, vocal symbols which permit all people in a given culture, or other people who have learned the system of that culture, to communicate or to interact. (Finocchiaro 1964, 8)*

These definitions suggest for us that:

- language is systematic
- language is generated by human beings
- many humans in many cultures learn language in similar ways
- language comprises a set of arbitrary vocal symbols. Over time, visual symbols have been developed to represent these vocal aspects of lan-

guage. These visual symbols have become standardized. The meanings of words formed from these visual symbols have become standardized

- language is used to communicate
- language is a tool by which humans interact
- language is shaped by the culture in which it operates
- communication can be verbal and nonverbal
- verbal communication is language. One type of nonverbal communication is gesture.

These simply stated definitions have resulted from theories of language acquisition, which influence today's educational practices.

Language Acquisition Theories Which Guide Current Educational Practices for Language Learning

No one theory explains all phenomena related to language acquisition. There are, however, two major theories of language learning that appear in the literature over and over again and make the process easier to understand: the behaviorist theory and the nativist theory. Both of these have influenced the research viewed earlier in this chapter.

The Behaviorist Theory

According to the behaviorist theory, language is observed and produced speech that occurs via the interaction of speaker and listener (Skinner 1957). Thinking involves perceptions and ideas and particularly what human beings do internally to process language.

Through interactions in the environment, language and thought are initiated. Language is internalized and when sufficiently stimulated the child talks. Interactions with parents and others provide a model for children to imitate. The imitations are encouraged by positive adult reinforcement. Skinner's principles, applied to language learning, are illustrated when we think about the infant who says "ma-ma" and receives enthusiastic reinforcement for the random verbal behavior. The caregiver picks him up and pats his back. She speaks to him and sometimes rewards that language behavior with food. The caregiver provides pleasurable experiences for the child (usually nine months old), who learns to associate those pleasures with the sound "ma-ma." The child learns the condition in which to make this babble, that is, in the presence of the caregiver. Language is acquired, according to behaviorists, when adults provide models (words, phrases, actions) in an environment where children imitate behaviors. The imitation must be reinforced by the adult. The reinforcement (pats, smiles, etc.)

encourages further attempts to make sounds that come closer to the modeled behavior.

This theory seems appropriate for describing how children learn words and actions. It does not explain the human ability to arrange and rearrange sentences without instruction, the human ability to combine and condense sentences, and the fact that children create forms of words, phrases, and sentence structures that they have never heard (i.e., goes, foots, etc.)

Scholars who realized a need to explain these phenomena developed the nativist theory. This theory of language originated with Noam Chomsky (1965) and was reinforced by researchers such as McNeill (1966), Lenneberg (1967), and Brown (1973).

The Nativist Theory

Noam Chomsky (1965), considered one of the founders of present day linguistic theory, presented a very different view of language acquisition. Language, according to Chomsky, is an innate human process. The human mind has incorporated into its structure a device from which language is generated. This device, referred to as LAD (language acquisition device), makes possible the ability to develop rules for manipulating and arranging words in creative ways. This subconscious internalization led Eric Lenneberg (1967) to extend Chomsky's theory to include a biological aspect of language growth. His justification for this extension was based on the following reasoning: if language is specific to humans, then normal children no matter where they live in the world can speak; if language is specific to humans, then normal children have the equipment necessary for creating language; if language is specific to humans, then normal children develop the ability to speak at approximately the same age.

If we accept these statements, then we are able to accept Lenneberg's (1967) notion that there must be a biological aspect to language learning. Language is part of the natural development of human beings and, except for some severely handicapped youngsters, is acquired by most children. There is a natural motivator within children that makes language learning a natural happening.

Several have considered the nativist's view of language acquisition inadequate for explaining the phenomenon (Bloom 1970; Brown 1973; Golinkoff and Gordon 1983). Reviewing the theory persuades one to question the lack of consideration for the context in which language is used. According to this theory, the child is able to generate syntactic structures (sentences) without context or in spite of the environment. Chomsky's theory, as presented in his writings, does not address the development of meaning and the functional uses of language. Although the theory does not speak to the role of the adult as a model for learning, the theory does provide for consideration of the interactive, communicative concept of the development of language, which is important to the thesis of this text.

Early Language Acquisition

Although differences exist between the theories of Skinner and Chomsky, together their thinking enlightens the process of language acquisition by reinforcing the existence of the learner's own innate language learning device and by acknowledging the need for models. The work of many psycholinguists sheds light on the oral language development of infants, toddlers, and young children. Facets of this development, central to chapters 4 through 10, describe and define specific developmental characteristics of early years.

Overall, infants advance from cooing, to babbling, to single words, to two-word utterances, and onto longer and more complex sentence constructions. Infants appear entranced with the sounds they make; they play with these sounds and soon learn that the sounds can function for them. The sounds affect their caregivers who then hold, change, or feed them. The infant, toddler, and young child take a surprisingly active role in oral interactions with an adult.

The forty-four different sounds of our language, given a normal vocal tract, are mastered in a predictable fashion from bilabial sounds /m/, /p/, /b/ to consonant clusters /pl/, /str/. If Chomsky's (1965) and Lenneberg's (1967) theories are supported, then we can accept the premise that sounds are strung together and words are formed, sentences are built, and the rules governing their structure and the order of language are internalized innately and intuitively.

The single words, followed by the two-word utterances of toddlers into which is compressed so much meaning, give way to the simplest of kernel (basic) sentence structures, such as, "He runs." Chomsky's (1965) transformational-generative description of language identifies and explains how these simple sentence patterns can be transformed into questions and negative or passive forms. The theory also demonstrates how various forms can be embedded into kernel sentences, modifying and enhancing their meaning.

During early childhood, language works to socialize the child, to induct her into her community (Garvey 1984). The early "bye-bye" and "hi" of the infant initiate such socialization.

Concomitant with oral language development, the child's awareness of print develops. The more books shared with him, the more signs and labels noted and identified, the more print-alert the young child becomes, the quicker letter/sound relationships are discovered. When the young child's squiggles become scribbles, the scribbles become letters, and the letters become words, invented spelling appears which mirrors the child's perception of the letter/sound system. In nurturant environments, this relationship is largely untaught, but its development is clear in invented spellings. Children's logical and analytical abilities are strongly related to the development of this relationship (Calfee and Calfee 1981). The young child demonstrates an understanding that sounds are represented by symbols.

In order to spell words, young children must develop a concept of what a word is; they must possess the ability to think about words (Morris 1981). Spelling words means that a child can say the word mentally to herself. She can hear when one word ends and another begins. She can sort through her repertoire of letters and find ones to match the sounds of the word in her mind. She can write down the letter or combination of letters she has chosen and recite the word again and again in her thoughts. The child, when writing a word, can eliminate the sound (phoneme) she has just spelled and locate the next sound to be spelled and letters or combination of letters which match it. She continues this process until all of the sounds, as she hears them in the word, are written.

Chomsky (1971), Sowers (1988), and researchers Burns and Richgels (1989) have found that spelling develops through stages like oral language and, eventually, these stages culminate into conventional spelling (Gentry 1982; Morris 1981). These findings suggest that, although nonconventional, children's spellings are systematic. Children who invent their spellings know what they are doing, and they are able to explain their own spelling (Read 1971; Temple et al. 1988).

We believe that the transition from the oral to the written code truly exemplifies the process of emergent literacy. It must be kept in mind that the sounds of language and invented spellings, which represent children's oral language, together provide information about children's comprehension of the sound system of their native language.

Thought and Language Acquisition

The relationship of thought to language usually provokes controversy. Scholars have debated for decades the chicken or the egg concept. Which comes first, thought or language? If thought comes first, then adults responsible for children's learning should emphasize the teaching of thinking. On the other hand, if language comes first and facilitates thought, then education must focus on literacy.

Without question, Jean Piaget (1951, 1952, 1955) has advanced the most sophisticated theory about children's thinking. Perhaps the reason his theory has had such impact on education is that Piaget communicates a tangible sense of what children's thinking is. The following description provides evidence of the convincing nature of Piaget's research. It describes Lucienne, Piaget's eighteen-month-old daughter, playing a game which involved hiding a watch chain inside an otherwise empty box. The adult closes the box far enough so that the chain stays inside even if the box turned over, but the box is open enough for the child to see the chain.

> *She looks at the slit with great attention; then, several times in succession, she opens and shuts her mouth, at first slightly, then wider and wider. Apparently, Lucienne understands the existence of a cavity subjacent to the slit and wishes to enlarge the cavity. The attempt to representation, which she thus furnishes is expressed practically, that is to say, due to inability to think out the situation in words or clear visual images, she uses a similar motor indication as "signifier" or symbol. (Piaget 1951, 338)*

Lucienne opening and closing her mouth represents the process of getting the chain out of the cavity. Children's actions are physical representations of ideas and, therefore, a system of sign.

Piaget's Theory

Piaget believed that development of thought evolves in stages which he labeled the sensorimotor period, the preoperational period, the concrete operational period, and the formal operational period.

The sensorimotor stage spans the period from birth to approximately age two. At birth, the child's thoughts are limited to motor reflexes. But within a few months, the infant develops a more sophisticated system. During this period, children learn that words are tied to activities. The preoperational period, which spans the ages two to seven years, is marked by the youngster's use of symbols to represent objects or experiences. Blocks may represent buildings, dolls, or people. Scribbles represent words that symbolize people and objects. The ability to draw deliberately emerges during this stage. The child develops the skill of forming mental images with the help of drawings. Vocabulary develops one-hundred-fold, with the greatest growth between eighteen and thirty months (McCarthy 1954). The use of words and their arrangements in sentences become increasingly complex.

Children in the concrete operational stage (ages seven through twelve) can think about ideas from more than one point of view. They can transform sentences. For example, "Quickly the boy ran" can be transformed to "The boy ran quickly." They can understand that the same letter, "e" for example, can appear at the beginning, the middle, or the end of words. Earlier, most children believe that there is a different "e" for each of these positions in a word. Formal operations, abstract reasoning, are attained for many after the age of twelve.

The child moves through these stages, according to Piaget, using three processes: assimilation, accommodation, and equilibration.

Assimilation occurs when the child incorporates information from an experience into his memory. A two-year-old, who sees a pony for the first time, shouts, "Dog, doggy." The pony and the dog for the child have the same features. The child, therefore, perceives the pony and other four-legged animals as a dog.

Children during this stage (birth to two years) have a strong desire to learn language. They repeat words over and over again, even when alone. Even when adults say "stop saying that," they continue. Unlike the behaviorists, who believe that external rewards are initially necessary to motivate repetition, Piaget believed that the reason for repetition (or rehearsal) is the personal satisfaction from using the language.

Accommodation occurs when children adapt their thoughts and actions in order to include new information. The child is told that a pony is different from a dog. The child, when told, also sees the animal. The language and visual information together guide the youngster into adapting his previously perceived image of a pony by accepting the new one.

Equilibration, Piaget suggests, takes place in three phases. First, the child achieves satisfaction in an activity. Subsequently, needs arise. When this occurs, the child is forced into a state of disequilibrium or dissatisfaction. When the needs are met, equilibrium is achieved once more. The child who believed that all four-legged animals were "doggies" was in a state of equilibrium. Once he was informed that the pony did not fit that class, he felt dissatisfaction. The new information caused disequilibrium. Once the child adopts the idea that other animals have four legs, a state of equilibrium is again achieved.

Although Piaget believed that language does not initially contribute to the development of thought, he recognized language as a tool used for cognitive development.

Piaget's theory does not explain language acquisition. However, many scholars who study language acquisition have used Piaget's developmental stages of thinking to explain language acquisition. Those who believe that Piaget's theory has validity for language acquisition observe that language in itself provides children with experiences that help them build strong mental structures for understanding (Furth 1970).

Vygotsky's Theory

According to Vygotsky (1962), children learn by maturing and, at the same time, by being stimulated by interactions with human beings. He believed that humans' innate biological needs are met in conjunction with social interactions.

Vygotsky refers to the child's external speech as the mechanism for planning and conceptualizing. This is the way children develop the ability to think. Vygotsky discovered in his research that even when children grow, they revert to external speech to help them understand difficult problems.

Vygotsky believed that communication was an important ingredient in the young child's growth. He believed that adults provided names, instructions, and suggestions and gradually children needed fewer models in order to produce language. Vygotsky was quite clear about children's language learning. He believed that language learning is, in part, biological, but that children need instruction in the zone between their independent language level and the level at which they can operate with adult guidance. Children function somewhere between the place where they speak in monologues and the place where they have dialogue with adults. Parents, teachers, or older siblings are the facilitators for children's conceptual growth. Language is the major stimulant for conceptual learning, and conceptual growth is dependent on interactions with objects and people in the environment. The adult's instructional role in children's learning is critical and contrasts with Piaget's point of view. Also in contrast are children's monologues. External speech, for Vygotsky, represents the first step toward the development of internalized thinking. For Piaget, monologues represent current thought and are not used by the child to stimulate further growth. It is important to note that adults, according to Vygotsky, are the major force for stimulating children to expand beyond their current functioning. Adult interactions guide children to extend their language.

Agreement among Theorists
Although differences exist, this brief explanation of theories illustrates similarities between Piaget and Vygotsky. Both scholars believe that thought processes are developmental. First, the child responds to objects and events in somewhat haphazard ways. Then each child develops responses that are consistent (invariant), building stability for further learning. Finally, the child develops the ability to abstract, or reason, without the need for objects. Both Piaget and Vygotsky believe that thinking processes grow from within the child's system. The learner constructs rules resulting from interpretations of experiences. Piaget's theories, particularly, have encouraged today's researchers to examine children's language productions for evidence of their understanding of the tasks they perform.

Philosophical Theories and Past Practices in Early Literacy
Several important philosophers and the educational practices resulting from their theories must be mentioned in order to establish a historical perspective. Past ideas and past practices influence current ideas and pedagogy.

Rousseau, Pestalozzi, Froebel, and Dewey have contributed to today's educational practices with respect to the child's development. Rousseau

(1962) might be considered the father of natural literacy learning and individual instruction. He believed that children ought not to be pushed into learning anything before they are developmentally ready. Rousseau and his advocates believed that a prescribed curriculum just does not work. An innate desire to learn about the world causes the child to use her curiosity to unfold, almost like a flower, and learn. Natural learning needs to be stimulated by appropriate instruction. Rousseau, however, was probably the first to suggest that respecting children was good educational practice.

Pestalozzi (Braun and Edwards 1972), a follower of Rousseau, developed instructional guidelines to enhance learning naturally. These guidelines or lessons helped the child manipulate objects and ideas in a natural environment. Guided interactions, he believed, would help children learn to read and write as easily as they play and eat. Pestalozzi's work represents a beginning point for early childhood education and the kindergarten movement. His theories, illustrated by a deep and loving concern for children, influenced Froebel, who visited Pestalozzi's school.

Froebel (Lilley 1967) believed that child's play, a form of instruction, was necessary in order for one to mature. He designed objects, referred to as gifts for children to examine, to guide them into using their senses to understand concepts of number forms and measurements. His materials and ideas were the first early childhood curriculum. Froebel believed, like Rousseau and Pestalozzi, in the natural development of the mind. He stated, however, that planned direction was necessary in order to achieve the fullest benefits for each child. It is Froebel who first used the word *kindergarten* (child's garden) to describe his classroom settings. The child, he believed, was like a plant in a garden. With proper nurturing, the child would grow and bloom to productive maturity. Current preschools and kindergartens use many of Froebel's practices. Doll corners, blocks, and show-and-tell time provide structure with freedom for children to explore in order to learn.

Dewey (1966) must have built on the concepts of the philosophers and educators mentioned previously. His ideas led to the child-centered curriculum we speak of even today. Dewey believed that learning in school must be built around children's interests. Like Froebel, he believed that play was the means for learning. Like Vygotsky, Dewey viewed interaction as the vehicle for learning both content and skills. Learning was an interactive activity, rather than a series of activities, that involved directed instruction to master isolated skills. Dewey's work, although important in American education, does not address formal instruction in reading or writing. However, his holistic view of children's development—particularly the interdependence of social and cognitive growth—strongly support much current thinking about early literacy.

Summary

Current ideas about literacy learning inform us that children who are literate in the early years in school are brought up on literate interactions. All of the components of literacy, the umbrella for reading, writing, and oral language, result in the facilitation of communication. Communication results from a need to function socially and culturally.

All activities that involve communication facilitate literacy growth, but the single most influential activity for the caregiver is reading to children. Reading to children develops print awareness and also fosters feelings of love. The sharing of print in a loving manner creates an emotional bond and facilitates successful formal and informal literacy experiences.

The current knowledge used to identify and build environments and a curriculum for literacy learning could not exist without the support of theories from the past, which offer explanations for the acquisition and development of language. There is no one theory that explains these intricate processes, but culling from several such theories helps psychologists and educators to explain this human ability. No matter which theory of language acquisition and learning one adopts, one may conclude that language learning is specific to human beings and occurs as each person interacts with others to function purposefully in society. Language changes with time, as do cultures and values. The reciprocal nature of communication—speaking and listening, reading and writing—necessitates concurrent learning of these language components. Thought and language are developmentally intertwined.

Neither nativists nor behaviorists nor Piaget nor Vygotsky have the answers. But all answer some questions about how and why children learn to become literate.

2

Foundations for Becoming Literate

Roles of Families, Teachers, and Children

This chapter reviews ideas concerned with roles of families and the home and teachers and the school in the development of literacy, as well as the role of the learner. The following questions are addressed:

- What roles do families and the home environments play in literacy development?
- What roles do teachers and school environments play in literacy development?
- What roles do learners play in their literacy development?

What Roles Do Families and the Home Environments Play in Literacy Development?

Concepts of the development of literacy have changed in recent years and so has the role of the family. Emergent literacy appears to have replaced, preceded, or subsumed beginning reading. With its concentration on the very early years of the child, in fact, from birth to the time conventional literacy begins, it views the roles of the family and the environment of the home as especially vital and critical. Field research that focused on homes, families, and developing literacy has confirmed the power of the home environment and the family group in building foundations for becoming literate (Crago 1975; Taylor 1983).

Leichter's (1964) studies of the family helped him conclude that:

> *The family is an arena in which virtually the entire range of human experiences can take place. . . . Since almost everyone has had profound experiences within one or more families, judgments of the family are often felt and charged with emotion. (p. 1)*

An unusual example of a relationship rooted in literacy is the one Doctor Morton Botel shares. He had just become a grandfather. As he tells it, "I walked up to the nursery, and my son-in-law helped me put on a surgical gown and mask. We went into the nursery. Holding Lara the first time was so exciting. I took out the T. S. Eliot poem that I'd saved to read to my first grandchild and read to her." "She smiled," Dr. Botel said joyfully, "I knew then she'd be a reader." Although many attribute a baby's smiling at several hours of age to colic, Dr. Botel attributed the facial expression to the interpersonal communication between his granddaughter and himself. He had begun to build a relationship rooted in literacy by using reading as the vehicle. The values of the relationship and reading were intertwined. Lara is now in high school, and each time Dr. Botel speaks of her, he shares the many times they read and write and share ideas about books and their values together.

Environments of infancy and early childhood are also shaped by cultural values (Baghban 1984; Bissex 1980). Learning to value books and print begins at birth. According to an anthropologist (Hall 1959), culture shapes its members in many ways, occurring more covertly than overtly. Cultures in which reading, for example, is done consistently and delightedly are more likely to make young readers.

The Role of Grandparent as Educator for Literacy Learning

Our society has changed rapidly and so have the roles of grandparents in families. Margaret Mead points out that "American cultural style is based upon immigration . . . a style which may also be called tentativeness" (1946, 346–48). This need to move caused a decrease in grandparents' presence and influence (Mead 1977). In old settled American families where a sense of lineage was strong and in poor families where grandmothers cared for children of mothers forced to work hard in fields and factories, the influences of grandparents were strong. The more prosperous middle and upper working classes placed less value on intergenerational family life. Many of these families working upward in the class system were ashamed of their parental heritage. Many new Americans tried desperately to identify with the culture of their new home and new language. If children were cared for by grandparents who were not English-speaking, parents stopped the children from speaking the language spoken by their grandparents, since this was, and sometimes still is, cause for embarrassment (Mead 1977, 68).

Three hundred years have passed since America began. In her work, Mead discovered that, unlike families in other countries, Americans expect minimal closeness between grandparents and grandchildren, except in certain ethnic groups (p. 68). These groups include those parents dependent on the grandparent for care while they work.

Some poor families maintain three-generation homes; some very affluent families maintain vacation homes where children and grandparents visit each other during holidays. Telephones have replaced the family correspondence. Gifts, via mail, also tend to substitute for conversations.

The lack of interaction between grandparent and grandchild has deprived new generations from learning about cultural traditions of the past. This was well illustrated when a twelve-year-old boy chose to interview his grandmother about her childhood and heritage for a school report. A first-generation American, the youngest daughter of a Russian immigrant herself, she is the only surviving maternal grandparent. She was without a father early in life. When her father was alive, he was too ill to share stories about Russia. Her mother was a working woman, struggling to support five children and a sick husband. The twelve-year-old wanted to hear about his great-grandmother, for as he said, so astutely, "When Mom-Mom dies, I won't have any record of my family history." This young boy was asking for stories about his family in order to solidify his understanding of his culture and heritage. He asked an adult important in his life to help; that is, to extend his information about his family (Snow 1983). Information about families develops most effectively through shared efforts. These efforts and experiences are the content for oral communication, which provides a way for grandchildren to gain knowledge, understanding, and pride in their lineage (Pflaum 1986). Particularly during infant years, grandparents can help grandchildren develop language abilities. Social interactions become a force for verbal transactions and language learning. Grandparents provide environments that help children accumulate resources (stories) for reading and writing. Stories are told and retold lovingly, with personal intimacy. Generation gaps are closed and vocabularies expand.

Although current literature in early literacy attempts to address the role of grandparents in the learning process, there is little research to report. We know that it is important for grandparents to mentor their grandchildren. Family stories enhance the children's development and desire to read and write.

The Role of Parent as Educator: Past Views

Parents and families are essential to the learning to read process. Although we know this intuitively, educators in the past have encouraged parents to facilitate only the growth of oral language. Reading instruction was to be left to the school. Language development was considered a natural part of home life, but reading and writing were learned only with teachers in formal school settings. A form of "turfism" operated with a "hands off" attitude about teaching, particularly teaching reading at home. Such turfism is exemplified in an incident that occurred more than forty years ago. A concerned mother of a seriously ill six-year-old child went to school and asked for the reading instructional materials. Her goal was to help her child learn to read. Returning to school after a six-week illness without instruction in reading, the mother felt, would be a hindrance to further reading development. The teacher's response to the mother's request was, "You do the upbringing, I'll do the teaching of reading. Your child will learn the wrong way if you interfere."

The practice of separating roles and activities encompassed most of the ideas about curriculum for the teaching of literacy in the United States for years. To learn to read and write, a child built upon sequential steps learned in a correct way in planned instructional sessions. Can you imagine teaching children to speak by providing a step-by-step approach to talking? The assumptions underlying a step-by-step instructional curriculum are outlined by Hall (1987, 2). We have selected the following as most meaningful:

- children are not ready to learn to read and write until they are five or six years old
- children have to be formally taught to be literate
- the teaching of literacy must be systematic and sequential in operation

These assumptions controlled the way educators and parents dealt with literacy. Parents had little to do with the process. The teacher was the most valued influence on children's road toward literacy. This professional, a trained specialist, had learned how to teach the process. Skills had to be taught in a systematic manner in a prescribed sequence. Underlying the teaching was a set of rules which described the relationships of one rule to another. Those who believe that reading is learned one skill at a time believe, too, that if the order and sequence of learning were disturbed, children would fail. The skills became the focus, not the learner. The materials used for instruction determined success or failure.

Thoughts about children's literacy development in the past gave no consideration to the ideas that reading also included learning to write, that talking served as a companion to reading and writing, that literacy develops in real, not artificial, situations both in school and out, or that children who are brought up in literate societies are literate and begin to learn to read and write as infants and toddlers.

Traditional notions deny the continuous nature of the literacy learning process. There is little consideration of the fact that language learning has social and cultural contexts. Today's researchers have dramatically demonstrated that an unnatural view of learning to read was a serious mistake (Durkin 1966; Holdaway 1979; Taylor 1983; Jewell and Zintz 1986).

We know that parent and child conversations are major vehicles through which children become literate (Sigel 1982). Conversations shape many aspects of the child's intellectual functioning, as well as linguistic and semantic understandings. Verbal, as well as nonverbal, behaviors of parents have potent impacts on the way children use language to communicate (Sigel 1982, 2).

The Role of Parent as Educator: Current Views

We now view learning to read and write as natural parts of the growing/learning process at home. The family begins the process, and school extends and expands the process. Case histories of early readers illustrate that young children, even some three-year-olds, can learn to read before going to school, without formal instruction, and sometimes even without direct intervention from caregivers (Butler 1979). A nurturing home environment is, however, essential. Jean-Paul Sartre, who learned to read before the age of six and was the product of an unusually literate environment, talks in his biography *The Words* (1964) of the books in his grandparents' home where he and his mother lived. Both written and spoken language were valued in that household. Oral recitation was respected and Sartre remembers making grown-up remarks, realizing later that these were far beyond his years. These remarks and poems had no meaning to him, yet he liked to "borrow whole sentences from grown-ups and repeat them" (p. 31). He was praised for his imitations of adult language, which encouraged him to imitate the adults in his life even further.

Sartre tells of his jealousy of his mother's ability to read. Imitating her, he sat down in a storeroom with a book entitled *Tribulations of a Chinese in China* and pretended to read. Much fuss was made by his family over this imitative behavior, and all decided that Jean-Paul was ready to learn the alphabet (p. 48). The magic of words and adult language, even without much understanding of the materials, and the encouraging, reinforcing environment of the home, built in Jean-Paul an irresistible desire to read like his mother and grandparents (Glazer 1980).

Literature in human growth and family literacy tells us that parents are children's first and most important teachers. (Baghban 1984; Butler 1979; Crago 1975; Taylor 1983; Teale 1988). They provide the environmental essentials necessary for becoming literate in global ways. These include:

- routine activities
- sensitivity to the child's need for response
- sensitivity to the child's capacity
- activities that meet the child's capacity in a challenging and successful way
- interest in communicating with the child
- interest in helping the child understand language
- respect for children's language utterances and meanings
- objects and activities that encourage communication
- challenges that drive children to make meaning for themselves

Once these essentials are established, exchanges of language must occur. The exchanges require parents to understand:

- how important communication is
- how much intervention is necessary to help children expand their language (modeling)

- how to help children answer their own questions about learning
- what amount of redirection is necessary
- what amount and kind of support is necessary
- what kinds of questions children ask and what they mean
- how to respond to questions
- when oral language interaction is important
- when nonverbal interactions are important
- what sorts of activities help children communicate

All of these elements involve some form of conversation between parent and child. Conversations are major vehicles through which parents act as teachers of children, affecting not only language acquisition but intellectual functions. It is during these conversations that parents demand that children separate themselves in ways to anticipate outcomes and recall objects, people, and events (Sigel 1982). It is through healthy playful conversations that children become thinking, problem-solving individuals who use language effectively.

Parents serve as models for helping make children's first experiences with language and print satisfying and pleasurable. Babies receive pleasure when they talk and then receive responses to their language. Children are satisfied when they ask questions and receive complete attention, when they recognize objects and labels, and when parents show appreciation for their comprehension of the English language. Parents brought up in homes where literacy was important will make literacy activities important in their homes (Durkin 1966; Clark 1976; Hansen 1969). Parents, on the other hand, who have not experienced a rich language environment themselves, will probably have difficulty creating one for their children.

The Role of Siblings

A review of the literature reveals that the role of sibling influences on literacy development has not been sufficiently investigated. However, practical thoughts about the influences that sisters and brothers have on one another are convincing enough to draw some conclusions. Siblings exert influences upon one another because they spend time together. They serve as models and sources of evaluation for one another. Meeting the standards of older and younger brothers and sisters presents challenges, which often become facilitators for learning.

Contacts are usually intimate, but informal and straightforward. Children learn from each other how to solve conflicts, how to cope with criticism, and how to become intensely involved with another human being. They learn to share responsibilities and confront issues of rights. They learn these aspects of living by negotiating issues using forms of language. The day-to-day negotiations probably have significant educational influences on siblings. This is well illustrated in a story about a wonderful family of four children, all boys, ranging in age from four months to twelve years. The three older children, ages six, nine, and twelve, were enrolled in an after-school reading enrichment program. Their parents traveled twenty miles to bring them to the program and took the four-month-old brother along. The three older children continuously talked to their infant brother. They showed him the books they selected from the library, and they shared their stories with him. One brother could be heard saying, "Quiet, Bobby, I want to tell Josh [the infant] my story first. You did it last week." Those young boys, their mother said, insisted that their infant brother know everything that happened. "I am positive," she said with assurance, "that this baby will speak before any of the others because of the older boys."

In another family, a fifth grader related the family's weekly meetings to discuss and decide, jointly, family concerns such as how to spend money and where to vacation. Everyone from the youngest sibling (a three-year-old) to the parents was involved in discussions and given time to express his or her views and justify them. The child's unusual skills in organizing her peers at a class meeting in the production of a newspaper and other activities were probably influenced by these family discussions, particularly those concerning scheduling. Years of such parent/sibling modeling and participation were certainly mirrored in this fifth grader's skills in literacy and in leadership.

The role of the family in literacy learning is paramount. Educational encounters range from conscious systematic instruction to moment-to-moment influences with marginal awareness of happenings. These educational experiences are profound since interactions and experiences with families are intimate, intense, and continuous. Judgments of family members are deeply felt and charged with emotion. They are shaped by cultural and social values and morals. Families—grandparents, parents, and siblings—plant the seeds that develop the roots of literacy.

What Roles Do Teachers and School Environments Play in Literacy Development?

Amazingly, the roles of the family and teachers and school are similar. Historically, however, these roles have been quite different. Teachers and schools have looked at literacy instruction as the teaching of reading. It was assumed, as mentioned earlier, that detailed sequences of skills and a specific way to teach these skills created readers. Systematic materials, developed for teaching reading, were adopted by entire school districts and included controlled vocabularies written specifically to teach word recognition. The materials included reinforcement activities in workbooks that required children to respond to items by marking correct answers. Criterion reference tests prepared by publishers were administered periodically to determine learning. Home influences were not considered part of reading development. Teachers functioned as managers of materials and delivered information from these to children. Because materials were controlled, they were thought to be "teacher and child-proof." Children of all ages and stages, these advocates agreed, would learn to read from teachers, either good or poor ones. The books, not teachers and learners, controlled literacy activities.

The literature cited thus far in this text supports a change from this sort of literacy learning. The concept of learning to read has broadened and the roles of teachers and parents have altered. Reading behaviors are multifaceted, involving all modes of communication. Social and cultural aspects of children's lives are considered important for literacy learning. Healthy environments shape children's attitudes, helping them to think of themselves as readers and writers.

The current views of reading and literacy processes necessitate a change in the roles of professionals involved in instruction in schools. The change in the role of the teacher might best be described as a movement from a prescriber of behavior to a describer of behavior. Teachers have become models, facilitators, and observers. Teachers need to have knowledge of human growth and development and apply that knowledge to behaviors they observe in children. Observations provide the necessary data about children. Teachers can then plan appropriate activities and instruction to meet individual academic, emotional, social, and physical needs.

Teachers describe behaviors in response to questions they ask as they look at children as they work and play. "What helps the child want to learn? What specific strategy helps the child demonstrate what he remembers after reading?" are two of many important questions used to focus observations. Unlike formerly prescribed curriculums for reading, instruction is based on data collections and is tailored to meet individual growth and needs. Data include children's drawings, transcriptions of tape recordings of their reading, and their written and oral stories. Data also include objective note-taking about children's behaviors. Assessment is a continuous, ongoing process. Teale (1990) states that "systematic observation and recordings of children's behaviors in classroom activities, keeping collections of work samples, and periodic performance samples of children's reading and writing gathered in one-to-one or small group settings that maintain an ecological validity of literacy activities hold great promise for providing teachers with information that informs their teaching of individual children" (p. 53).

Systematic collections of these sorts of data, over time, bring together teaching and assessment in classrooms and in homes as well. Data collecting occurs in environments that permit children the time and space to manipulate and create drawings, oral and written stories, and more products. Products are produced in naturalistic environments, similar to the home environment where children first learned to speak in natural settings. The child and teacher work, together, as did mother and child in the earlier years. Teachers model behaviors and children follow their guidance. As teachers watch, they create mental and written notes about learning. They guide and assess many times within one activity. Shifts from instructional behaviors to assessment procedures occur constantly. Like the mother, who cared for and observed needs for food and love, the teacher becomes observer or researcher, and, at the same time, is an integral part of the environment for learning. The teacher guides instruction but also acts as an outsider looking at behavior from another point of view (Glazer and Searfoss 1988, 27).

This sort of research/instructional paradigm has existed for years. Mothers have collected observational notes about children and stored them in baby books, diaries, and journals. Glena Bissex in her book *Gyns at Wrk* (1980), illustrates how such research works. She writes:

> *When I began taking notes about my infant son's development, I did not know I was gathering "data" for "research;" I was a mother with a propensity for writing things down. . . . I was particularly interested in my son's language development; and, as an English teacher just retrained in reading, I wanted to observe his learning to read. When Paul started spelling, I was amazed and fascinated. Only somewhat later did I learn of Charles Read's research on children's invented spelling. Excited by his work I started seeing my notes as "data."*

Dr. Bissex defined her role as observer and, at the same time, a supportive model for her son. Like Bissex, our role is researcher/teacher observing our children at all times in the environment where we are also participants. Our goal is to learn from children how they become effective communicators. Once we collect data, we can alter environments, modify actions and reactions, and provide appropriate materials and intervention for further learning.

The role described herein is supported by research and also by the recommendations of the Early Childhood and Literacy Development Committee of the International Reading Association (1986). These recommendations suggest that professionals:

- build instruction on what the child already knows about oral language, reading, and writing. Focus on meaningful experiences and meaningful language rather than merely on isolated skill development.
- respect the language the child brings to school and use it as a base for language and literacy activities
- ensure feelings of success for all children, helping them see themselves as people who can enjoy exploring oral and written language
- provide reading experiences as an integrated part of the broader communication process which includes speaking, listening, and writing, as well as other communication systems, such as art, math, and music
- encourage children's first attempts at writing without concern for the proper formation of letters or correct conventional spelling
- encourage risk-taking in first attempts at reading and writing and accept what appear to be errors as part of children's natural patterns of growth and development
- use materials for instruction that are familiar, such as well-known stories, because they provide the child with a sense of control and confidence
- present a model for students to emulate. In the classroom, teachers should use language appropriately, listen and respond to children's talk, and engage in their own reading and writing.
- take time regularly to read to children from a wide variety of poetry, fiction, and nonfiction
- provide time regularly for children's independent reading and writing
- foster children's affective and cognitive development by providing opportunities to communicate what they know, think, and feel
- use evaluative procedures that are developmentally and culturally appropriate for the children being assessed. The selection of evaluative measures should be based on the objectives of the instructional program and should consider each child's total development and its effect on reading performance.
- make parents aware of the reasons for a total language program at school and provide them with ideas for activities to carry out at home
- alert parents to the limitations of formal assessments and standardized tests of prefirst graders' reading and writing skills
- encourage children to be active participants in the learning process rather than passive recipients of knowledge, by using activities that allow for experimentation with talking, listening, writing, and reading*

* Reprinted from "Literacy Development and Early Childhood (Preschool through Grade 3)" a joint statement prepared by Early Childhood and Literacy Development Committee of The International Reading Association.

What Roles Do Learners Play in Their Literacy Development?

Why look at the child's role? Because it is time that children take responsibility for their own learning. Traditionally, parents and teachers have taken the responsibility for children's learning as the following incident shows. A second grade teacher recalls two separate discussions with two different sets of parents. One child, Anita, was doing well in school. Her parents' joy was reflected in their conversation with her teacher. "Oh," said Mrs. Fisher, "I expected Anita to do well. Her father always did well in school and you must be a good teacher." The second child, Kathy, was not achieving as anticipated. During a parent conference, her mother remarked, "Gosh, I guess you don't know how to teach her. She did well last year." In both instances, parents held the parent or teacher responsible for the success, as well as the failure. Not once did either parent consider the child's role in the learning process. Not once did the parent or the inexperienced teacher realize that little can be learned by children without active participation.

Observation yields much data about children's involvement in the process of language learning. On one particular day, three second grade teachers came to visit seven-year-old Laurie's classroom. They followed the school's policy of becoming a learner in the setting. An experienced teacher sat next to Laurie who was writing a story. Laurie's paper was divided into two columns as shown in Figure 2–1. Each time she wrote a line or two, Laurie stopped, put her elbows on the table top, and rested her chin in her hands. She asked herself questions and then wrote more text. The questions were concerned with the line or two which she had just created. Questions seemed to help Laurie compose the next segments of her story. They were used to hypothesize and predict what should come next in her draft.

The story, on this day, was about her trip to the store to buy a Halloween costume. She wrote, "Today, I am going to the store for a Halloween costume. I will buy one." At this point, Laurie stopped and asked herself, "Now, what kind of costume do I want?" Then she wrote, "An angel costume."

The visiting teacher sat next to Laurie and listened. Her facial expression illustrated her confusion about the talking-to-self behavior. She sheepishly said to Laurie, "What are you doing when you talk?" "Oh," said Laurie, "I'm telling myself what I'm thinking about." This seemed to confuse the teacher even more and she asked, "What do you mean?" "Well," said Laurie, "I think about what other kids will want to know about when they read my story. Not all of the kids who read my story know about the store that has costumes. And, they don't know what kind of costume I want, so I want to

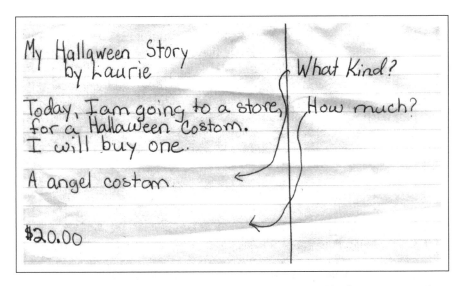

My Halloween Story
 by Laurie

What Kind?

Today, I am going to a store,
for a Hallaween Costom.
I will buy one.

How much?

A angel costom.

$20.00

FIGURE 2–1 **This seven-year-old is moving naturally from manuscript to script.**

tell them." "Oh," said the teacher, as she took her own piece of paper in order to record her observations.

Laurie, at the age of seven, was aware of the purposes and processes needed to create text for an audience. Asking questions of herself was the strategy she used for writing effective text. The visiting teacher seemed in awe of Laurie's ability to say what she was doing and what she wanted to accomplish. "How does she know about these things?" she asked. Laurie was able to talk about what she was thinking because the teacher had deliberately guided her to ask herself questions. Laurie has been fortunate, for adults responsible for creating environments for learning have helped her to:

- become actively involved in the teaching/learning process
- make decisions about her learning
- read and write with purpose
- listen and respond
- take risks in learning environments
- continuously evaluate herself in order to notice strengths and needs
- continuously receive specific praise which focuses on the desired behaviors (i.e., "I love the way you tried to write that story," or, "It is good that you write about things you have done")

Children who become involved with their own learning, who learn to understand how they are thinking, assume responsibility for their activities.

Children learn how to learn when they work in apprentice roles, i.e., they learn by doing. Children learn to talk by engaging naturally in purposeful conversations. Susuki's method for teaching children to play the violin emphasized the learning-by-doing philosophy. Montessori's self-activity approach, using specific materials, respects "learning for self" (Montessori 1965). Frank Smith (1978) believes that one learns to read by reading, and one learns to write by writing. He stresses:

> *One of the most important skills of reading—is knowing the right kinds of questions to ask for different kinds of text. To read we must ask questions, implicit questions, not ones that we are aware of, just as we must ask implicit questions to comprehend spoken language. . . . If we do not know the right kinds of questions to ask of a math text or knitting pattern then, obviously, we will not be able to read a math text or knitting pattern. And if we present children learning how to read with materials they cannot possibly ask questions of—because they find it boring, beyond their understanding, or simply because it is unequivocal nonsense in any case—then we should not be surprised if they cannot read. (p. 107)*

Children take responsibility for their own learning when they interact effectively with materials and ideas. They will create new language within already familiar frameworks. The song "Go tell Aunt Rhody, go tell Aunt Rhody, the old gray goose is dead" has been the stimulus for the creation of many original verses. One seven-year-old wrote: "Go tell your teacher, Go tell your teacher, Go tell your teacher, It's almost time to go." Children will do this with walking, talking, reading, and writing as well. To develop children who will be responsible for their own learning requires an environment and activities prepared and created by adults who understand that children will:

- construct their own rules for language use and behavior
- create text, oral and written
- hypothesize about text and rules
- accept challenges and meet them
- learn the language necessary to express ideas, if they are expected to
- form their own expectations

Children must learn how to create change in their lives and they must be willing to do so. Children must be willing to observe, participate, play, and, as they do so, manipulate ideas and materials in constructive ways.

Mentally healthy children construct ideas creatively, actively making decisions in order to control their worlds.

Summary

Constructing and maintaining the foundations for literacy lie in the hands of communities of families, teachers, and children. Each participates in active purposeful ways creating and responding to language. Families, including grandparents, parents, siblings, and other caregivers, help the learner to expand knowledge in his life, extend information, and clarify questions about living. Learning happens in environments where language is exchanged effectively. These exchanges require adults in the home to understand when and how much intervention is appropriate.

Roles of teachers today have changed and will continue to change. Teachers must observe children in order to determine their strengths and needs in language learning settings. Today's observational procedures have matched the current research data which support maternalistic environments for learning. Teachers are expected to know how to create environments that stimulate language production. Teachers, as professionals, are expected to guide parents in understanding the relationships between children's behaviors in and out of school. Teachers carry out these expectations by serving as models for children and parents. Appropriate uses of time, space, and materials are necessary to facilitate growth in language in school.

Children must take responsibility for their own actions. They must be guided to know that they need to tackle and solve problems in order to meet their own expectations and those of others. If appropriate expectations exist, children will learn how to make decisions, take risks, and evaluate their own learning. They will learn, too, how to look upon errors as stepping stones and guides to further learning.

Learning to become literate is a community endeavor. Families, teachers in schools, and children must work together toward this goal.

3

Frameworks for Observing Growth and Needs

Studying young children's behaviors means observing growth. Observing growth is the basis for assessment in environments where all aspects of language work interactively for functional meaning. Looking at children as they emerge as literates, understanding how they emerge, and clarifying the roles adult caregivers play in this emergence are the foci of observation of this text. Current assessment procedures require that reviews of performance occur in the environment where children grow and learn. Reviews are ongoing, cumulative, and based on data from children's behaviors and productions as they engage in their daily activities.

In order to carry on a naturalistic review of behavior, frameworks for looking must be used. The teacher, who is a researcher of children's behaviors, selects a framework for observing and recording growth and needs.

This chapter will focus on several frameworks for observing and reviewing children's actions. The selected frameworks will guide descriptions of behaviors in literacy activities. We will answer the following questions:

- What theoretical model for learning helps us to guide children to become literate?
- What framework guides observations of children's ability to use oral language as a tool for communicating?
- What framework guides us to observe children's ability to use written language as a tool for communicating?
- How do frameworks guide holistic assessment?

The works of Don Holdaway (1979), M. A. K. Halliday (1975), and Marie Clay (1975) provide frameworks that encompass and enlighten most of the observations in classrooms. These models make sense when holistic perspectives are the goal for classroom environments. They help children and adults to observe developmental aspects of growth. These tools can be used for children from birth to age eight in most environments. They provide the knowledge base for reviewing most behaviors included throughout this text.

What Theoretical Model for Learning Helps Us to Guide Children to Become Literate?

Watching children is fascinating. Knowing what to look for to determine growth and needs is an art. Looking at behavior through frameworks provides parameters for reviewing the appropriateness of the instruction (intervention) and the environment created by caregivers.

Holdaway's (1979, 1986) child-centered model for learning is an appropriate tool for looking into natural holistic environments. Dr. Holdaway refers to the learning process as a "sort of formal dance of participants which displays a primitive structure universal to all environments." His model has four distinct stages: demonstration of an activity, the learner's partial participation in activity, the rehearsal or role-play period where the child "rehearses the dances" he will use later in life, and the learner's performance. This model can best be described by using Holdaway's (1986) illustration for making a sandwich. The activity occurs in the home environment regularly.

Stage one: the child observes the adult demonstrating (modeling) the activity. The adults are important to the child and ones to whom the child is bonded. The activity is not performed for the child but for all family members and is a valid (real) one, for it is routine. For example, members of a family need a school lunch. The mother makes the lunches daily as the child observes the activity for months before becoming seriously involved in the activity. Facial expressions, gestures, and oral language tell the observer that the child is expressing his feelings and is in stage one of the learning process. He is an active, participant-observer in a natural environment. He sees the repetitive behavior, important to the setting and people who exist in his life. The child observes demonstrations of this purposeful activity carried out by those he knows. The motivation to be part of the sandwich-making process is being fired up.

Stage two: the child partially participates in the activity. He becomes compulsively attracted to the center of the activity, by approaching and wanting to help. Whoever is making the sandwiches may allow some helping or may even place a hand over that of the toddler as the complexities of spreading are explored. Lots of talking about the activity helps the child explore. The desire to learn is intense; the need to learn is real. The natural form of instruction—observing and clumsily attempting to engage in the activity—is fostered by the adult mentor, a significant person in his life. He or she helps the child and praises even fumbling incorrect responses. The child has partially participated in the activity under skilled guidance in a natural setting.

Stage three: rehearsal occurs during this stage. When, says Holdaway, "the coast is clear," our potential sandwich-maker gathers what is necessary and tries to make a sandwich. There is great absorption—probably a small tongue pokes out in concentration—and the most difficult parts of the skill, such as spreading with the knife, may be abandoned in the interests of completing what may be viewed as a whole, real sandwich. The job is invariably botched. A high level of frustration may be self-imposed in role-playing the skill—a level which would not be tolerated by the learner when there is a critical audience (p. 58).

Stage four: performance culminates the learning process. The child, who has learned how to make the sandwich, seeks approval and voluntarily displays competence. There is a turning outward to find an audience—"Hey

Mom! Look at my sandwich!"—and the important other person—the skilled one—now becomes the observer, offering praise and often a little friendly advice or even good-humored admonishment—"Oh! Look at what you've done!" The social and rational sequence has come full circle. The child is mentor/teacher, the adult, the learner. There is a natural drive that forces each of us to show what we have learned. There is an inner voice that wants to shout, "Look at me, Look at me. I can do what you do!" (p. 60)

Holdaway's model provides adults with systematic parameters for watching children and serves as a framework for drawing tentative conclusions about children's growth. His paradigm suggests that adults must:

- become part of the learning environment
- create activities that are natural ones—part of the everyday environmental structures in which children live, eat, sleep, and grow
- serve as models for the expected behaviors
- provide appropriate intervention to facilitate children's attempts to master and achieve understanding of skills
- assist youngsters on the spot, when needed
- leave the scene so each child has time and space to rehearse over and over again
- understand that absences permit natural motivations, frustrations, and problem-solving attempts to occur (absence means leaving the room or moving away from the child)
- be ready to shift roles and become the learner as the child displays newly acquired behaviors

Holdaway's model for describing how children, and in fact all people, learn requires that caregivers engage in productive language exchanges in functionally meaningful ways. It is the adult who must continuously review the effectiveness of the environment for facilitating growth.

The Guide in Table 3–1 is organized to follow Holdaway's stages of learning. It should serve as a tool for looking over the environment.

What Framework Guides Observations of Children's Ability to Use Oral Language as a Tool for Communicating?

M. A. K. Halliday (1975, 7), an English linguist, is well known for his theory of language development. He describes the theory as one which defines the process by which children "learn how to mean." This theory suggests that children learn that language is a tool that serves them when sharing ideas and feelings in life. They find out that language helps them direct daily

TABLE 3–1 Examining Environments to Determine their Effectiveness for Facilitating Language Learning

	Comments
Physical Setting Spaces are visually attractive.	
Pleasant sounds are associated with the environment.	
Objects are attractive and appropriate for the child's age and stage of growth.	
The environment abounds with materials that facilitate a desire to read and write.	
Observable Activities Learner can rely on consistent human models for language learning.	
Learner can rely on consistent routines.	
Learner can rely on natural "nurturing" into literacy activities.	
Learner can rely on consistent praise.	
Participation Activities Materials are available that encourage participation and observation simultaneously.	
Ample space is provided for attempts at activity.	
Ample time is provided for rehearsal with assistance.	
Ample space permits peer support and mentoring.	
Role-Play Time is provided for independent rehearsal.	
Physical space is provided for independent rehearsal.	
The environment generates feelings of trust to try and try again.	
Materials for rehearsal are placed in inviting spaces and in enticing ways, so the learner seeks them for role-play.	
The learner knows that rehearsal (role-play) is part of learning.	
The learner has vehicles for self-evaluation of progress.	
Performance The environment provides time to display behavior.	
The teacher makes time to watch.	
The caregiver watches in order to learn about the child's strengths and needs.	

functions of living. Halliday (1975, 19–21) has identified seven functions found in oral language of young children: instrumental language, regulatory language, interactional language, personal language, imaginative language, heuristic language, and informative language.

Instrumental language is used to satisfy needs to get things done. At the earliest stages, it may be satisfying personal wants, food, love, or shelter; at later stages it takes the form of polite requests or persuasion. "Gimme that," represents instrumental language of young children. Skilled, more sophisticated speakers request their needs with expressions such as, "It's so pretty, I'd love to have it."

Regulatory language controls the behavior of others. The language is used in competitive, rule-governing situations. The bully or bossy child might say, "You get it" or "Don't you dare do it." Positive regulatory language can help an administrator, foreman, shop owner, president of a club, or student council member. Positive regulatory language is also cooperative, for example, "You really know how to select a good book; please find one for me."

Interactional language helps children build a bond with others. The language defines social relationships and may include negotiations or expressions of friendship. Telling jokes and the small talk adults use before formal meetings represent this function. It is language often used to establish "we-ness" (Temple et al. 1988).

Personal language is used to tell about oneself. Strong feelings and emotions comprise this function. Phrases such as, "I love you," or "I hate vegetables," help children establish their identities and build self-esteem and confidence.

Imaginative language is used to pretend, to make believe, to have fun. Fantasy demonstrated through drama, poetry, song, and stories incorporates this function. Imaginative language is used naturally by most children. It must be nurtured by caregivers in order to guide children to use it throughout their lives.

Heuristic language helps children to explore the environment. Children use it to find out about things. The term *heuristic* means to discover things. The function helps children to figure things out and to satisfy the curiosities of life. When we feel that "aha" sense of knowing, we have used heuristic language.

Informative language is used to communicate information to others. It is the language associated with school (Pinnell 1985, 59–60).

The guide in Table 3–2 has been developed to help caregivers observe and review children's functional uses of language.

Halliday believes that oral language is sometimes learned before its meanings. According to this theory, language learning precedes functional uses in many instances. Caregivers and teachers, when watching and

TABLE 3–2 Language Function Guide

	Comments
Instrumental Language Child uses language that controls others and says, for example, "Gimme"; "please"; "may I? pretty please." Child will cry, whine, or pout to get what he or she wants. Example of Child's Language:	
Regulatory Language Child controls others and says, for example, "Give me that"; "You do it"; "I'll be your friend if you give me your toy." Example of Child's Language:	
Interactional Language Child uses language to define social interactions and will say, "You're my friend, so you can play with my toy"; "You can have my cookie"; "Do it with me." Example of Child's Language:	
Personal Language Child tells about self and says, for example, "I hate to go to sleep"; "I feel sad when my Mom goes away"; "The music sounds nice." Example of Child's Language:	
Imaginative Language Child pretends and says, for example, "I'm a fairy princess. La, dee, dah, de dah, dee dah." Child repeats language patterns, as in songs, for example, "Go tell Aunt Rhody, go tell Aunt Rhody, go tell Aunt Rhody."	

Continued

TABLE 3–2 *Continued*

Example of Child's Language:	Comments

Heuristic Language	
Child wants to find things out and says, for example, "What is it? It's like a dog, but it has a bill like a duck."	
Example of Child's Language:	

Informative Language	
Child wants to let others know something, and might say, "Apples are red and sometimes green"; "July 4th is the birthday of America"; "It is cold out, and I'm wearing a coat."	
Example of Child's Language:	

listening to children, can determine their conceptual understandings about language by asking the following questions:

- Is language used intentionally to meet a goal (or purpose)?
- Is the child effective in accomplishing the goal?
- Are notions about meaning appropriate?
- Would most people interpret the child's language similarly?

What Framework Guides Us to Observe Children's Ability to Use Written Language as a Tool for Communicating?

Marie Clay (1975) has developed a series of principles that provide a framework for examining the development of children's writing. The principles define and describe the perceptual development of young children's writ-

ing. These include: the recurring principle, the directional principle, the flexibility principle, the generating principle, the inventory principle, the contrastive principle, and the abbreviation principle.

The recurring principle demonstrates reasons for repeated drawings that create patterns (1975, 20). When children begin to write letters and words, they will write the same words and syntactic patterns again and again (Figure 3–1). The repetitions provide practice and "a wonderful sense of accomplishment" (p. 21). They create a visual consistency that provides a sense of empowerment over written text. This same principle describes young children's oral language. Children repeat sounds, words, and rhymes over and over in the early years.

The directional principle explains the use of space and the conventions that must be followed in order to share language using space in written form. Evidence for explaining the use of direction on space occurs when we hear a youngster say, "Read it to me and point to the words when you say them." Further evidence exists when we watch two-, three-, and four-year-old children tell the story in a book using their own words (Figure 3–2). The oral language is characterized by story language with appropriate pitch, stress, and juncture to illustrate the story's plot, theme, problem, and resolution. The child moves his head from left to right, indicating that he knows how print moves on the page. He turns the page and proceeds by first looking at the left side of the book. Again, as if reading a line, the youngster begins moving from left to right, returning to the left once again.

The flexibility principle explains other stages of this directional principle and is represented by random representations of letters on pages (Figure 3–3). Children seem to have a need to experiment with written language

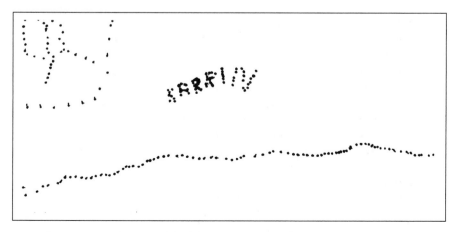

FIGURE 3–1 The Recurring Principle

FIGURE 3–2 The Directional Principle

symbols. They reverse letters, invert letters within words, and place patterns in different order often deliberately to achieve their goals.

The generating principle is illustrated by recurring letter elements (Figure 3–4). Often teachers and parents show delight when young children copy words and letters correctly. Although this demonstrates well-developed small motor skills, it does not provide information about the child's linguistic knowledge.

The inventory principle addresses children's information storage. Observing young children writing or drawing illustrates that they arrange or order the things they have learned into inventories. Children will make exhaustive lists of all the letters they know, all the words they know, and all the combinations of letters they have learned (Figure 3–5). They often use information to invent or create order or structure. These organized inventory systems serve to reinforce their written language and also to help children discover that they can create codes.

The contrastive principle guides youngsters to compare ideas on paper. Children often make a list of items and subconsciously ask themselves, "Are

FIGURE 3–3 The Flexibility Principle

they the same?" They construct letters using lines and angles contrasting one with another (Figure 3–6).

The abbreviation principle is often used to record a child's awareness of signs that present whole words or ideas. These attempts to abbreviate are usually deliberate and are observed in children's writing in the elementary grades (Figure 3–7).

Table 3–3 is based on Clay's principles and can be used to review children's written language development.

The information provided by Clay and others mentioned earlier represents the strong relationships between the development of oral and written language codes. These relationships suggest that:

- major caregivers must be actively involved in their children's development of oral and written expression
- written as well as oral expression are often part of the child's world even from birth. Specific stories, words, and book formats are part of the child's print environment

FIGURE 3–4 The Generating Principle

- when children learn to talk, they seem to develop a set of rules that permits them to produce and understand the language. When children begin to put scribbles on paper, they make marks that appear to be rule-generated. These are repeated, and children can identify what their code says. As children grow, correct forms of letters, words, and spellings are conceptualized and refined.
- children learn to talk without direct or formal instruction. They learn to write naturally without formal instruction, too.
- children learn to talk to meet personal needs and to adjust language when these needs change. They learn, too, that writing serves different functions and that how and what they write can be adjusted based on their goals and needs.
- all human beings collect information about talking and writing that is stored in memory. Each person develops a series of rules about how to construct language, oral and written, and how to use it functionally. Most rules and ideas about language are learned in environments that encourage language production. Language is not taught formally; there-

FIGURE 3–5 The Inventory Principle

fore, written expression is learned informally in environments where print is necessary for communication. We are unaware of the knowledge that each child has in his or her head. We can watch, however, the behavior and the products that result from that knowledge and try to determine how functional the child's language productions are for him or her. We do that by observing children at their work, which is also their play.

How Do Frameworks Guide Holistic Assessment?

Human beings must communicate by reading, writing, talking, and listening interactively in order to emerge literate. Reviewing children's ability to talk, write, and read simultaneously has recently surfaced as a major problem in schools. The cause of such a problem is the contradiction between the holistic development of these communication skills and the "atomistic"

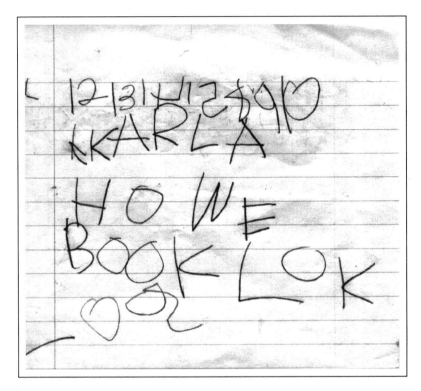

FIGURE 3–6   The Contrastive Principle

sequential subskill development. In the past, subskills have been taught one at a time. The assumption was that each step was the groundwork for the next skill, which led to specific instructional procedures. Results of these procedures necessitated evaluation. Children took reading tests, spelling tests, and writing tests in isolated settings. They were expected to respond correctly in a setting unnatural for them. Current researchers and theorists in the field of early literacy are speaking out about such procedures. We, and others, recommend that tests be viewed as only one part of the assessment process. The continuous collection of data—performance samples and observational notes—about children's language productions in various settings constitutes a vast amount of other material for assessment. Holdaway, Halliday, and Clay have helped to bridge the gap between assessment and instruction by providing the models mentioned earlier for looking at children as they work and play in natural environments. Parts of these models can be used to look at a child's drawing, for example, from more than one

FIGURE 3–7 The Abbreviation Principle

viewpoint. Two of the models can be used to describe children's written messages. Holdaway, Halliday, and Clay have guided the development of assessment alternatives. These tools provide systematic ways to observe children. Observations generate the data that justify changes in literacy activities.

There is much to observe. Time and space for looking and collecting data about each child in classrooms are limited. Teachers must, therefore, make decisions about:

- the goals that foster systematic observation and data collections
- the children who need to be systematically observed, over time
- the academic areas in which systematic observations are needed for each child
- the numbers of performance samples needed in order to identify children's strengths and needs (e.g., stories written by children, oral transcriptions of retellings of stories heard or read, or children's drawing in response to an event)

TABLE 3–3 Aspects of Writing Development

	Comments

Recurring Principle
    Does the child repeat the same moves, creating
        "recurring" text?	

Directional/Flexibility Principles
    Does the child move his hand or head, first to the left
        side of the text and then to the right?
 	
    Does the child point to the left column as he or she
        attempts to read?
 	
    Does the child draw, first on the left side of the page
        and then direct his movements to the right?
 	
    Do you notice "creative" attempts to place letters or
        words on paper?	

Generating Principle
    Does the child seem to use letters in patterns?
 	
    Does the child use a series of consistent patterns?
 	
    Does the child use a sentence pattern over and over,
        changing only one element of text (i.e., Last word
        of sentence: I like *dog*, I like *cats*, I like *me*)?	

Inventory Principle
    Does the child write and rewrite groups, series, or
        "bunches" of words or letters?
 	
    Does the child seem to "take inventory" of what he
        can write over and over again?	

Contrastive Principle
    Does the child write "contrasts" (i.e., small letters
        next to capital letters)	

Abbreviation Principle
    Does the child draw a picture or lines that represent
        an idea?
 	
    Does the drawing or writing stand for something
        other than what it looks like?
 	
    Do written attempts resemble familiar signs (i.e.,
        billboards, advertisements) available to the child?	

Our resources for deciding that alternative assessment is necessary come from three types of research: empirical studies based on children's comprehension of stories, ethnographic or diary-type studies carried out by parents, and the development studies already cited.

Empirical studies of children's story comprehension tell us that children learn to comprehend stories when they integrate what they hear when read to with their own sensory perceptions (Mandler and Johnson 1977; Rumelhart 1975); construct meaning for themselves (Paris 1975); internalize structures of stories as a result of hearing them, and use these structures to help them process other stories (Stein and Glenn 1975, 1977). These results came from systematically constructed research in which stories were read to children in controlled environments.

Diaries, unlike systematic research, are personal memoirs of parents' story-sharing experiences with their children. They are, in a sense, a less sophisticated form of this text's illustrations of child development. These are usually written in chronological order and consist of a series of incidents, in these cases a series of parent-child-storybook incidents, which document the powerful influence that books have on children's lives.

The first of these accounts, published more than three decades ago, is considered a pioneer work. Dorothy White (1954) wrote as a parent and also as a librarian. Probably the most important aspect of White's diary, for our purposes, is a description of herself as an adult reader and the important role she played in the relationship between her child and books. This relationship significantly affected her child's attitude toward stories and books. The fact that the major adult in a child's life plays a significant role in a child's understanding of stories, in the processes involved in hearing and reading them, and in reading itself is crucial.

White's (1954) work led others to record early literacy experiences of their children at home (Sanders 1976; Butler 1979). Butler's (1979) account of her granddaughter, Cushla, begins when she was four months old and extends over a three-year period. The book *Cushla* records the profoundly positive impact daily experiences with books had on her granddaughter's physical and perceptual impairments. Story book interactions provided Cushla with opportunities for language development and for imaginative and visual development through activities within the warm security provided by home and family.

Diaries can be considered a major portion of assessment. Data about growth are collected and recorded based on real actions and reactions of the child and those in his or her environment.

These decisions and data collections mirror each child's growth over time and define children's performances in literacy activities. Such data collections, when reviewed, reflect consistencies in performance. We can learn when to guide, how to prompt to push children a step further, and when to back away to permit rehearsal to occur. The important relationships between the development of the oral and written language coding systems support the need for data collections. We have identified and provided materials for facilitating this process.

Summary

The use of frameworks to describe and guide literacy development illustrates clearly that oral and written language must be considered together. Models, or frameworks, help us notice and describe children's behaviors in consistent ways so that appropriate decisions are made about environmental changes to help children grow. We know that we can review only one piece of data at a time. Synthesizing the information, however, provides a holistic view of the child's literacy skills. Children talk to each other and we observe their language. They write and draw and we look at the results of interactions.

The use of ongoing assessment data is supported by research, which illustrates that:

- children begin to develop literacy skills long before they start formal instruction. They use reading and writing skills informally at home.
- oral and written language grow together. Children learn to listen as they learn to speak. They learn to read as they learn to write. The notion that one skill must be learned before another is a misconception.
- children become literate in real-life settings when involved in real-life activities. There is a real need to learn in order to function.
- children learn about written language by exploring print and modeling the behavior of adults
- children learn about literacy at different ages via common stages. A sequence of instructional procedures to guide growth denies individual development (Teale and Salzby 1986, xviii).

4

The First Year of Life: The Foundations of Literacy

The first months of life are so critically vital for preparing the child for learning. Therefore, we will provide an extensive overview of this growth period.

This chapter will answer the following questions:

- What growth patterns characterize the first year of life?
- What activities and materials foster literacy?

The first year of life is a period of remarkable growth and development—many miracles of nature happen in such a short period of time. Within twelve months, a cooing uncontrolled bundle turns into a toddler who communicates and waddles about, making his or her place in the world. A child grows and changes dramatically physically, emotionally, socially, and cognitively during the first year.

What Growth Patterns Characterize the First Year of Life?

Physical Changes

The infant, Ben, spends most of the first three months of his life eating and sleeping, waking only because of hunger or physical distress. As the year progresses, he sleeps through the night and naps during the day. The year begins with meals every three hours and ends with three meals during the day. Ben is four months old before his muscles are strong enough to enable him to hold up his head.

As the months advance, Ben uses his eyes to explore the environments in which he lives and grows. At approximately sixteen weeks, Ben begins to grasp objects. By six months, he can take hold of an object and let it go. When he begins, at four months, to roll over intentionally, crib sides must be fastened tightly to assure that Ben will be safe.

It is fascinating to see Ben begin to hold his own bottle at six months of age. We know Ben is teething when he chews on the nipple with his first tooth.

What a difference one-half year makes: Ben is now able to sit alone, turn over, and recover his balance. He even raises his body at about nine months, pulling himself to a standing position. By one year, a hand-in-hand walk down the street may be a reality.

Special safeguards must be provided when children begin to crawl at six months and to creep at ten months. Cabinets and drawers, for example, must be closed tightly to protect their contents from Ben and Ben from their contents.

Ben explores and learns much from his sense of touch—reaching out, feeling, and trying to grip whatever is in sight.

Emotional Changes

Ben responds to discomforts including hunger, coldness, and wetness by crying. He is using the infant form of instrumental language to communicate basic needs. He expresses emotions during the first year with overall body movements. He kicks and waves his arms furiously—showing by movement and facial expression his discomfort and his pleasure. By six months, Ben has learned how to show affection. He begins to kiss and hug. Fear is another emotion evident during the first year. Preferences, too, are forming: Ben pushes away food, toys, and objects that he does not like.

Social Changes

The newborn is asocial. But within four months, Ben smiles, clearly enjoys being jostled around, and recognizes and responds to his major caregiver. He is fun to watch as he observes and plays with his own hands and feet.

During this first year, Ben plays alone and with others. The attachment to the major caregiver is strong, whereas responses to strangers can be negative. Peek-a-boo and pat-a-cake are favorite games, and these support Ben's growing socialization. Ben begins to imitate the actions modeled by those around him and becomes more and more a part of his environment.

Cognitive Changes

Ben's cognitive development is strongly supported by his active curiosity. He will inspect things for long periods of time. He demonstrates an awareness of the association between objects and activities by opening his mouth when a box opens and shutting it when the box is closed. Ben learns to differentiate between people and objects in this first year; identifying mother (or the major caregiver) and, later in the year, other familiar faces in his environment. Ben searches for hidden objects, imitates actions of others, looks for things in their proper places, and begins and ends actions correctly. Amazingly, too, one-year-old Ben can remember events that happened earlier in the day.

Language Changes: The Foundation for Literacy

All aspects of growth affect literacy development but, assuming normal hearing, learning to talk plays the critical role in this process. It is the foundation of literacy development. Hearing and talking the language are integrally related to reading and writing the language. Caregivers of young children know this. They use talk extensively to socialize the child and to induct him or her into the world and the community (Garvey 1984). Adults know this, and interestingly, babies know it too, for they become absorbed with their new capacity to use words and explore what they can do with these words. Children learn to talk because they are physically able to do so and find they need to. Learning to talk comes as naturally as walking, eating, sleeping, or playing.

Ben talks for many reasons. The development of talk during the first year of life is an amazing process to observe. Babies move through predictable stages and, as they do, they discover rules that tell them how language works. Quite naturally, they learn about the sounds of language (phonology), the rules of language (syntax), and the meanings of words (semantics).

By the end of their first year, young children themselves become absorbed with their new mastery of language and enthusiastically experiment with words and still more words. During his first months of life, Ben plays with sounds. He cries when uncomfortable. When happy, he can make a delightful array of sounds. Caregivers are able to distinguish these cries from the sounds Ben makes to signal his needs. Parents easily learn which cry means, "I'm hungry," and which means, "I'm full." Ben, young as he is, learns easily to use instrumental communication. He cries and makes sounds to get what he wants. Nonverbal communication is used, as well, during the early months to make wants and needs known.

At about 6 months, Ben's babbling seems to become more differentiated. Ben combines sounds in systematic ways—in ways he has heard. He does not need teeth to bring his lips together and create "ma." He likes what he feels and hears and repeats the sound again and again: "ma-ma-ma-ma-ma-ma-ma."

It is at this stage that Ben's parents believe he is learning to say real words. Ben's mother is delighted with "ma-ma" and his father with "da-da." Ben's repetitive language behavior and his parents' joyful responses help him to remember the word. Ben will continue to say "ma-ma" to secure the pleasant hug and sounds he receives. Ben is learning that specific sounds bring specific results.

By the time he is eight months old, Ben's ability to understand language has increased enormously. His understanding will surpass his ability to produce language for some time. First words are learned during these last four months of the first year. "Mommy," "Daddy," "bye-bye," "no," "cookie," and "up" are among Ben's first words. When used, each often represents an entire sentence. "Up," for example, might mean, "Pick me up," or "I want the cookie that is up there," or "I want to be on top of the table," or "Hold me."

The child, in a year's time, moves from a creator of random sounds to a user of language to fulfill specific purposes. Ben's ability to talk is helping to socialize him. His ability to label many new things is giving him control of his world.

What Activities and Materials Foster Literacy?

Birth to Six Weeks

In the first days of life, Ben sleeps fifty-seven minutes out of every sixty; he and his agemates are alert about three minutes an hour during the day and less at night. This alert behavior increases over the next month to an average of six to seven minutes an hour.

Newborns shift easily from a state of irritability to a state of apparent comfort. Quick mood changes persist for months. These persisting shifts are dramatic reminders that infants probably experience life quite differently from adults. Their will exceeds their physical ability. When angry, therefore, they manage to propel their bodies the entire length of a crib by repeatedly digging their heels into the mattress surface and thrusting out with their legs.

Ben, in his first weeks of life, is unusually sensitive. He will startle and cry at any abrupt change in stimulation. Bright lights are bothersome; Ben will try to avoid them. Toward the end of the first month of life, Ben will notice, with interest, features of the caregiver's face.

The major concern of newborns seems to be comfort or the absence of discomfort. Since Ben is easily and regularly discomforted, he is often restless and distressed. Hunger, changes in sounds or temperature, or a disturbance from sleep create an urge for the infant to seek relief. Although newborns are asocial, two simple signs of sociability emerge during the first six weeks of life: Ben may look into the eyes of the person holding him and appear to smile while doing so.

Probably comprehension of language does not exist this early in life. However, Ben can hear. He can discriminate among an impressive range of sounds, even during the first weeks of life. Loud noises are likely to startle him especially when he is awakened by them. Oftentimes, crying follows startled behavior, then Ben needs comforting.

Communication during early months of life is tactile. The newborn needs to be held and hugged and petted frequently. It is important that the major caregiver be an "object for touching." When Ben cries, an immediate response by the caregiver is both desired and desirable. The caregiver must check frequently to see if the infant is distressed.

There are few specific skills that Ben will develop during the first few weeks of life. However, if placed on his stomach several times each day, he can begin to develop the muscles necessary for head-raising. Toward the end of the first month, visual interest seems to appear. Ben will look at simple mobiles again and again.

Literacy Materials and Activities for This Period

Talking and reading to Ben are vital for his development. Although his responses will be minimal, the caregiver's oral communication and affection are essential for healthy holistic development. Talking to Ben during feeding time, reading and singing to him while holding him, and taking care of his needs build good feelings. These actions create the environment necessary for nurturing the roots of literacy.

Reading should occur consistently at similar times each day—after feeding, for example. Language is associated with feelings of comfort during eating. Singing to the baby while rocking him to sleep, reading, or saying and chanting the same poems, rhymes, songs, or lullabies over again build security. Repetition shapes a familiar environment and results in a sense of knowing, which leads to a feeling of security. The following books are representative of those needed to build a foundation for literacy.

Brown, Marc, collector and illustrator. (1985). *Play Rhymes.* New York: E. P. Dutton. Note especially, "John Brown's Baby Had A Cold Upon Its Chest," p. 6. Use words and melody at first. Later, illustrated hand and body motions that accompany all lyrics will be useful.

dePaola, Tomie. (1985). *Tomie dePaola's Mother Goose.* New York: G. P. Putnam's Sons. Note especially "Bow Wow Wow," "O Where O Where Has My Little Dog Gone," "Hickory, Dickory, Dock," and "Diddle Diddle Dumpling." All of these verses are brief and rhythmic and they begin and end with the same line.

Fox, Dan, arranger and editor. (1987). *Go In and Out the Window.* New York: The Metropolitan Museum of Art and Henry Holt. Note particularly for the infant "Hush, Little Baby," "Lavender's Blue," "Rock-a-Bye, Baby," "Oh, How Lovely Is the Evening," and "Twinkle, Twinkle, Little Star." This is a songbook illustrated with art treasures. This treasury could be the beginning of a lifetime library.

Francine. (1985). *Francine Sings a Keepsake of Favorite Animal Songs.* Berkeley, Calif.: Lancaster Productions. This is an audiocassette and song book. For the infant, particularly note, "Once I Saw a Little Bird."

Yolen, Jane, ed. (1986). *Lullaby Songbook.* Illustrated by Charles Mikolaycak. New York: Harcourt Brace Jovanovich. Here are bedtime songs from around the world—some new, some familiar—accompanied by beautiful illustrations.

Six Weeks to Three and One-Half Months

Ben at six weeks is showing a genuine interest in the many things in his environment. He is alert and awake more often; he smiles a lot. Learning is still minimal because of limited skills and minimal control over movement. Still, this age may be the period of the most rapid rate of development. Although Ben cannot yet turn over, reach for objects, or turn his torso, there is more coordination than previously. He can now hold his legs up together and his arms, as well. At the end of three and one-half months, Ben can move his head freely from one side of the crib to the other when lying on his back.

The most remarkable kind of growth in this period is Ben's ability to socialize. At six weeks, Ben's behavior is asocial but at three and one-half months (11 weeks), Ben smiles a lot and appears to study faces. This may occur because there is a dramatic change in his vision. During this period, Ben's vision develops so that his eyes can focus on objects at a distance. He can also focus on objects that are very close (three to four inches away) better than adults with normal vision. It is estimated that a baby at three and one-half months of age has near-mature visual capacity. His ability to see and his insatiable curiosity prod Ben to a continuous exploration of his new-found world.

Ben explores with his hands. Feeling things, reaching, grabbing, and moving them back and forth intrigues Ben. When rattles and small toys are brought near for Ben to examine, his curiosity is intensified. Ben is interested in the human face, in hand movements, and in touching objects. Mobiles must be sturdy for touching. There seems to be a striking increase in Ben's desire to find out everything he can about his environment. His bright glances and alert responsive manner demonstrate an eager curiosity. He appears to be "all eyes."

Ben at three and one-half months is interested in sounds, even his own. He likes to hear records, radios, and the caregiver's voice—in songs and stories. In addition to producing sounds, Ben uses his mouth and gums to explore objects. Fingers are sucked as are objects small enough to grasp and pop into his mouth, so caregivers need to be constantly alert.

Literacy Materials and Activities for This Period

At three and one-half months the caregiver should continue to sing lullabies and songs such as those previously listed to Ben. It is also the time to begin to associate songs with certain movements and to read, associating language with a book. Many small, soft books that can be easily managed by the caregiver while holding Ben are made just for the young child. Chunky books with thick pages should be shared so that Ben and his caregiver can hold the book together. This satisfies Ben's need to grasp. Books with hard, sharp corners should never be used since they may end up in Ben's mouth.

It is important that the same books be read over and over again. The repetition helps Ben and his agemates to build associations and expectations—elements necessary for reading much later on. Books to be read and handled in the bath, the crib, the playpen, or the carriage are usually small; those for the caregiver to share may be larger.

Language in these books should guide adult activities. Caregivers can rock to rhyme to lull the baby to sleep. Folk songs and poems may help when Ben is being bathed.

Playing records and tapes and singing to Ben can begin at this age. In these early excursions into the world of rhythmic sound and song, Ben is delighted and intrigued.

Following are a few of the many books and records available and appropriate for the child who is three and one-half months of age, in addition to the books and tape previously mentioned.

Ahlberg, Janet, and Ahlberg, Allan. (1982). *The Baby's Catalogue.* Boston: Little, Brown. The caregiver should point to the pictures and label them.
Aliki. (1968). *Hush Little Baby.* Illustrated by author. Englewood Cliffs, N.J.: Prentice-Hall. Sing this book.
Hart, Jane, compiler. (1982). *Singing Bee!* Pictures by Anita Lobel. New York: Lothrop, Lee & Shepard Books. Note especially "Bye, Baby Bunting," "Lullaby" (Brahms), "Now the Day Is Over," "Rain, Rain," "Merrily We Roll Along," and "London Bridge."
Langstaff, John. (1974). *Oh, A'Hunting We Will Go.* Illustrated by Nancy Winslow Parker. New York: Atheneum. This song suggests rhythmic movement of caregiver and infant.
Langstaff, John. (1985). *What Do Babies Do?* Photographs selected by Debby Slier. New York: Random House. A "Cuddle Book"—a board book that caregivers can turn to again and again and infants can hold and see themselves in action.
Prelutsky, Jack, selector. (1986). *Read-Aloud Rhymes for the Very Young.* Illustrated by Marc Brown. New York: Alfred A. Knopf. Note especially "The Frog on the Log," "Good Night, Good Night," "Higglety, Pigglety, Pop!" "Little Wind," and "There's Music in a Hammer."

Three and One-Half to Five and One-Half Months

The three and one-half- to five and one-half-month-old child is a delight. His increased bonding with his major caregiver is obvious and joyous. Ben now smiles at his mother and to himself much of the day. During this period, he even laughs and giggles and enjoys exercising his large muscles regularly, turning his torso from side to side. When he is on his stomach, he can lift his head and hold it up for longer and longer periods of time. Small muscles, too, receive much exercise. Ben, at this age, uses his hands as tools to explore—clothing, bed sheets, fabric on the bed bumpers, and other things within reach. Watching Ben watch is fascinating. He is able to concentrate for longer periods of time. He explores not only with his hands but with his eyes, his mouth, and his ears. He clearly listens to nearby sounds and enjoys the sounds he makes himself. He spends a good deal of time exercising and rehearsing motor skills. He responds to people when they are nearby.

The end of the fifth month might be considered a turning point in Ben's development. The social interactions between the caregiver, usually a mother, and the infant are most crucial. Ben is alert to human faces and voices and movements particularly to those of his major caregiver. Ben is learning to respond to expressions and signals. He is learning that particular sounds he makes can get him what he wants; he is (according to Halliday) employing the instrumental function of language. Ben also uses language to regulate behavior (regulatory function), to relate to others (interacting function), and to reveal himself to those in his environment (personal function). Even infants like Ben know they must communicate.

Literacy Materials and Activities for This Period

Environmental preparations and the activities in which Ben engages are determined by his interests. At this early age, we can only assume from observation what Ben's interests are. Table 4–1 describes Ben's behavior and suggests a corresponding, appropriate behavior for the caregiver.

The following list of books and recordings can be added as part of the starter library for the three and one-half- to five and one-half-month-old child.

Degen, Bruce. (1983). *Jamberry*. Ancramdale, N.Y.: Live Oak Media. Here is a merry rendition of the Degen rhythmic, rhyming "berry" wordplay. Infants will respond to the music of the words.

Dijs, Carla. (1987). *Who Sees You: On the Farm*. New York: Grosset & Dunlap. This is a "pop-up and peek" book—sturdy and small with an animal (with a moving part) on each two-page spread. Caregivers should share and demonstrate and set aside for repeat demonstrations. Infants will be fascinated, but it is too early for them to handle the book without acting on the movable parts.

Hopkins, Lee Bennett, collector. (1988). *Side by Side: Poems to Read Together*. Illustrated by Hilary Knight. New York: Simon & Schuster. Note especially the "ABC Song" and "Wee Willie Winkie."

Smith, Jessie Willcox. (1986). *The Jessie Willcox Smith Mother Goose*. Illustrated by author. New York: Derrydale Books. This volume contains 750 nursery rhymes including "Heigh, Diddle, Diddle," "Yankee Doodle," "Pat-a-Cake, Pat-a-Cake," "Bye Baby, Bunting," and "Eye Winker."

Tafuri, Nancy. (1983). *Early Morning in the Barn.* Illustrated by author. New York: Greenwillow Books. All the farm animals are pictured in color and the sounds they make are shown. Caregivers need to cheep, quack, oink, gobble, and cluck.

TABLE 4–1   Observation of a Child's Behavior and Appropriate Response of a Caregiver: Three and One-Half to Five and One-Half Months

Ben's Behavior	Caregiver's Behavior
Wants to socialize.	Play with the child regularly.
Responds to people. Seems to feel intensely about whatever he is doing.	Enjoy the child and many experiences with him or her.
Enjoys the nurturing of one caring adult.	Show affection.
Likes to hear the voice of the major caregiver.	Play talking games while loving the child. Use repeated phrases e.g., upsy daisy, u-u-up-ps-s-y daisy.
Shows excitement in everything seen. Becomes involved in and explores everything within reach of hands and eyes.	Provide a nonglass mirror for the child, placing it about six to seven inches from the eyes.
Is beginning to control his or her torso and head.	Select an infant seat that is sturdy.
Is interested in exploring the world around him, but also interested in new power of turning and reaching—increasing physical strength.	Provide crib toys for kicking, hitting, or pulling.
Enjoys eye-hand exercises. Will take an object and pull it close to him or her. Enjoys the power of controlling objects—will shift an object (rattle) from hand to hand. Likes using hands and watching what can be done with them.	Provide well-constructed books made of tagboard or of cloth. These ought to be touchable with both hands and safe if the child places them in his mouth.
Turns body toward sounds. Begins to repeat sounds for the first time.	Sing and chant songs or verses again and again. Repeat pleasing sounds during play, feeding, and bathing.

Five and One-Half to Eight Months

During the next three months, Ben gains greater command of his body. By the end of this period, he is able to crawl and to satisfy his growing curiosity. In general, Ben is a happy baby.

Peculiar to this age is an interest in small particles. Crumbs, raisins, pieces of thread, and other small things on surfaces spark an intent interest. Playing with small objects is fun. Ben wants to see what will happen if he pushes a ball or shakes a rattle. Ben wants to know what will happen when he drops his toys down from the high chair so he drops and throws them to the floor as often as he can get someone to retrieve them. Dropping, throwing, and banging reflect Ben's interest in the effects of motor actions on objects. Gradually, activities shift from interest in objects to interactions with objects.

In the first six months, cause and effect relationships are not understood but within the seventh month, Ben will become aware of some of these relationships. Memory, an important part of intelligence, is probably limited during this period, but it is developing.

At this time, Ben begins to exhibit abrupt mood changes, moving quickly from one mood to another and apparently at times unable to remember why he had been unhappy. He may require coaxing before he stops crying and starts smiling. During this period, Ben may become shy or apprehensive. He will bond more closely with people within his immediate environment.

Probably the most dramatic and important happening for Ben during this period is the emergence of actual language. Meanings of words will probably be acquired by the end of the eighth month. Ben will know, for example, what the "cookie" looks and tastes like. He will learn that "Mommy" means his mother, and not an aunt, sister, father, or grandfather.

The rate with which Ben acquires language is awesome. Ben and his agemates will respond to many words but not say them until they are one and one-half to two years old. During his sixth and seventh months, Ben's love of sounds grows, and he will indicate his delight with gestures and expressions. It will not always be clear how much he fully understands. He might respond when hearing his name but, often, during the sixth month, it is the intonations of the voice to which he responds, rather than the meaning. By the end of the eighth month, however, this changes. Clearly, Ben begins to respond to specific words.

First words, usually include the name of the major caregiver, "ma-ma" or "da-da," and words such as "bye-bye," "baby," and more. Other first words learned between eight and twelve months are those upon which the child acts. If Ben can see it or do it, he is more likely to learn it (Dale 1976). Words usually comprehended and produced between eight and twelve months include: Mommy, Daddy, other family members' and pet's names, bye-bye, baby, shoe, ball, cookie, juice, and no.

Literacy Materials and Activities for This Period

Ben is now mobile. He will crawl, creep, and get into things. There will be much for the caregiver to cope with.

This is also a period of helping and watching. Observation is critical to guiding Ben appropriately. Observing with the knowledge gained from child development research permits comparisons so caregivers are able to interpret information more accurately and form reasonable expectations. Table 4–2 describes interests and suggests activities for the child at five and one-half to eight months of age.

The following books and recordings meet the needs of the five and one-half- to eight-month-old child. Add these to books previously mentioned.

Demi. (1987). *Fluffy Bunny.* Illustrated by author. New York: Grosset & Dunlap. This is a soft and furry board book cut in the shape of a bunny with front and back covers of soft, furry material. The child will like to feel and hold the book and look at and hear about the bunnies hopping, jumping, and sliding through the pages.

de Regniers, Beatrice Schenk, selector. (1988). *Sing a Song of Popcorn.* Illustrated by nine Caldecott Medal Artists. New York: Scholastic. Time is needed to study the pictures. Share poems "Four Seasons," "There Was a Crooked Man," and "Rain, Rain Go Away."

Hart. *Singing Bee!* Note especially "Sally, Go Round," "To Market, to Market," "The Bus Song," and "Row, Row, Row Your Boat."

Hoban, Tana. (1985). *What Is It?* Photographs by author. New York: Greenwillow Books. Full-page photographs of familiar objects (one to a page) invite children to identify everyday objects.

Mitchell, Cynthia. (1978). *Playtime.* Pictures by Satomi Icikawa. New York: Collins-World. There is much to see in these active pictures and to hear in the active "doing" words (two to a page).

Pomerantz, Charlotte. (1984). *All Asleep.* Illustrated by Nancy Tafuri. New York: Greenwillow Books. Pictures can be viewed and poems softly shared, especially "All Asleep—I" and "All Asleep—II."

Wildsmith, Brian, illustrator. (1983). *The Nest.* New York: Oxford University Press. This is a wordless picture book that allows caregivers to point to and to label branches, nest, leaves, birds, eggs, worms, and deer.

Eight Months to One Year

This period, the beginning of the toddler years, is difficult to manage and difficult for many to understand. In this period intimate relationships are

TABLE 4–2 Child's Interests and Caregiver Activities That Promote Literacy: Five and One-Half to Eight Months

Child Behavior: Interests	Caregiver Behavior: Activities That Promote Literacy
Exhibits curiosity. Likes to look at small objects and take them out of and put them into containers. Will be occupied with this activity for long periods of time.	Provide time, a mat or blanket on a floor, and a variety of small objects and containers in which to put the objects.
Likes to drop, bang, and throw small objects.	Provide a number of dropable, bangable, safe, throwable objects but avoid small objects that might be swallowed.
Wants to know how things work.	Provide stacking objects such as cups that can be placed one atop the other. Provide objects and space for moving things out of the way.
Wants to be loved. Seeks meaningful interaction with caregiver. Responds to and enjoys sounds.	Play hide-and-seek or peek-a-boo. Talk to the baby when involved in activities; e.g., when feeding, talk about the event; when changing diapers, talk about the process by pointing to and naming the items—pins, Pampers. The best talk is about concrete things that are in the immediate environment and activities that are currently occurring. Make a habit of reading aloud to the child, preferably at the same time each day, for example, before naptime. Stories should be short, simple, and full of rhythmic language.
Moves about and explores constantly.	Provide "walkers" to permit the mobility the child needs to explore and exercise. Supervise this mobility.
Likes to solve problems.	Begin to use language that involves simple instructions such as, "wave bye-bye," "give kiss," and "get up."

beginning to form, strong feelings are shared, and experiences are enjoyed or disliked by child and adult. It is the period in which communication to establish bonding plays a major role in growth and development. Children in this period learn how to manage their social relationships through language. They begin to learn both verbal and nonverbal forms of language for sharing ideas, feelings, desires, and needs. These are the foundations for literacy. The conditions, therefore, in which children learn and grow during this period influence greatly their achievements later on in school (White 1975, 107).

Intellectual and social development are of special concern at this stage. Intellectually, children need continuous nurturance of their intense curiosities and their development of language. Both curiosity and language contribute to social development.

Intellectual development is shaped by the eight-month-old child's interests, which include bonding with the major caregiver, mastering motor skills, and exploring the environment. These interests are prompted by an incredible curiosity, the fundamental drive that prompted his or her learning. Curiosity drives the child to find out the why of everything in his or her environment.

Eight months may be a turning point for learning language. The child is beginning to produce, as well as understand, language. The two, language comprehension and production, begin to come together as the child approaches the first year. At eight months, he or she is beginning to understand: what he or she can and cannot do; how much he or she can "get away" with; how to interact with people in his or her life; and how to be a comfortable, delightful, or difficult companion. Some children are not as socially alert as others. But other variations and combinations of behaviors are exhibited by children during this stage.

Some cautions need to be taken during this period. The child during the next fourteen weeks learns to walk, talk, and interact socially. Amazing changes happen in this relatively short period of time. Adults unaware of the stages of development are often both surprised and distressed by the eight- to twelve-month-old child. Because children are inadequate masters of their bodies, they can easily get into trouble. Eighty percent of all accidental poisonings involving children take place between ten and thirteen months of age. It is not surprising that the major caregiver, whose stress may increase as the child's mobility increases, becomes anxious.

Also stressful is the actual damage that babies can do to the environment. They are clumsy, unaware of the value of objects, and controlled by their curiosity. They are also forgetful. For example, a twelve-month-old child will accept the challenge and climb a flight of stairs. Half-way up, the child may stop to investigate an object that has caught his or her eye, forget that he or she is on a flight of stairs, look down, and fall.

Sibling rivalry often appears at this time. Deep-rooted feelings of anger and dislike sometimes result in nasty behavior and attempts by the older child to hurt the younger sibling. These feelings usually become more prevalent in the second year of life.

Literacy Materials and Activities for This Period

Ben's remarkable curiosity includes a continued interest in his own body. He delights in and practices new motor skills. Ben will crawl, climb, stand, and attempt to walk by holding onto objects, and he will stand and stare at objects for extensive periods of time. He will label them with language and gestures if he can. Table 4–3 includes interests of the child during this age and activities related to the development of literacy and growth in general.

What Specific Activities and Materials Should Be Used During the First Year?

We know that children learn to love literature when someone important lures them into the wonderful world of books. Oral language and books

TABLE 4–3 Interests of the Child from 8 Months to 1 Year of Age

Child Behavior	Caregiver Behavior
Shows strong interest in the major caregiver, usually the mother. Makes first requests from him or her, usually for food, or something to suck.	Be available to guide the child. Note when he or she is motivated; provide materials, settings, and time, to facilitate interests.
Expects major caregiver to respond.	Respond to the child with supportive language (if she brings a toy dog, say, "He is a dog like Sandy, our dog. He has big ears like Sandy"). The language is not as important as the attention the child receives.
Likes to focus on objects for long periods of time.	Begin to read to the child. Read books over and over again. Books should have pictures of single objects or letters, or one word in large print, for focusing. Books without words, with large pictures of objects, animals, or people are also recommended.

must be part of the child's life from birth. Book selections and activities that accompany them should be based on the developmental patterns discussed earlier in this chapter. The books, themselves, are less important at this stage than the activities they generate. When the child is seven months old, it is important to begin to focus on the interpersonal nature of activities with books. The child at this age likes to be enticed by adults into activities that satisfy his or her intense curiosity. In part, this means guiding Ben and his agemates to become more aware of their surroundings, including books and print. Activities ought to provide the child with a model for interacting with humans via language, books, and print.

Models for using books and language are necessary for Ben, so he will develop a desire to seek books and interact with them. The major caregiver must read in front of the child, modeling behaviors for the child to imitate and providing books for him or her to hold and see and play with.

Reading sessions with picture books might begin after each feeding. During these sessions, the baby should be held on the caregiver's knee. The baby's back should be supported by the front of the caregiver's body, and the book to be read held at a distance from the baby's eyes. (The most appropriate distance is established by observing the child's focusing behavior.)

The major caregiver should always begin the session with the beginning of the book. Each page is turned as the baby watches. The caregiver can use the index finger of her dominant hand to point first to the left side of the book and, after reading the text, to the right side. If possible, the caregiver should point to an object on a page and name it.

It is important to begin to carry the baby around the home and also out of doors. As the baby is carried, the caregiver should point to objects they pass and name them. Within the house, paintings, photographs, mirrors, lamps, and other large objects attract the baby. Such objects can become the focus for the baby's attention. Outside, cars, trees, plants, garden furniture, and flowers entice the child. When the caregiver labels these, learning is facilitated.

Two kinds of books are recommended for children between the ages of seven and twelve months: books in which an object dominates a page and rhyme-type books.

Object Books

"Object" books recommended here offer one object and its label per page. The infant can hold the book and point to and stare at the objects for long moments.

Bruna, Dick. (1980). *My Toys.* New York: Methuen. Here are many different toys to be recognized and named.

Hill, Eric. (1984). *Spot's Toys.* New York: Putnam. This is one of the many books about Spot, a popular dog character. Here Spot and his toys are pictured on each page.

Lynn, Sarah. (1986). *Clothes. Food. Home. Toys.* New York: Macmillan. Clear, brightly colored board books present familiar objects and their labels. Infants will recognize the objects, point to them, and wait to hear the names.

Mathiesen, Thomas. (1981). *A Child's Book of Everyday Things.* New York: Putnam. Here are many brightly presented, everyday objects infants see inside and outside home.

Oxenbury, Helen. (1981). *Dressing. Family. Friends. Playing. Working.* New York: Simon & Schuster. These are wordless books that invite one- and two-year-old children to name familiar objects on the page and the younger child to recognize the object and wait to have its name supplied.

Rhyme-Type Books

Says Eileen Burke, "Nursery rhymes trigger much verbal activity" (1986, 89) and "All that young children love about literature resides in nursery rhymes" (1990, 108). Although the child in the first year does not use formal language, the seeds for using that language are planted. The repetitive format of rhymes makes them rote-able. Repetition is a strategy for learning with pleasure. Expectancies are set up and gloriously materialize. The desire to hear more is intensified.

There is a strong connection between the child's motor and language development. Catchy language in rhyme and song encourages the child to produce body language and oral language. The language of rhyme becomes easily fixed in memory; it can become part of a child's linguistic and intellectual resources for life. The following list of books of songs, rhymes, and chants can be used as a starter library for the one-year-old child.

The rhythm of such books will facilitate body language and the rhyme in many of them will initiate echoic responses to the last syllable of each verse. These are in addition to pat-a-cake and peek-a-boo and songs like "Down by the Station."

Chorao, Kay, selected. (1984). *The Baby's Bedtime Book.* New York: E. P. Dutton. Here is a compilation of verses meant for naptime and bedtime sharing.

Hayes, Sarah, editor. (1988). *Clap Your Hands: Finger Rhymes.* Illustrated by Toni Goffe. New York: Lothrop, Lee & Shepard. Infants are too young to follow the directions for finger movements here, but they will listen to these 23 rhymes with glee, flex their fingers, and point to the cartoon art.

Hennessy, B. G. (1989). *A, B, C, D, Tummy, Toes, Hands, Knees.* Illustrated by Wendy Watson. New York: Viking Kestrel. A mother and child enjoy time together in this illustrated rhyme book. Caregivers will find many opportunities here to excite curiosity and to satisfy it.

Wright, Blanche Fisher, selected and illustrated (1916, original). *The Real Mother Goose.* New York: Macmillan. Checkerboard binding identifies this collection of a great many rhymes; illustrated and ready for lap sessions.

Zuromskis, Diane S., illustrator. (1978). *The Farmer in the Dell.* Boston: Little Brown. Rhythm, repetition, and illustrations keep infants going on toddlerhood fascinated and bouncing.

A group of single nursery rhyme books and compilations of rhymes and songs follow. All inspire vocalization and movement.

Aliki. (1974). *Go Tell Aunt Rhody.* Illustrated by Steven Kellogg. New York: Macmillan.

Brooks, Leonard Leslie. (1977). *Ring O'Roses.* New edition. New York: Frederick Warne.

Glazer, Tom, editor. "Children's Greatest Hits" Volume 1 and Volume 2. Mount Vernon, N.Y.: CMS Records. Audiocassettes.

Kovalski, Mary, collector and illustrator. (1987). *The Wheels on the Bus.* Boston: Little, Brown.

Langstaff, John. (1974). *Oh, A'Hunting We Will Go.* Illustrated by Nancy Winslow Parker. New York: Atheneum.

Lobel, Arnold. (1978). *Gregory Griggs and Other Nursery Rhyme People.* Illustrated by author. New York: Greenwillow Books.

Pearson, Tracey Campbell, illustrator. (1984). *Old MacDonald Had a Farm.* New York: Dial Books.

Quackenbush, Robert. (1975). *Skip to My Lou.* Illustrated by author. Philadelphia: J. B. Lippincott.

Rae, Mary Make. (1988). *The Farmer in the Dell: A Singing Game.* New York: Viking Penguin.

Spier, Peter. (1967). *To Market, to Market.* Illustrated by author. New York: Doubleday.

Spier, Peter. (1985). *London Bridge is Falling Down.* Illustrated by author. New York: Doubleday.

Tripp, Wallace. (1976). *Granfa Grig Had a Pig and Other Rhymes Without Reason from Mother Goose.* Illustrated by author. Boston: Little, Brown.

Yolen, Jane, editor. (1986). *Lullaby Songbook.* Illustrated by Charles Mikolaycak. New York: Harcourt Brace Jovanovich.

How Do Holdaway's and Halliday's Models of Learning Apply to the First Year of Life?

Four of Halliday's (1975) language functions may be fostered with the activities described in this chapter. They are instrumental language, with which the child satisfies needs; interactive language, with which a bond is built between the caregiver and the child; imaginative language, with which the child amuses himself; and, finally, regulatory language, with which the child controls the caregiver's behavior. In the first year, imaginative language will probably take the form of motor behavior (swinging legs and arms to the beat of a poem, song, or rhyme).

The following description of a reading experience demonstrates the functional uses of language, described in terms of Don Holdaway's learning stages.

Setting

An eleven-month-old child has picked up a book from his crib floor. The picture book pages are colorful and bold. Each page has one word and one animal on it. The word labels the picture. The child makes some sounds. These sounds are, obviously, directed toward his mother, who is standing at the sink scraping carrots for the dinner meal. As the child uses his regular story language which is directed at the mother, the mother stops her activity, and walks over to the child in the crib. She says, "O.K. I'm coming to read you the book." She bends over, picks up the baby, and takes the book from the child's hand. As she takes the book, she says, "Book. I will read the book to Ben."

Stage 1: Observation

A soft armchair holds mother and child. Ben sits on his mother's lap with his back resting on her chest. The mother's arms stretch around the child as she holds the book. She reads, "Brown bear, brown bear, what do I see? I see a red bird looking at me." She runs the fingers of her right hand along the line of this page and other pages. Halfway through the book, Ben places his hands on his mother's hands, and permits himself to enjoy the motion caused by moving her hands along the line of print from left to right. Mother and child seem relaxed, engrossed in the language of the story, and contented. Bill Martin, Jr.'s (1983) *Brown Bear, Brown Bear* is being shared in an environment that makes language and print mesh with love and relaxation.

Stage 2: Partial Participation

Ben, after being placed back into his crib, crawls to the book, *Brown Bear, Brown Bear.* He takes it in his hand, holds it up, and makes some sounds facing toward his mother, who is in the room. His mother, aware of the cue she is receiving from Ben, walks over, picks him up, and settles down in the armchair once again. As she cradles her baby, eleven-month-old Ben takes the book, opens it, and motions as if to say, "Take it and read it to me." His mother does. Ben puts his hand on each page as his mother reads. His mother, as before, follows the print and her voice with her hand, moving it under each line as she reads. At the end of the story, Ben, who obviously enjoyed the book, hits the book with his hand, indicating that he wants to hear the story once more. His mother reads it again.

Stage 3: Role-Play

As his mother reads in her armchair, Ben attempts to do the same in his playpen. He has taken his book, *Brown Bear, Brown Bear,* and is resting himself against the side of his playpen. The book is open and in his lap. He moves his arm in a sweeping motion over a page and moves to the next and does the same. As he moves his arm, he makes a consistent sound, "ahhhhh." This continues until he has come to the last page in the book. He puts the book down, creeps to the other side of the playpen, and looks up at his mother who is still reading. He looks down at the book, back up at his mother, and then begins the activity described above once more.

Stage 4: Performance

Ben makes some sounds directed toward his mother who is in his bedroom. He also picks up his book and shakes it at her. His mother moves toward the child and, as she does, Ben takes the book and begins to point, making sounds and turning pages. Mother watches and smiles as Ben continues until the book is completed. Mother smiles, applauds, and says, "I like the way you read your book. Hurrah!" (as she claps her hands together). Ben laughs, hugs the book, puts it down, and motions to his mother to lift him up. His mother lifts Ben, kisses him on his forehead, and places him in the crib with his book.

Ben's behavior as seen through Holdaway's frame permits teachers and caregivers, alike, to describe knowledgeably the child's interactions with language. It permits adults and children alike to speak about actions, reactions, behaviors, and learning trends from the same point of view.

Summary

Growth during the first year of life is phenomenal and dramatic. Random babbling blossoms into single words or two-word phrases. Crawling and creeping are transformed into standing and, perhaps, an unsteady step or two.

Some of the mysterious sounds made by the infant's caregivers are now understood, and twelve-month-old infants are ready to repeat those sounds—the ones that function for them. They can even create fresh combinations of their own.

Infants at twelve months enjoy rhythm, rhymes, and songs. They demonstrate this enjoyment with body movements, facial expressions, and, later, with sounds. Increasingly alert to the environment, infants begin to focus better, to move in the crib, and then around the playpen, and, eventually, around the room with more agility. They examine everything within the range of eyes and hands. They learn, too, what their own actions can do; e.g., when some objects are pushed, they fall or roll.

An environment complete with love, talk, space, and materials nurtures infants' development. They can attend for longer periods of time and respond to their surroundings by staring and by exercising their increasing motor strength; they test everything and see that they can control certain objects by the ability to kick, hit, push, and pull.

Language is getting infants what they want. They are learning to use certain words that cause caregivers to respond to their needs. They are beginning to see how certain words and actions of theirs generate actions by others. In small but consistent ways, the infant begins to control certain objects as well as the actions of certain people through sounds that represent words.

The infant needs to hear language—to be stimulated by both words from mouths and words from books. Although the infant cannot produce many words, he or she is beginning to understand a growing number of them.

Caregivers of children of this age help development by preparing an environment that meets the infant's needs but also by observing them closely. The role of loving guide-observer best guarantees the infant's wholesome development because it assures the needed bonding and the consistent watching that enlighten planning.

Caregivers concerned about literacy sprinkle the infant's day with functional and funny language. They share pictures and talk. As they bathe and diaper the infant, they name the objects they use. They share daytime and nighttime stories. They fill the infant's day with language and listen carefully to the language the infant begins to share with them. They answer the infant's questions and show their happiness in doing so. They wean infants into the language that furthers socialization, e.g., "bye-bye," "hi," "mommy," and "daddy."

The socialization and intellectual development of infants of this age are very much bound up with language development; each feeds the other. Curiosity about things, their labels, and about people generates more questioning looks, more staring, and more appropriate words—all of which increases curiosity still further. Finding that they can do and say more and more, that they can make some things happen, and that some people respond to them bring to infants feelings of success.

The infant is growing in every way and clearly, on the whole, enjoys it. The upcoming second year of life has its own phenomenal dramatic change.

5

The Second Year of Life

This chapter addresses the following questions:

* What growth patterns characterize the second year of life?
* What activities and materials foster literacy?
* What is the role of the caregiver in nurturing the child's growth toward literacy?

What Growth Patterns Characterize the Second Year of Life?

Sarah is walking and talking; her world is expanding. Walking and talking greatly facilitate such expansion. Sarah's insatiable curiosity guarantees it. Early on, Sarah can explore the playpen and later the room and other areas in her home. Little by little, Sarah gains independence and she becomes less dependent on her caregivers.

From "Da" and "Ba" for Daddy and ball, Sarah's language will grow to "Daddy" or "Dadda" and "Sarah ball." Sarah is learning more and more labels for objects in her world. Such naming is the foundation of categorizing which, in turn, is the beginning of intellectual control of her environment. Sarah's endless mobility combines with her ever-present curiosity to encourage her to see, touch, hold, push, poke, pull, bang, hit, drop, and test every object within reach.

A principal road to literacy for young children is play. The place of play—free-play, pretend play, sociodramatic play, academic play (planned activities), and the more specific block play, sand play—has been much discussed.

Play invites the practice of new skills and behaviors, helps to assure focus, fosters creativity, appreciation, and manipulation of symbols, and self-motivates learning. Play does all of these in a relaxed atmosphere. Play helps problem solving. It is a way of learning.

Rogers and Sawyers (1988) speak of a much cited problem in research. A group of children in free-play realized that by joining devices they can link sticks together, creating one very long stick to secure an out-of-reach article. In an array of such experiments, children in free-play handle the problem better than those who are given a demonstration of how to use the joining pieces. In this case, free-play led to high-quality convergent thinking.

Play appears to support divergent thinking too, that is, the thinking that generates many possible solutions to a problem. [Kogan, 1983]

Whether play is the actual cause of better convergent and divergent thinking needs to be further researched. Certainly, however, there is little argument that play facilitates social development. Not only is it a prime vehicle for the expression of many emotions, but it is also the vehicle for rehearsing real-life roles necessary as children grow in their ability to communicate.

Clearly, not enough has been said about play for the sake of play. In its own right, play provides opportunities for emoting, for appreciating, for socializing, and for feeling. These sensations and the honing of them are not only the heart of childhood, but they are also the focus of all creative efforts of life. Play certainly facilitates the young child's ability to decenter—to think about more than one viewpoint or thing at a time. Role-play (stage 3 of Holdaway's learning model) fosters this ability, a basic life skill.

A balance of free-play and guided play for young children makes sense. Freedom to select, freedom to experiment, and freedom to imagine and pretend are vital. Such free times give rise to new words, new concepts, and fresh alternatives. When children play, they tend to group themselves. Although these groupings are tentative, guided group activities for one- to two-year-old children are vital to things such as safety, social development, sharing of playthings and caregiver's time, and, later, conversing. Rogers and Sawyers (1988) summarize the need for play. They say, "Although play is not a necessary condition for learning language and literacy skills, play is probably the best environment for these abilities to thrive" (p. 64).

During the time from twelve to twenty-four months, Sarah's play will involve turn-taking or peek-a-boo and the joining in on some parts of nursery rhymes and hand rhymes. Sarah likes "Diddle, diddle, dumpling, my son John . . . " and she will try her best to be timely as she joins in. Although she cannot follow the complete story of the three kittens who lost their mittens, she knows when the "me-ows" are appropriate and will join the chant or at least the first syllables. If the caregiver says the first "diddle" and waits, Sarah will offer the second. Through such interactions, Sarah participates in the speaker-listener turn-taking which is the basis of linguistic and most social development. The caregiver's role in this nurturance is clear.

The use of stories such as "The Three Pigs," "The Three Bears," and others like them provoke practice in verbal interaction by young children. Games like "What does the dog say?" and "What does the cat say?" facilitate an awareness of the question-answer form that a considerable amount of dialogue assumes. During these early years, shared stories and poems and songs may not be completely understood. The more the child participates in these, however, the greater the awareness of the need to wait one's turn and listen.

In addition to nursery rhymes and chants, this is the time for Sarah's caregivers to share more name-the-object books. Sometimes such books come in chunky widths because the pages are boards of heavy paper. With one or two simple, clear figures or objects to a page, Sarah begins to identify and label what she finds in these boardbooks, such as Lawrence DiFiori's

The Farm, a boardbook small enough for a young child's hands. On each page is one farm animal or tool for the young child to name.

Dick Bruna's clear, bright, simply drawn figures and objects facilitate Sarah's identification and labeling. The Random House "cuddle books" help young babies see other active babies doing things they normally do. These books offer clear photographs on board pages and invite babies to label the photos and smile.

Twelve to Fifteen Months

Physical Development
At the start of this period, Sarah may still creep or crawl, but she is also beginning to fight her way toward an upright position. By fifteen months, she attains it and delights at her accomplishment especially since her caregivers provide instant praise for each successful try. Of course, say some parents, from that moment on, nothing is safe in the house. Indeed, some time is now spent in child-proofing the house and house-proofing the child.

There are observable increases in Sarah's mobility and an increase in all sorts of experimentation. Sarah can now pick up the small toy that has dropped to the carpet while she supports herself with one hand. She is beginning to stoop and to stand easily and sometimes even gracefully. Sarah grins delightedly as she climbs the stairs on hands and knees. She can climb other things, too—sometimes to the dismay of her caregivers who watch as the rocking chair will not stay in place when Sarah tries to climb it. They know Sarah sometimes resists physical restraint so they hover nearby ready to catch her if the chair goes one way and Sarah the other.

Creeping, crawling, and walking around the floor of the room are far preferable to Sarah than being in the playpen especially since, when she tosses objects out of the playpen, she finds it difficult to retrieve them. She seems to enjoy, whether voluntarily or involuntarily, plopping down from a free-standing position.

Sarah delights—sometimes endlessly—in putting small balls or round objects through rings. She manipulates small objects better than she did a few weeks before, obviously relishing the act of dropping them into containers. She is also quite happy flinging small toys about. Sarah is as mobile and active as her physical development will allow, and her play is becoming more and more diversified.

Since the motor area of the brain controls muscles and is one of the most mature of all functional areas at birth, Sarah early-on can exercise control over her own movements. She delights in testing herself in all sorts of motor activities. Locomotion greatly increases her ability to investigate everything, which she loves to do. Everything Sarah can pull, push, poke, or prod will be hoisted, thrust, punched, and jabbed. Sarah is also learning to turn the pages of books and magazines. As she turns pages, she points to pictures she finds, proudly naming the objects in those pictures.

Sarah loves rhythm and she will move or sway to the primary beat whenever the caregiver provides counting songs. The rhythm in books like *17 Kings and 42 Elephants* or *Crocodile Beat* and the Rhyme books of Marc Brown match this age group's love for strong rhythm and rhyme. The text brings physical and language activities together.

Matching movement to sound may have actually started at infancy. Infants twelve hours old have been observed moving heads, toes, hands, and legs in time with segments of adult speech (Condon and Sander 1974).

Language Development

Sarah bears out the truism that the twelve- to fifteen-month-old child understands many more words than she can produce. Between eighteen months and three years, Sarah's language will grow from certain basic sounds such as /p/, /m/, and /b/ to several hundred words. Sarah responds to all sounds and to many words she herself cannot yet produce.

Researchers Lindfors (1987) and Lieven (1978) tell us that children, even those as young as Sarah, are highly active in shaping the dialogue in which they engage; this is a newly recognized role for the young child. When adult and child verbally interact, the child is as much the shaper of the language and the situation as is the adult. Sarah's "dada" and "ba" may instigate an adult's question, an answer, a direction, or even a hug and lift-up. When she says "Mommy read," she may generate all sorts of verbal and nonverbal behavior. Sarah is clearly active in molding this interchange. This active role continues when she is being read to and when she first begins to scribble. She will raise questions about the reading and remind the reader of missed words; she will also explain what her writing "says" and expect that it will be understood. Sarah loves to scribble; she may start with "back-and-forth" jabs at the paper (McGee and Richgels 1990) to sprawling scribbles (Baghban 1984) to connected circles (Baghban 1984). Sarah may not yet appreciate Crockett Johnson's mini-classic *Harold and the Purple Crayon* about a boy who draws himself some exciting experiences, but Sarah is certainly adventuring with her crayons.

Cognitive Development

As her curiosity is both satisfied and spurred, Sarah and her agemates begin to make associations. At times, it takes an astute caregiver to probe the origin of these associations. The deVilliers tell of their thirteen-month-old son, Nicholas, and what they call an "exotic overextension." Nicholas applied the name of Nunu, the family dog, to the pitted black olives that stared at him from the salad plate in a restaurant. His parents were puzzled but could see, after thinking about it, that their hairy dog had beady dark eyes that probably could be linked to the pitted olives in the salad (deVilliers and deVilliers 1979). Another analogy Nicholas identified was the relationship between his own protruding toes from his all-in-one pajamas, with the turtle who pokes his head from his shell. Nicholas called the protruding toe, "turtle." Nunu, turtle, ball, dog—are all labels for tangible things, the elements of language (nouns) most often found in early talk. Caregivers who take time to name objects in the environment and to repeat those names feed the young child's word hunger. These interactions help to nurture Nicholas' and Sarah's and Ben's new-found ability to associate and organize their experiences.

Emotional and Social Development

Sarah demonstrates her emotions at this stage by using two-word sentences that carry much meaning. She continuously seeks the attention of the caregiver and sometimes becomes aggressive, demanding it. It is now that caregivers have a problem (Garvey 1984).

As Sarah develops socially and emotionally, her personality is formed. "As far as we now understand, personality is grounded in the emotional history of an individual," says David Bleich (1975, 4). Certainly social and emotional development is closely related to personality formation. It is during the second year of life that self-awareness, basic to self-concept and the formation of personality, emerges (Kagan 1981). This is, therefore, a critical period in the development of Sarah's selfhood.

Success and competence contribute to strong self-concept. As Sarah retrieves the toy or stacks the rings or names the object, she strengthens her view of herself. Playing peek-a-boo—taking turns—yields social pleasure, and Sarah will want more social play and social talk in order to enjoy these pleasures.

Babies' facial expressions and gestures generally "tell it all." As Sarah grows, she exhibits more and more emotions. At fifteen months, Sarah is growing in assertiveness, in exhibiting affection, in imitating caregivers, and in displaying negativism, sometimes strongly. Some of these behaviors lay the foundation for the label, "Terrible Twos."

At thirteen to fifteen months, Sarah exhibits the five emotions—disgust, distress, surprise, interest, and the neonatal smile (Izard 1979). She also displays other more complicated emotions through facial expressions, motor activities, and gestures. At this time and earlier, social play with the major caregiver is crucial to the bonding vital to early health and to the development of emotional stability.

The simple miming and chanting of nursery rhymes, bouncing to the beat of "The Duke of York Went up the Hill" or matching movement to the poem "One, Two, Button My Shoe," bring movement, words, and, possibly, melody together.

Toys can become important links in nurturing social contact, but play-things can also become the basis for contention. It is difficult for Sarah at twelve to fifteen months to share (Sarafino and Armstrong 1986). She may offer an agemate a toy especially if that nearby child is crying, but Sarah will quickly want it back (Holmberg 1980). Quick changes of interest are the rule not the exception for Sarah; attention flits from object to object.

At twelve to fifteen months, Sarah may pay attention to the child next to her by looking at and touching her. This is the very beginning of social awareness and development.

Research on the negative impact of separation from the caregiver is voluminous (Ainsworth 1973; Bowlby 1969; Freiberg 1977). Such a negative impact is particularly serious in children from three months to three years of age. The penalty paid by the child who is separated from the caregiver is strongly documented when institutionalized infants are studied (Campos et al. 1983).

Continue the use of song books and nursery rhyme collections cited earlier, and add the following to the twelve- to fifteen-month old child's library.

Literacy Materials and Activities for This Period

Brown, Margaret Wise. (1947). *Goodnight Moon.* Illustrated by Clement Hurd. New York: Harper & Row. A small rabbit bids everything goodnight before retiring. Toddlers will do the same.

Galdone, Paul, reteller (1979). *The Little Red Hen.* Illustrated by reteller. New York: Clarion Books. This story invites participation, role-play, and much discussion. Toddlers quickly learn when to join in with "Not I."

Hoban, Tana. (1986). *Red, Blue, Yellow Shoe.* Illustrated by author. New York: Green-willow Books. This is a chunky board book, colorful and simply designed, that compels the toddler to hold, look, point, and name.

Miller, Margaret. (1989). *My First Words.* Illustrated by author. New York: Thomas Y. Crowell. Also, *In My Room, At My House, Me and My Clothes, Time to Eat, More First Words, Every Day* (1991).

Oxenbury, Helen. (1981). *Family.* Illustrated by author. New York: Simon & Schuster. Also, *Dressing, Friends, Playing,* and *Working.* These are simply-designed, sturdy, small board books about everyday events and routines that babies can easily relate to.

Fifteen to Eighteen Months

Physical Development

At eighteen months, Sarah can walk rapidly without falling and runs awk-wardly. She can climb into an adult chair and turn around and seat herself.

Manipulating all kinds of dials and wheels and opening boxes and other containers fascinate her. Radio and television dials are easy to manage; buttons on appliances are easily pushed.

At sixteen months, Sarah can scribble, deliberately imitating others, and at seventeen months she is likely to show some hand preferences. At the end of this period, she can jump off the floor with both feet. When playing ball, she will use her whole arm, and she can stack more and more cubes or blocks. Sarah constantly experiments; her developing gross and fine motor control facilitates such experimentation which develops still further motor control.

Like other fifteen- to eighteen-month-old toddlers, Sarah still likes to poke, pull, prod, pound, dump, and fling. At eighteen months, her delight is to walk with a pull toy. She begins to show preferences in playthings. She is also becoming adept at stringing large colored wooden beads, dramatizing with a play phone, and blowing bubbles.

Language Development

Somewhere between fourteen and eighteen months, Sarah combines two words and these two-word utterances are packed with meaning. An analysis of these early word combinations reveals that the child who is almost two combines words to express major relationships such as:

Relationships	Language
Existence or labeling	See dog
Nonexistence	No more milk
Recurrence	More cookie
Attribution	Stove hot Bobby mean
Association	Daddy hat Mommy shoe

(Lindfors 1987; Slobin 1979; Brown 1973; Miller 1982; Bloom 1975). Sarah expresses the relationships noted above using varied syntactic structures as she grows. Sarah is also starting to notice that when people act, there are results. She talks of locations ("Mommy here"; "Ball box"). Relationships like sequence and causation are not yet apparent. Caregivers who listen conscientiously may chart the growth toward these more complicated relationships by using a checklist (Table 5–1).

TABLE 5–1 Expressing Relationships in Oral Language

Relationships	Example of language
Existence or labeling of objects	("See dog," "My hat," "Funny baby") Your child's language: _____
Nonexistence of objects	("No more milk," "All gone," "Went bye-bye") Your child's language: _____
Recurrence	("More cookie," "Up, up" (with actions to illustrate "pick me up again") Your child's language: _____
Attribution	("Stove hot," "Bobby mean," "Ben bad," "Sarah eat") Your child's language: _____
Association	("Daddy hat," "Mommy shoe," "Ben cookie") Your child's language: _____

Your child's age when data are recorded: _____
Language caregiver will use to model relationships: _____

What growth patterns are noticed after modeling over period of _____ (time span).

Emotional and Social Development

Sarah at fifteen to eighteen months continues to demand attention. She is easily distracted and gives toys to a caregiver but wants them right back. She may hit out at adults and does not hesitate to say "no." Sarah is illustrating her awareness of the need to gain control over her environment. She understands "taking" better than "giving". She may pinch or poke other agemates but will hug her caregiver, stuffed animals, and dolls. She can be a show-off.

During this period, Sarah has little tolerance for frustration. She claims what she wants as her own and is oftentimes catalyzed into a temper tantrum because of anger or anxiety or tiredness.

Usually children of eighteen months, like Sarah, can look at themselves, say their own names, and label more and more parts of their environment.

Literacy Materials and Activities for This Period
Object books, song books, and nursery rhyme collections cited earlier are useful with toddlers. The following titles may be added to the fifteen- to eighteen-month-old child's library.

Ginsburg, Mirra. (1980). *Good Morning Chick.* Illustrated by Byron Barton. New York: Greenwillow Books. This bright, simply drawn, full-color story of the chick who leaves the egg to explore matches toddlers' own desires.

Hague, Katherine. (1984). *Alphabears: An ABC Book.* Illustrated by Michael Hague. New York: Holt, Rinehart & Winston. A group of active bears journey through the alphabet. Their antics invite much comment.

Hoban, Tana. (1978). *Is It Red? Is It Yellow? Is It Blue?* Photographs by author. New York: Greenwillow Books. Through attractive photographs of everyday objects, the primary colors are introduced.

Oxenbury, Helen. (1985). *The Helen Oxenbury Nursery Storybook.* Illustrated by author. New York: Alfred A. Knopf. These nursery tales, including "Goldilocks," "The Three Pigs," and "Three Billy Goats Gruff" are retold simply and are colorfully illustrated.

Tafuri, Nancy. (1984). *Have You Seen My Duckling?* Illustrated by author. New York: Greenwillow Books. This book is fun for toddlers. Mother Duck has lost a duckling, which the reader can see but mother cannot. Young children keep advising mother and at last she seems to take their advice.

Eighteen to Twenty-One Months

Physical Development
This is an especially active period. Sarah jumps, runs, throws, and climbs. She can walk downstairs if someone holds her hand, and she can climb upstairs with both feet placed on each step. Climbing up onto and down out of chairs is not a problem. Sarah can kick a big ball. She loves to move to the rhythm of words and music.

Sarah is mastering some daily routines. She can easily handle a mug or cup. She can take off her clothes if they are unzipped. Buttons, however, can be a problem. Sarah very much wants to help do things—all kinds of things, such as cleaning, sweeping, or dusting.

Language Development
Sarah at 21 months, can communicate her food and toilet needs and can point to some parts of her body and name those parts. She delights in using the toy telephone, and she engages in humming and singing and repeating syllables. She enjoys hearing rhymes chanted, and she can sing-song her words.

During this period, children create more and more two-word sentences and experiment with longer combinations. Chomsky's theory (1965) explains how children do this. In their creations, they overgeneralize or overextend words ("They runned away" or "He drinked it.") Such overgeneralizations, though unacceptable in adult speech, demonstrate an awareness and logical thinking about certain language patterns.

In cognitive as well as language development, young children overgeneralize. All round things are balls or balloons, and all animals are dogs.

At this age, children enjoy literature to hear and to feel. Dorothy Kunhardt's classic *Pat the Bunny* and the later *Pat the Cat* (E. Kunhardt) offer tactile experiences. Sarah recognizes some of the objects and figures in Peter Spier's *Crash! Bang! Boom!* and will jab the page excitedly as she shouts the name. She dearly loves the caregiver who will render dramatically every sound in the text so that each "crash," "bang," "thump," or "ugh" is given its full power.

Cognitive Development
The eighteen- to twenty-one-month-old child succeeds in placing blocks of various shapes into a frameboard. Sarah can match puzzle pieces to a form outline. She can place pegs in a pegboard.

Children of Sarah's age are fascinated with small things. They can spend many minutes staring at small moving insects. Karla Kuskin's and Aileen Fisher's bug poems are ones they can appreciate. They will share their observations of bugs, snails, and small woodland animals.

Sarah enjoys staring at picture books and delights in identifying whatever she can in each picture.

Sarah is easily distracted by environmental sounds—bells, cleaners, clocks. She loves to handle things and succeeds at putting together two-, three-, or four-piece puzzles. She may even be ready to enjoy such books as *Animal Walk* (Dreamer), a combination of book, toy, and puzzle.

Emotional, Social, and Personality Development
Sarah is anxious to communicate and will try to share experiences even if her vocabulary is insufficient. She is happier with familiar people and, therefore, seeks them. She continues to play near but not with other children. She talks to herself as she works. Characteristic behaviors of this period include acting out an adult role or fantasy character; playing in water, sand, and dirt; scribbling with crayons; and hugging familiar adults, not strangers.

At this time, Sarah is beginning to understand that favorite adults may have to divide their attention among several children. During this period, Sarah will repeat an action demonstrated if told to "Do this." In fact, Sarah enjoys turn-taking and I-do-you-do games.

Literacy Materials and Activities for This Period
Add the following books to Sarah's library at eighteen to twenty-one months to increase her love of language.

Bruna, Dick (1972). *b is for bear.* New York: Methuen. This bright, clear, and simple alphabet book presents a letter and an appropriate object on each set of two pages.

Eichenberg, Fritz. (1952). *Ape in a Cape: An Alphabet of Odd Animals.* Illustrated by author. New York: Harcourt Brace Jovanovich. These zany animals and rhymes must be seen and heard.

Potter, Beatrix. (1902). *Tale of Peter Rabbit.* Illustrated by author. New York: Frederick Warne. Peter's punishment for disobedience was not as bad as it might have been. All toddlers breathe a sigh of relief at this. This is a tale toddlers easily relate to; talk abounds.

Sendak, Maurice. (1962). *Chicken Soup with Rice* (Nutshell Library). Illustrated by author. New York: Harper & Row. Here is the happiest of calendar songs; it must be heard and sung. Available in record.

Sendak, Maurice. (1962). *Alligators All Around* (Nutshell Library). Illustrated by author. New York: Harper & Row. This is a mini-alphabet book. On each page is a capital letter, a comical picture, and an alliterative phrase.

Spier, Peter. (1972). *Crash! Bang! Boom!* Illustrated by author. New York: Doubleday. Full of everyday objects and environmental sounds, this book is ideal for pointing to, labeling, and sounding out. Toddlers delight in hearing the sounds and will try to mimic their caregiver's efforts.

Ziefert, Harriet. (1987). *Where's the Cat?* Illustrated by Arnold Lobel. New York: Harper & Row. Also, *Where's the Dog? Where's the Guinea Pig? Where's the Turtle?* The toddler can follow the everyday antics of the cat, dog, turtle, or guinea pig, and then, happily, find the animal under a flap at the end of each book.

Twenty-One to Twenty-Four Months

Physical Development
At almost two years of age, Sarah can walk up and down the steps alone. She almost never falls. She runs with a fair measure of coordination, pedals a small tricycle, strings more large beads together, and piles more and more blocks on top of each other. Sarah is able to imitate by copying circles and vertical lines. She continues to delight in pushing large wheel toys and bounces and sways to the music, even "dancing" a bit.

Language Development
This period is characterized by greater use of pronouns, many echoed words, and the beginning of a personal repertory of favorite nursery rhymes and chants. Sarah responds to stories like *Ask Mr. Bear* (Flack), *The Little Red Hen* (Galdone), *The Three Billy Goats Gruff* (Galdone), enthusiastically participating by joining in and saying repeated phrases. Children at almost two

years can point and name familiar people and label more and more familiar objects. Sarah can tell you her full name, and she uses descriptive terms like "pretty," "dirty," and "yucky." Sarah loves to hear "The Wheels on the Bus Go Round and Round" and "London Bridge Is Falling Down."

During this period, Sarah is comfortable using language to talk about things out of sight. She giggles at onomatopoeia and alliteration. Excursions in cars, to parks, to malls, and to grandparents' homes result in Sarah's acquiring more words to label things. Games like "Ring Around the Rosy" and dances like the hokey-pokey help facilitate the development of listening skills. These and other games prove that Sarah understands many more words than she can produce. Sarah likes to talk about her experiences. In fact, she just likes to talk and often talks to herself as she plays.

Cognitive Development

The child of almost two mimics words, imitates writing, and can copy the counting behavior of adults. She will apply number names to cookies or toys, giving early evidence of a budding understanding of counting behavior. Sarah manipulates playthings with more skill and control than before and takes great pride in telling others "Me do."

The attention span of the almost two-year-old child is brief. She moves quickly from one activity to another. She is more interested in discovering and, to some extent, exploring than she is in fully savoring an experience. Holdaway's sequence for literary experiences (1979) discussed in chapter 3, namely discovery by observing, exploration when partially participating in an activity, or rehearsing alone, and independent experience/expression, is developing. Sarah discovers the melody and cadence of words. She explores the book or poem by participating in the repetitive sections of the story—moving, humming, clapping, acting out, and saying the words as the song or poem is shared again. Eventually Sarah experiences the book independently, seeking the book, thumbing through its pages, staring at the pictures, pointing, and talking as she turns the pages. Sarah enjoys picture books for longer periods of time and can now turn the pages smoothly for herself. Sarah's ability to follow the natural learning sequence described by Holdaway is not yet a behavioral pattern. She finds stories about the everyday world particularly interesting; she can point to and label things in pictures and she wants her favorite tales shared again and again.

Emotional, Social, and Personality Development

As has been noted, the nurturance of the child's self-esteem and healthy ego needs to start early. Play is important and fantasy play, which permits Sarah to function for a time without the need to conform to reality, can be a strong support to healthy personality formation.

Sarah's understanding that the caregiver's time and attention must be shared is growing slowly but surely. She will try to engage in all sorts of activities and household tasks to be near her caregiver and to demonstrate that she is growing up and "can do it herself."

Although Sarah still needs and seeks approval, her chief caregiver may be absent for a time without Sarah staging a tantrum as long as another familiar adult is present.

The profusion of "no's" of earlier months may be declining, and an adult may smile to see a child, trying to follow the "rules," engage in telling others to "shh" or "too noisy." According to Garvey (1977), the two-year-old still has a great deal to learn about how to play with others.

Literacy Materials and Activities for This Period

Add the following books and songs to the library shared with the twenty-one to twenty-four-month-old child.

Bruna, Dick. (1968). *I Can Count.* Illustrated by author. New York: Methuen. The simplicity of the format keeps the young child's attention.

Francine. (1985). *Francine Sings a Keepsake of Favorite Animal Songs.* Audiocassette and songbook. Berkeley, Calif.: Lancaster Productions. This collection includes "Bingo" and "Once I Saw a Little Bird." Sarah is ready to learn more animal songs from this collection, previously mentioned.

Galdone, Paul, reteller. (1981). *The Three Billy Goats Gruff.* Illustrated by reteller. New York: Clarion Books. Toddlers may shudder at the fearsome troll but delight in his comeuppance. This must be enacted.

Martin, William, Jr, and Archambault, John. (1989). *Chicka Chicka Boom Boom.* Illustrated by Lois Ehlert. New York: Simon & Schuster. Here is visual, verbal fun. Toddlers will want to look at it again and again and hear it over and over.

McCully, Emily Arnold. (1984). *Picnic.* Illustrated by author. New York: Harper & Row. In this wordless book, a lost mouse child is happily found.

Pearson, Tracey Campbell. (1986). *A Apple Pie.* Illustrated by author. New York: Dial. This book folds out to eighteen feet to accommodate the twenty-six hungry children who devour the pie.

What Activities and Materials Foster Literacy and What Is the Role of the Caregiver in Nurturing the Child's Growth toward Literacy?

For the walking and talking child of twelve to twenty-four months, the physical environment must be free of obstacles she might trip over. Many objects, however, must be available for Sarah so she can experiment in order to develop further oral communication and the beginnings of writing. Sarah feels secure in an environment that offers safety, space, and developmentally appropriate objects that are manipulative.

Materials seem to make a difference in terms of symbolic play, that solitary pretend-play that precedes representational thought. Representational thought, according to Piaget, is the first level of cognition. It is nurtured by play with real materials—a real spoon or a real bottle—even if the objects are on a smaller scale. It is these materials that help children best in forming the symbols and images of the real world—the symbols and images needed for representational thought.

This is a time of increased exploration. Sarah needs to test and create, watch and imitate, and pretend and move about. Space must be provided so Sarah can manipulate objects, look at scenes and pictures, hear the sounds of language, and test the new knowledge gained from new experiences.

As oral language develops and differentiates, Sarah moves from purely heuristic language (searching for information) to instrumental, interactional, personal, and imaginative talk (see chapter 3). In an environment nurturant of these functions, caregivers tend to the "I want's" of the toddler, respond and question in order to facilitate interactional talk, acknowledge and sometimes share personal anecdotes in response to the personal language of the child, and may greet imaginative speech with delight and even some drama. Sarah's environment serves her well if all of the items in Table 5–2 are addressed. If Holdaway is right, " . . . there is a wealth of evidence . . . indicating that literacy skills develop in the same 'natural' way as spoken language when the conditions for learning are comparable" (1979, 20).

The question is whether or not the environmental conditions are always comparable. Spoken language is developed informally. Situations trigger its use; how language is used depends on its intended function. Clearly, an environment to nurture literacy capitalizes on spontaneity. Healthy language environment provides for risks that can be taken without encountering abuse or rebuke. In a sense, risks are the stepping stones for growing.

Success comes from trying and failing and trying again. Settings are warm and nurturant. They invite chatting and chanting and humming and dancing. They also nourish the toddler's growing ability to use symbols to communicate and understand his world. Chants and rhymes are repeated because Sarah takes joy in that repetition. Caregivers hear the growth from unidentifiable chanting to clearly understood humming sing-song. It is the trial and trial again that guides the growth of Sarah's oral language.

Preparing the environment begins with the nurturing process of bonding, attaching the child emotionally to the principal caregiver. This is crucial to the young child's well-being, for it is the undergirding of positive social and emotional development. Although differences exist concerning the definition of the most critical period for establishing a loving bond, certainly the early months and the second year of life figure strongly in such estimates (Ainsworth 1973).

TABLE 5–2 Creating an Environment That Nurtures Growth Toward Literacy

Environmental Conditions	Comments
Preparing Space There are places to store toys, books, and objects to manipulate. Some storage space is open so a child can see and select objects for himself or herself. There is space to pull and push toys and objects. There is space for chairs. There is space for adult and child to share together, when appropriate.	
Preparing Time Caregiver spends time demonstrating how to look at books. This adult models the behavior by doing what the child is learning to do. Caregiver makes time for the child to look at books on his or her own and in the presence of the caregiver. Private times are available for pretending. Time is available for listening to the child ("I want," questions, imaginative speech, etc.). Time is available to respond to all questions, even those that seem unimportant. Time is arranged so that the child can expect to interact in a special way (i.e., pretend play, sharing a book or experience, play with push-or-pull objects, etc.)	
Supplying Real Objects The environment includes spoons, forks, spreaders, plastic dishes, stuffed animals, stuffed toys representing book characters, dolls, pull toys (including trucks or cars, animals, wagons, or doll carriages), and containers with and without lids to put things into and take things out of. Containers are included to store small real objects.	

Continued

TABLE 5–2 *Continued*

Environmental Conditions	Comments
Supplying Materials to Nurture Literacy The environment has books, including picture books with rhymes, repeated words; named objects; animal stories with simple plots; songs; wall pictures and posters that remind the child of recent stories heard; familiar objects in the child's world; records or tapes of stories and songs; crayons; paper without lines; chalk; and large pencils for writing and drawing; simple puzzles; and blocks.	

The personality characteristics of the caregiver are critical to establishing bonding. Mothers, for example, who lack confidence may be rather tense and irritable, disinterested in and insensitive to the child's needs. These characteristics create anxieties in their children (Egeland and Farber 1984).

Caregivers who assure the young child easy access to toys and people, who restrict the child spatially as little as possible, and who help the child play on his own (Frodi, Bridges, and Grolnick 1985) are nurturing the development of competence and positive self-concept. Building a sense of personal and positive self-concept is probably the most important human variable in terms of a child's holistic and literacy development. When the caregiver says, "I really like the way you put the toys in the box," he is shaping a desire to do that again. Statements like "Put it in your way" encourage experimental manipulation. In such building, caregivers spread both physical and psychological safety nets for the toddler—nets that support rather than smother the child's development.

To serve the toddler best, a caregiver must also be a careful observer. Such a mind-set may appear antithetical to bonding, but the caregiver can preserve a close bond with the child while observing her behavior and noting additional needs. Supporting the child's continuous reach for independence can be accomplished while carefully watching the child; i.e., a balance can be preserved between the bonding and the observing tasks. The following caregiver's behaviors provide the foundations for nurturing the toddler's growth toward literacy:

- talking and listening to children. In addition to the need to hear language, young children must become accustomed to the turn-taking that interaction requires and full communication necessitates. As the caregiver responds to the child's one- or two-word utterances, she learns to wait for a response to the words she has said. Curiosity then propels a fresh statement or question and another response is activated. The caregiver's inclination for expanding the child's language is doing what comes naturally. This practice may cause the child to reinterpret her surroundings and revise or reorder her perceptions.

Certainly, the caregiver who exposes the child to much meaningful language by responding to her statements and questions and shows enthusiasm for them is reinforcing the development of oral communication. As the young child responds, she too shapes the direction of the dialogue. Caregivers nurture communication when they verbalize their actions as they play games with the toddler. ("I am dressing my baby. First I put his socks on. . . . ") As the child and caregiver open and close the lid of a box while acting out the movements, they can verbalize "open" and "close." The touch, sight, and sound merge. Caregivers nurture the development of literacy when they show delight and when they sing, chant, mime, and move with children.

- chanting and singing to and with children. Movement is a natural accompaniment to chant and song; this, along with enthusiasm, yields new wordplay and new chants.

   Cassette renditions like *Favorite Animal Songs* offer young children a marvelous group of songs from "Where Oh Where Has My Little Dog Gone" to "Bingo" and "The Bear Went over the Mountain." Their endless verses are useful throughout preschool and the primary grades for inviting children to repeat melodies and lyrics. Audiocassettes plus books (in this case, with simple piano accompaniment) will also nudge children to repeat melodies and to create diverse movements in response to the lyrics. Using Marc Brown's Rhyme series—*Play Rhymes* and later *Hand Rhymes* and *Party Rhymes*—caregivers encourage both listening and participating by chanting and moving appropriately with the rhymes. This is the start of echoic (echo-type) reading behavior. Singable and rhythm and movement inducing, such activities lead to happy rote-learning and chanting by young children.

- filling the home or nursery school with objects to poke and prod, stroke and swing, fit through openings, test, hold, and talk to. Dolls need to be mothered, soothed, hummed to, talked to, hugged, and scolded. Caregivers see that all sorts of containers are placed around the room to fill up and empty while "full" and "all gone" label the actions. Large crayons and large sheets of paper are available. Engrossed in the act of creating, Sarah draws a mouse and calls it "mouse" as she maneuvers her crayon and deliberately fashions more squiggles. This might be considered the beginning of writing.

Playing catch provides "to-you—to-me" cooperative activity while it helps the development of gross motor coordination. Caregivers who say names with each throw help to accent the verbal throw-catch and give-take basic interaction pattern of communication.

Giving young children their own choices in selecting an object to play with requires the instrumental language Halliday defined—the "I want's."

- sharing books, stories, and poems. Caregivers carry poems and stories in their heads and fill the home and nursery with jolly picture books and posters. Language is generated when pictures are viewed. Large figures and small details are noticed and commented upon.

The language of story and song should fill the air. When reading to Sarah and Ben, the caregiver is modeling book behavior. Page turning, left-to-right eye movement, and top to bottom of page—all of these are noted by the child. Later, the two- to three-year-old children themselves enjoy turning book pages and detecting new things to label. Young children imitate the singing and join in.

From any one of many nursery rhyme compilations or poem anthologies such as *Side by Side* and *Read-Aloud Rhymes for the Very Young*, the caregiver can select rhymes to fill the ears of young children with rhythmic, rhyming, sometimes alliterative, and onomatopoeic speech. Cassettes and records abound in a story corner. In preschools this corner announces the special place stories hold in programs. Stories, of course, can be shared anywhere. In schools and day-care centers a story hour or special time set aside for sharing tales and poems is essential to assure the child that story sharing is important. In no case, should stories be limited to the hour set aside.

At home, a very special routine time for the toddler is just before sleep when delightful end-of-day tales can be enjoyed by child and caregiver. Margaret Wise Brown's *Goodnight Moon* is a classic. Eve Rice's *Goodnight Goodnight* or a poem from Lee Bennett Hopkins' *Go To Bed! A Book of Bedtime Poems* will interest and soothe young children at day's end; through such tales all sorts of words will be added to the listening vocabulary of young children. Aliki's *Hush Little Baby* may instigate some participation initially but, as the caregiver reverts from song to hum, toddlers will begin to nod.

Unlike bedtime stories, during-the-day stories should have lots of action and accompanying movement.

- the caregiver in nursery school or the day-care center understands that children at almost two years can play close to, but not necessarily with, other children. The young child is unpredictable in associations with other children and will just as soon quietly watch them as ignore or push them. Caregivers must be particularly watchful to support but not to force sharing. The sociodramatic play (i.e., pretend play which reflects social experience [Garvey 1977] and in which very young children respond to the imagination of others) probably comes later at about three years of age (Fein 1983). However, the beginning of such imaginative role-playing may be apparent after two.

- young children begin to understand that there is, whether in home or center, a time to sleep and a time to snack, a dress-up time, and a clean-up time. The caregiver guides actions natural to such times: the use of spoon and cup, the zipping and snapping in and out of clothes, the listening-to-story posture. With guidance, the young child grows to manage her world.

- the toddler needs guidance in saying and gesturing "hi" and "bye-bye," finding hidden objects, marching rhythmically, stacking blocks, and threading big beads. The guidance and activities help her toward independence and social ease, resulting in a feeling of control and competence. Daily success in an array of major and minor challenges supports self-esteem and independence in a way that nothing else does. The successful labeling of "cat," "dog," "bead," and "ball" in a book sends a smile to the young child's face.

An enthusiastic, caring, observing adult is the greatest asset to any young child's environment. This caregiver is the someone who is always "on call"—ready to listen, respond, and guide.

The checklist in Table 5–3 will help parents, grandparents, day-care center caregivers, and others to monitor their actions in order to enhance the child's environment for language learning.

Sarah Acts and Role-plays

Sarah and her agemates need the freedom of large paper and large writing tools to draw their messages. They also need to learn to fit one- or two-piece puzzles into place accurately. Young children may work with blocks all alone for some time, but they need to know, perhaps by quiet modeling, that blocks can be placed several different ways. They also need to know that the blocks are for everyone's use.

Sarah is given materials and space to scribble and to build with blocks, and she talks as she works. Her senses—taste, smell, sight, hearing, touch—help her to play. The more her senses are stimulated, the greater is the intensity of experiences and the greater urge Sarah has to talk about these if only to herself.

Playing with objects, with words, and with games and acting out real-life roles in dramatic play are all conducive to emergent literacy. Objects

TABLE 5–3 Building Self-Confidence and Language Together: A Self-Monitoring Guide for Caregivers

Caregiver Action	Comments
I reward desired behaviors by using direct praise, that is, naming the behavior. Examples include: "I like the way you put the doll in her bed," "I like the way you went to the potty all by yourself," "I like the way you finished all of your dinner."	
I know when to let the child play, and solve problems on his or her own. I know when to help avoid frustration in order to preserve the desire to solve the problem.	
I look at and listen attentively as the child talks to illustrate the "wait-response" activity of interactive language behavior.	
When the child uses one or two words to describe or express ideas, I expand on the language in order to provide a model for learning. "Sarah eat," would be expanded to "Sarah is eating her dinner," for example.	
I identify actions as they happen. When, for example, a box is opened, I say, "open." When it is closed, I say, "closed."	
I repeat action rhymes and do the actions simultaneously.	
I engage the child in cooperative-type play activities. Playing catch and using a pegboard together are examples of such activities.	
While I do my work, I also chant and say favorite rhymes, poems, and sing-songs. This continuous exposure enhances the joys of language.	
I read books that accompany routines. Bedtime stories are by the bed; stories about the doctor and the zoo are in the child's library.	
Routines—naps, meals, storybook reading, and getting dressed—are scheduled at the same time daily. Routine develops expectations and the child can predict what comes next. Anticipating forthcoming events (outcomes) is important for reading in school.	
I am "on-call" continuously, providing responses, modeling, and lending a listening ear.	

intrigue Sarah. At two, she picks up, holds, and turns blocks. She works with cups, saucers, and spoons, and by the end of this period, she can use them to achieve her purposes. She starts stacking blocks and placing them side by side and experiments with how they go together.

According to Garvey (1984), young children can begin to link action patterns with functional wholes. They do this when they role-play cooking and eating and cleaning up. Sarah will brush her hair and her doll's. As she brushes her doll's hair, she will note "Dolly hair messy." When she is finished brushing, she'll report satisfactorily "Dolly pretty." She may parody the cat's meow and the dog's bark as she plays with them. Later, Sarah will imagine she's stirring tea or coffee or baking a cake.

By acting on objects and talking along the way and by interacting with adults, Sarah engages in symbolic play, the predecessor of the development of language and abstract thinking. Diverse objects will spur different kinds of thought, so Sarah needs a variety of things to play with.

Sarah pretends; things like large boxes can become a "house" or the "bunny's house." Language accompanies pretense because Sarah has to tell her caregiver and others what this box really is. Then Sarah may go on to role-play the inhabitants of the cottage or begin to place her stuffed animals inside, regulating their behaviors by ordering them to "Stay there," and "Be good."

Later, between the ages of two and three, Sarah uses crayons and paper to scribble loops and draw vertical and horizontal lines. She is in the stage where recurring text is created. As she explores books, she turns the pages, names the objects on the pages, and tells her own picture stories. She must have cupboards and doors to close and open. She wants balls to roll and toss or drop into boxes. She needs beads to string and during rhythms, bells to ring.

Sarah at two can act emphatically. She can throw a tantrum, negate and reject, chuckle and cry.

Sarah engages in activities outside and inside home and nursery school and can name outdoor things like tree, bird, flower, and swing, as well as indoor things like chair, table, and sink. Because of her mobility and her daily reintroductions to words and actions, she remembers more names more often.

Sarah can count by rote. She can take some things apart and put them together again so she needs materials she can string and separate.

Sarah Listens and Observes

Sarah listens to sounds of the environment, to conversations, to directions, to lullabies, to stories, and to poems. She has beads to string. When they fall, they make a "ping" sound. Sarah says "ping" as she hears the sound. Sarah listens to the direction and drops the toy in the big box. She likes the "plop" she hears and does it again. Sarah listens to the audiocassette of "Old MacDonald Had a Farm." The observer sees and hears her join in at the end of each animal's sound. Sarah hears "snacktime" and moves toward the table. Sarah gets ready to "fall down" at those words in the "Farmer in the Dell" and to march up and down the hill as she hears "The Noble Duke of York."

Sarah lives in a world of sounds. Some of these sounds facilitate her desire to imitate for they are funny enough to try to say; some result in Sarah's acting or moving. Sarah differentiates the sounds and responds to certain words. The ability to discriminate and differentiate sounds is part of the exploration of the workings of language. Sarah is not only learning language but also is becoming conscious of paralanguage, the tonal features of language, and the suprasegmentals, pitch, stress, and juncture. She responds to a whisper; she responds to the stress and juncture of the accented beat of a march; she responds to the rising pitch of a question. She loves it when her caregiver dramatizes words and roars like a lion and growls like a dog or points to something in Peter Spier's book *Crash! Bang! Boom!* and imitates the sound. Sarah tries to follow along.

The sounds of the environment in which Sarah lives nudge all sorts of reactions from her. She is guided by certain sounds to a state of readiness for snacks and moves to the table. She mimics and echoes sounds she hears. She asks "What dat?" and waits for an answer. She moves out of range of the "swish" of a broom.

From all noises in the home or nursery classroom, Sarah learns and selects those noises meaningful to her. As the caregiver shares stories in big books, Sarah listens and sees her finger move under the words. Sarah is provided with actions that tell her that sound and finger movements are related. She is provided with guidance that begins to make her aware of print.

As the caregiver says, "Sarah," he points to a strip of paper with Sarah written on it. Sarah begins to recognize this as hers. Sarah sees the group of letters later on a birthday cake or birthday calendar and hears "Sarah" again. She sees them embroidered on a new sweater given to her by a friend. She learns to relate these letters to herself, to the word "Sarah."

Sarah Watches and Observes

Sarah lives in a world of sights as well. The big posters, friezes, and picture books are full of things she wants to know about. She points to these things and asks "What dat?" She knows these things have names, and she wants to be able to label them herself. She is telling her caregiver that she knows that words name objects.

Her nursery classroom and home are full of strange squiggles on pieces of paper that make people do things or make sounds. For example, the refrigerator door at home may have some of these. The black marks in the book the caregiver reads seem different from the squiggles on the refrigerator door, but the squiggles and the marks, wherever they are, make people say sounds or do things.

Sarah watches the caregiver say these sounds and move her finger from left to right, and when the sheet of paper has lots of marks, move down the sheet. Sarah knows "book" and she will, at two, turn the pages although not always from front to back.

As Sarah continues to watch her caregiver read, she notes that eyes and fingers move to the sounds. She likes what she hears, for the sounds are stories. It seems that writing and speech are related. Sarah watches further as the caregiver prints her name on the calendar and says, "Sarah."

After a while, Sarah begins to think she can make those sounds and squiggles and she picks up the crayon and starts talking as she does. Again, somehow she knows that writing and speech are related and that writing and speech relate to the stories she loves.

Sarah is hearing and seeing more words. She is seeking more words each time she uses language heuristically. She watches her agemates as they hide and then seek. She watches and hears and learns that she must take her turn at blocks, beads, and the sand pile. As she watches her agemates wait for the caregiver's attention, she is beginning to get a further sense of what "waiting your turn" means as well as the "your-turn, my-turn" interchanges of talking and listening.

Sarah lives in an appropriate, supportive environment rich in materials and caring. She is emerging toward literacy in such an environment. Her caregiver is not only caring but observing. Mother, father, and teacher structure the environment so that Sarah can play freely. Caregivers do not hesitate to guide Sarah and her agemates in small but flexible groups in various activities. Both caregiver and environment lay the foundations for literacy to emerge in Sarah.

Summary

At two, children participate in storytelling and know when to join in. They enjoy name-the-object books and the sounds of rhyme. They learn quickly that what they say does matter.

Two-year-old children delight in their increased mobility; they explore thoroughly the boundaries of their space—horizontally and vertically. They constantly engage in making associations and in exhibiting a range of emotions, and they continue to adjust to the turn-taking of talk and of games like peek-a-boo. One- to two-year-old children are dependent upon strong bonding with their caregiver(s). They seek closeness and affection and will consistently offer to help the caregivers in every way possible in order to attach themselves more strongly to these special people.

Motor control, at two, intensifies for both fine and gross muscles. The toddler can do more and so tries more, always experimenting and testing. Extensive experimentation also characterizes the toddlers' language development. Their two-word utterances are packed with meaning and are lengthening. They effectively continue to shape conversations with adults.

Environments nurturant of literacy for the one- to two-year-old are ample in space, rich in real materials and objects to manipulate, generous in time for pretend and real play, and resounding in language, talk, and song.

Caregivers who nurture literacy establish loving bonds with young children and provide easy access to toys and people. They comfort, praise, and demonstrate literacy behaviors by talking and listening, singing, and chanting with them. They share books, stories, songs, rhymes, and chants. They guide the formation of early social relationships, and they preserve stability while nurturing the toddler's freedom to choose among objects or types of play. They plan for the toddler's success in simple tasks.

Toddlers' experiments are important and valued and so are toddlers' scribbles and participation, verbal and nonverbal, in stories and poems. The caregiver's use of oral and written labels to accompany relevant and real activities underscores the toddler's growing awareness that things have names and that there are squiggles that are related to these names. The toddler observes that such squiggles make people talk and act.

The two-year-old child ventures into language activities through free-play and guided play. Caregivers watch the play and utilize what they see to facilitate more learning.

A beginning awareness of the sounds of language and a glimmering of the meaning-making processes are unfolding. Expansions of these processes in the toddler's life and development characterize the third year of life.

6

The Third Year of Life

This chapter addresses the following questions:

- What growth patterns characterize the third year of life?
- What activities and materials foster literacy?
- What is the role of the caregiver in nurturing the child's growth toward literacy?

What Growth Patterns Characterize the Third Year of Life?

The twenty-four- to thirty-six-month-old child is a buoyant, bouncy, robust toddler. Running replaces walking; exploring continues; questioning increases; fantasy and fact still confuse; everything seen must be touched.

Friendships are off-again, on-again. In the last half of the third year, determination and sometimes stubbornness and assertiveness justify the label "terrible twos." It may be that the child now has just enough command of locomotion and language so that independence appears attainable. In any event, this is the "I do it myself" period when caregiver intervention can be viewed as caregiver interference.

Ben, at three, needs guidance but does not always appreciate it. The caregiver role requires astute balancing and timing. The thrust toward independence demands nurturing, but caregivers must recognize when the inability to achieve it exists to cushion frustration.

Language is a symbol system. It is important to note that at about the beginning of this period—at twenty-four and twenty-five months—children can symbolize. For Piaget, this ability signals preoperational thought. Earlier, at about thirteen months, Ben began to understand that there is a relationship between a symbol and its referent and that the symbol can be substituted for its referent (Bates 1979). Symbolizing becomes a natural activity when Ben and Sarah hear and talk about folklore, literature, music, and art. According to Egner (1989), this symbolizing is manifest in imaging their own stories.

> . . . *if children have a rich variety of stories available to them and many opportunities to imagine and to place themselves in the roles of story characters, they are more likely to formulate clearly their own stories. . . .* (p. 244)

Ben listens to many stories and, for a time, becomes the Biggest Billy Goat Gruff, the Noble Duke of York, or Old King Cole. The stories Ben hears help him to imagine himself in a variety of settings and situations and provide a way for him to organize his own experiences.

During this period, Ben's self-concept is forming. Ben comes to realize that he can shape, even control at times, some parts of his environment and that he should do so.

Twenty-Four to Thirty Months

Physical Development

Throughout his third year of life, Ben's ability to command groups of muscles grows. Moving small muscles to write (Figure 6–1) or to hold a fork becomes effortless. The two- to two and one-half-year-old child is so mobile and so eager for greater mobility and muscular control that a good deal of the caregiver's time is devoted to the creation and maintenance of a safe environment. Medicine taken orally, razors, and rulers, for example, must be inaccessible.

Ben can hurry (somewhat) and still maintain balance, but he often bumps into things and people. He tends to balk at being carried or pushed or pulled. He throws balls clumsily, usually keeping a rigid stance. He

FIGURE 6–1 Writing Sample from a Thirty-Month-Old Child

begins to master the tricycle; he can walk up steps by alternating his feet. Ben climbs up whatever attracts him, but he finds it difficult to step down.

A toy that moves fascinates Ben. If he can push or pull it and it rolls or jumps, so much the better. Caregivers need to exercise care in selecting toys, for some may be inherently unsafe; others are unsafe for a two- to two and one-half-year-old child.

Ben's brain growth continues at a slower pace. Until three years of age an injury to the left hemisphere of the brain may cause temporary language aphasia. After age three, recovery from an injury is more difficult (Lenneberg 1967). Ben, like all his agemates, is vulnerable to falls and injuries.

Ben can turn doorknobs, remove jar lids, pile cubes or stack blocks into higher and higher towers, grip writing tools, and begin to use a fork. He can also discriminate among printed letters, and he can undress himself more easily than he dresses himself.

When Ben is given crayons, he can scribble many straight strokes and then spirals and curves, perhaps talking as he scribbles.

Ben requires good nutrition because at this age poor nutrition has tragic and lasting effects. During these early months, the results of infection and disease that follow malnourishment have been well documented worldwide (Bender and Bender 1982).

Language Development

The two- to three-year-old child is a talker. Utterances run beyond two words. Ben comprehends longer and longer utterances, but it is still too early for him to understand figurative language and most idioms. Words that label things, people, or actions predominate, but there is also an increase in words for self—pronouns like "me," "mine," and "I." The use by Ben of his own name in his talk is still common although it is lessening. Statements like "Ben fall down" are disappearing, for Ben is developing and internalizing a rule system that guides him to create new and more interesting sentences.

Ben often synchronizes his movement of body with verbalization; he talks as he moves. Ben likes to label what he does, what he touches, and what he sees.

Ben continues to play with words. This wordplay is often alliterative and rhyming; many times it is the extension of stories and rhymes read or chanted to him. "Turkey, murkey, lurkey, furkey," can wing off from the tale of *Henny Penny.* He responds well to simple stories about things he knows— his family and his surroundings. He still likes point-and-say books as well as simple plots from which he can predict what will happen.

Ben wants to communicate. Wanting to express himself is a powerful motivator for the use of language. Social situations in nursery school and at home provide impetus for Ben's absorbing words.

Role-playing occurs as Ben and his agemates play with blocks, put dolls to bed or feed them, or talk to toys. Such role-play advances the language development of toddlers.

This is prime time for stories. Ben hears many tales and begins to organize and tell his own tales. He begins to sense story structure and his thoughts become more and more organized. All sorts of imaginative notions creep into Ben's head between "once upon a time" and "the end." Creativity appears in the middle of Ben's tales; anything can happen between the beginning and the end—sometimes, just one sentence's worth.

The range of Halliday's language functions is more and more in evidence. In addition to these functions, some children tend to use language to express their personal feelings while others use it referentially to name things in their environment (Nelson 1973). What, if any, relationship this difference has to subsequent personality development is unclear, but there do appear to be distinctive differences in the use young children make of language. During this stage as with earlier ones, Ben understands more language than he can produce. The expansion of sentences and vocabulary by his caregivers continues.

Cognitive Development

As growth continues, perceptions, experiences, and associations increase and a memory base is formed. Ben can examine new situations on the basis of former associations and make decisions. He may use a small table as a support to stand, but as he leans on it, the table moves, then topples and so does Ben. Ben decides that he will not use the table as an aid to standing again.

Environments in which caregivers routinely share stories provide powerful bases for memory strengthening and for cognitive and language development. Memory, at least visual memory, seems linked to IQ with the length of time a baby looks at a new stimulus an indication of IQ. Strides have been made in predicting the IQ of infants with predictions sustained when these same children start school (*New York Times* 1989). IQ scores also indicate children's cognitive abilities, which influence reading achievement indirectly (Tunmer, Herrinan, and Nesdale 1988).

A nurturant environment would include much to look at, hear, and feel. Pictures and stories provide powerful bases for memory building and strengthening as well as for language and cognitive development.

Social Development

Ben between twenty and thirty months imitates the gestures and mannerisms of his caregivers. Indeed he has a very strong attachment to his primary caregiver and is much influenced by her.

Young children of twenty-four to thirty months are still mainly interested in themselves and their increasing desire to be independent. A willingness to share and play with agemates is beginning to develop. However, young children are still likely to parallel play (play next to each other). They also respond to musical rhythms and enjoy singing and moving to music together.

Emotional and Personality Development
Fears of separation, especially from the primary caregiver, surface at this time and fears learned from parents (a fear of thunderstorms, for example) can be noticed in young children. The "I can do it myself" attitude is intensifying as is a desire for ownership. Ben may tend to protect and hoard his toys, for example.

Literacy Materials and Activities for This Period
The following books are appropriate for Ben and his friends at this age.

Ahlberg, Janet, and Ahlberg, Allen. (1979). *Each Peach Pear Plum.* Illustrated by authors. New York: Viking. An I-Spy book that assumes children know the stories of Goldilocks, the Three Bears, Jack and Jill, etc. Caregivers need to be sure that nursery rhyme and nursery story figures are indeed known.

Crews, Donald. (1978). *Freight Train.* Illustrated by author. New York: Greenwillow Books. A freight train with a range of special cars dashes across the pages. Settings change. There are cars to label and much to talk about. Talking about trains or visiting one can be the result of, or initiate, such sharing.

Emberley, Barbara. (1967). *Drummer Hoff.* Illustrated by Ed Emberley. Englewood Cliffs, N.J.: Prentice-Hall. This is a brightly colored cumulative tale full of onomatopoeic words that toddlers will love. They will join in loudly to help the cannon discharge. Auditory memory will be stretched and dramatic fun will be enjoyed.

Freeman, Don. (1968). *Corduroy.* Illustrated by author. New York: Viking. This is the story of a stuffed bear waiting to be loved and a girl waiting to love him. *Corduroy* invites the sharing of stories about loved stuffed animals and the writing of these stories.

Galdone, Paul. (1984). *The Teeny-Tiny Woman.* Illustrated by author. New York: Clarion Books. This story is a bit scary, but toddlers will love it when shared by a caring adult. As momentum grows, the final words of the Teeny-Tiny Woman are not teeny tiny at all. Toddlers delight in joining in the final shout.

Thirty to Thirty-Six Months

Physical Development
Ben acquires his full set of baby teeth by age three. Ben can now jump and hop and balance on a beam better than he did a few months ago. Close to

three years of age, he has good hand and finger coordination and can stack seven or more blocks. He is also developing a hand preference. Ben feeds himself with more ease because he can now manage utensils like spoons and mugs better. In play, Ben can handle more materials—wood, clay, and under supervision, blunt scissors, hammers, fingerpaints, and poster paint. Overall, Ben is increasingly more mobile and dexterous. Such mobility intensifies his curiosity.

Language Development
Language development advances markedly in Ben and his agemates between two and three years of age (Garvey 1977). This is the time when caregivers notice a dramatic growth of language. Ben's vocabulary may grow from approximately 300 to 1000 words by his next birthday. He will understand at least twice as many words as he can use. Although Ben uses two and three words together that sound like he is dictating a telegram (referred to as telegraphic speech), the complexity of his syntax, the rules he uses to create sentences, continues to develop. By the end of this year, Ben will be able to transform and combine some sentences and later embed one into another. Ben begins to use words like he, she, and they (pronouns), and, but, and or (conjunctions), of, with, and to (prepositions), the, a, and an (articles), and Mommy's, hers, theirs, and mine (possessives) to express relationships. Chomsky's (1965) theory that the biological nature of language learning permits all normal children to learn the rule system of language during the toddler and preschool years is confirmed. Ben generates new sentences using these rules. The basic sentence patterns that Ben has begun to learn and will continue to master through his early years in preschool and the primary grades are:

- sentence patterns
  Subject-verb: She runs.
  Subject-verb-adverb: He runs quickly. She runs home. They run during the day.
  Subject-verb-object: I see the horse.
  Subject-to be verb form-complement: The girl is happy. The boy was home.
  Subject-verb-infinitive: I want to play.
  Subject-verb-indirect object-object: They gave him the candy.
  Subject-verb-object-complement: They named her captain.
- simple transformation
  Questions: Basic sentence: Sarah got a new dress. Transformation: Did Sarah get a new dress?
  Explicit negative: Basic sentence: Ben is a good boy. Transformation: Ben is not a good boy.

Passive basic kernel: Basic sentence: Ben and Sarah have a book. Transformation: A book was given to Ben and Sarah.
* embeddings (expanding or combining sentences)
Adding modifiers (adjectives and adverbial and adjectival phrases): Basic sentence: The boy is big. The boy wears sneakers. Transformation: The big boy wears sneakers.
Compounding (combining words, phrases, and independent clauses): Basic sentences: Ben skipped. Sarah ran. Ben ran. Sarah skipped. Transformation: Sarah and Ben skipped and ran.

Ben's and Sarah's use of diverse sentence patterns, simple transformations, and embedded forms will increase throughout their preschool years.

Observations of young children support the idea that experiencing an event or participating in an action creates a hunger for words. It is from Ben's daily experiences in social settings that he forms the concepts for which he seeks labels. Experiences make him label-hungry.

Between thirty and thirty-six months, Ben plays with words; he rhymes them, repeats them, and listens to his own inventions again and again. Ben not only creates "verbal fun" by his rhymes and chants, but he seeks labels for his fantasies. He invents the name of "Eljie" for the elephant on the poster in his room and, having heard someone say "ridiculous," he imitates with "didicklous."

In language development the value of stories for Ben and children older than he is lauded many times. In a study by Watson (1987) involving two preschool teachers who taught the word "protozoa" to their classes, one teacher defined the word and discussed the characteristics of protozoa; the other told the children a story about a fisherman who knew about protozoa. When asked afterward to indicate what the new word meant, the children who learned about protozoa through the story recalled its meaning much better than those who had not heard the story. Experiences and stories are necessary for language development and for the overall development of Ben and his agemates.

Cognitive Development
For the two and one-half to three-year-old child, linguistic development and cognitive development are tightly related and, in many ways, similarly developed. If experiences make Ben word-hungry, it is those same experiences that form his concepts and understandings. Many of these experiences are a result of Ben's curiosity and active, highly mobile exploration of his environment.

Ben at two and one-half still enjoys what toys teach him; i.e., by some action of his, the pull toy moves; by shaking the rattle, he hears a sound, or by pushing a bell, he hears a ring. Such toys help Ben to organize and integrate intersensory information. For his cognitive development, such integration is essential. Ben sees the bell, pushes it, and hears it ring. Ben's sight, touch, and hearing are involved. He is learning to deal with and to organize information that comes simultaneously from several senses. According to Abravanel (1968) and Blank and Bridges (1964), this intersensory coordination improves with age.

The ability to attend to and to discriminate among stimuli and the details within stimuli also improves with age. Ben at almost three can ignore some distracting stimuli or at least be bothered less by them. He can attend to the toy, the puzzle, or the food at hand. Ben has many years to go in focusing his attention for longer and longer periods of time.

Ben is developing perceptually. The ability to attend to certain aspects in his environment and to discriminate among stimuli is basic to his perceptual development. If Ben looks at and touches huge alphabet blocks, he probably feels the shape of M as different from that of O. He touches the pieces of a four-piece puzzle and notes the differences in their appearance as he decides how to place them in the frame. He plays with several such puzzles over time and sees that many frames have four straight sides and some pieces have one or two straight edges. Ben knows that the pieces when put together make a picture. These actions and prior knowledge document Gibson's (1969) differentiation theory. Ben, after feeling and seeing the huge alphabet letters, begins to differentiate the shapes; he notes the distinctive features of certain letters. In dealing with the puzzle pieces and the puzzle frame, he notes the general shape of the frame and the many different shapes of the pieces; he also knows what it means to complete the puzzle. According to differentiation theory, Ben is beginning to make discriminations among shapes, to detect invariant properties (the frame shape), and to understand relationships between stimuli via structure and rules, i.e., the pieces when fitted properly together should make a picture.

Clearly, Ben's perceptual and cognitive development, including abilities to integrate information from several senses working simultaneously is very much environment-dependent. (A nurturant environment is discussed later in this chapter.)

Ben's learning at this time is part of what he sees people do. If Brian, his older brother, enjoys playing with the family pet, Ben may pet the dog too. If Mary Kay, his sister, takes a cookie from the cookie jar without asking and is scolded, Ben is less likely to reach for a cookie without asking. Ben's behavior is very much conditioned by the rewards and punishments his models receive.

At about two, Ben is entering the second stage of cognitive development—Piaget's preoperational thought. Ben thinks intuitively rather than logically; he focuses on one aspect of a situation only. He thinks that inanimate things that move are alive. Ben understands the world about him only in terms of himself. Very often this egocentricity is obvious in human relationships. Ben is like David who, when a teacher recognized him as "Chuckie's brother," replied "Uh, un! Chuckie's *my* brother! (Rasmussen 1979) The second utterance illustrates the shift to self for the two-year-old child.

The degree of centered thinking, egocentricity, animism, and intuitive rather than logical thinking within the range of Piaget's preoperational thinking (two to seven years) is debatable, but the existence of these restrictions on logical thought is generally acknowledged and will be operative in Ben's development.

Concomitant with Ben's cognitive development is his moral development. At Ben's age, his moral thoughts are related to self-preservation. He simply wants to secure pleasure and praise and avoid punishment or pain.

Social Development
Ben's social development is very much a part of the relationships within his family. Family caregivers who coerce are likely to find Ben aggressive or sullen; family members who nurture are likely to find Ben amenable. Learning to communicate with his brother Brian and his sister Mary Kay is helping Ben relate to other children. Parenting behavior, the presence of siblings, and family routine affect the nature of Ben's relationships. According to Lieberman (1977), three-year-old children establish the most successful relationships with peers when they enjoy secure relationships with their mothers. According to Rheingold (1982), children of two and one-half volunteer to help their parents perform tasks more than fifty percent of the time.

Opportunities to play and interact with peers are critical. It is probably Ben's perception of his peers as being similar to him—"Here's somebody like me"—that is the thrust toward interaction (Rubin 1980).

Ben is more likely to behave aggressively toward others if he is prevented from achieving what he wants. Later, competition in addition to frustration may generate aggressive behavior. At Ben's age, this behavior is likely to be physical; he pushes or shoves the offender. Much later, Ben will probably resort to verbal aggression when thwarted.

Caregivers need to reflect on the way they themselves model frustration and the way they react to Ben's feelings of helplessness and constraint.

Ben's enjoyment of fantasy play seems to draw other children to him even if, due to short attention spans, he and his agemates do not sustain any one form of play for long periods of time. Ben's preference for fantasy play may well help him to develop the flexibility new situations require (Herron and Sutton-Smith, 1971).

Personality Development

Ben is learning to do things for himself, and he is justifiably proud of his independence and success. Caregivers must help Ben to set realistic goals. This is vital since failure to achieve goals may make Ben unhappy and less likely to approach the task another time. A nonconfident Ben is likely to be an unsuccessful Ben (and vice versa). The caregiver's guidance in goal-setting and generosity in praise-giving are critical to personality development.

Literacy Materials and Activities for This Period

The following are a few selected titles appropriate for Ben and his agemates of thirty to thirty-six months.

Aliki. (1984). *Feelings.* Illustrated by author. New York: Greenwillow Books. Faces showing a range of emotions abound. This book generates much talk about feelings. Via pictures, caregivers can help to stimulate talk from children who have difficulty expressing their feelings.

Carle, Eric. (1969). *The Very Hungry Caterpillar.* Illustrated by author. New York: Philomel Books. Here is a poke-able, readable, viewable presentation of the caterpillar-to-the-butterfly cycle. Young children and caregivers love it.

Ehlert, Lois. (1988). *Planting a Rainbow.* Illustrated by author. San Diego: Harcourt Brace Jovanovich. A variety of flowers—all colors in the rainbow—are planted in a family garden. Large print, vivid colors, and clear details invite children to identify each of them and then return to the garden again and again. Colors and form will fascinate the toddler. Some flower names, if reinforced by actual blooms, may be learned.

McPhail, David. (1984). *Fix It.* Illustrated by author. New York: E. P. Dutton. This is a real-life story toddlers understand about a broken television and a broken-hearted child. The video must be fixed. In the meantime, however, the child discovers that books are interesting too.

Sendak, Maurice. (1962). *One Was Johnny.* Illustrated by author. New York: Harper & Row. Nutshell Library. This is a miniature counting book focusing on Johnny, alone with a book. All sorts of visitors decide to enter Johnny's room, one by one. Johnny becomes increasingly disturbed by this intrusion into his peace and dramatically shouts that he will eat up these unwanted guests if they do not leave. *One Was Johnny* is easily adapted to dramatic play.

What Activities and Materials Foster Literacy?

Given the curious, mobile, independent, word-amassing Ben, the physical setting prompting his emergent literacy must guarantee space, diverse materials, and safety.

Space and Activity

Within the overall space, Ben and his peers move constantly. Opportunities abound to explore by crawling through tunnels or boxes; by climbing stairs; by sliding, rocking, pushing, and pulling toys; by stacking blocks; by tossing soft balls; by handling rhythm instruments; by solving wooden puzzles; and by filling up and emptying the contents of all sorts of containers. Ben experiments with everything and, as he does, he becomes more dexterous.

Not only do opportunities abound for movement but also for choice. Activity centers within the overall play area invite Ben to move in one of several directions. Ben may choose an article from a prop box for fantasy play and go on to rehearse many roles; he may select a puppet and begin to plan the puppet's behavior. He may dress up, look at picture books, sing along with some records, or march along to some music. When Ben announces that he is going to grandpa's, there are tote bags available for him to fill and prepare for the trip. He can reach for a stethoscope and a white smock when he is in a doctor mood. If Ben looks befuddled at all the possibilities, his caregivers need only mention two or three alternative activities and allow Ben to make his choice.

Ben becomes conscious of divisions within the overall space. Sometimes his caregivers use colored tape on the floor to signal to Ben just where he can mold the sand and strain it, scoop and dump it, or mix sand and water. Sometimes a table and chair set apart, a huge box, or a specially carpeted area invite a particular kind of activity. As he plays alone or works with others, Ben understands the organization of the play area, where things are and where they go; Ben learns to use his space in a variety of ways and to talk about different areas.

Talk and Materials

Ben talks to himself and his toys as he participates in some of these activities. He used the cookie cutter in the sandbox yesterday, but he cannot find it today. He does not know its name so he demonstrates to the caregiver what he wants by bringing her to the sandbox and showing her what "it" does with his hands in the sand. "Oh, you mean the cookie cutter," she says. He looks at her and repeats "cookie cutter." He nods his head. She reaches deeply into the sandbox, pulls out the cookie cutter, and gives it to Ben. He grins and walks away repeating "cookie cutter, cookie cutter." Expanding language, in this manner, is vital for the emergent literate.

The caregiver makes a mental note that she must cut cookies and bake them soon so that the cutter can be demonstrated and the name better understood.

In a similar way—from function to label—Ben learns puppets, cassettes, records, bubbles, spatulas, shovels, smocks, Legos, and innumerable additional words. The continued use of vocabulary to name play materials, functional as it is, becomes part of Ben's learning.

In addition to pets, some of the toys or games available to Ben especially invite talk—dolls; stuffed animals; bath toys; play toys; play telephones; prop box materials; wood, cloth, or rubber play families; participation books and games; and rhythmic music. Ben loves to match actions with words and he can render an emphatic "Pop Goes the Weasel."

In all areas, Ben needs to know that he can manage the materials and space safely and comfortably. Toys should not have sharp edges and painted objects should be treated so that when they end up in his mouth, they offer no threat to his health.

For circle, ring, and dance games, the large space is cleared. Children move freely. In effect, the area suits the activity.

Aesthetic Setting

Ben and Sarah need to grow aesthetically too. Caregivers' attempts to create settings that are pleasing to the eye deliver powerful modeling messages to Ben and Sarah about how the environment can be changed and made more attractive. Even toddlers can be asked questions like "Ben, where should we put the flowers Grandmother brought with her?" or "Sarah, how can we make this corner look prettier? Perhaps if we put the toys here and . . . What do you think?" Toddlers so challenged think about alternatives and express preferences, thereby involving greater use of personal and/or instrumental language (Halliday 1975).

The social/emotional setting most nurturant of literacy is one in which:

- there is much talk and much wholehearted and wholeminded listening. The caregiver's modeling behavior is critical. Ben knows he is being heard when his caregiver asks him questions about his experiences and smiles delightedly at his adventures.
- children's freedom of choice among ideas, suggestions, and materials is continuously supported. Ben may need help in selection, but he has a right to choose sand, water, block, prop, or paint play.
- Ben's inquisitiveness must be respected. He grows by asking "Why?" again and again.
- feelings are respected between caregiver and child and between child and child. The caregiver-observer watches carefully, alert to the easily bruised feelings of young children.
- role-play and puppet-play abound. Ben's involvement furthers his language development and his just-emerging social collaboration.
- the caregiver's manner is patient and calm throughout the day—helpful, as Ben rehearses a skill; dramatic, as Ben engages in fantasy play; sympathetic, when Ben needs a nurturing word.

Specific Activities to Nurture Literacy

Home and nursery school abound in opportunities for direct and indirect literacy experiences. Some categories of such experiences include identification, picture book probes and prompts, chant reading, and story creations.

Identification

Ben is involved each day in identifying the much-seen labels in the house on cans, bottles, boxes, newspapers, books, lists, and his own T-shirts. Outside the house, he notices signs and words on stores, restaurants, and gasoline stations. He names these correctly. This development of language growing in Ben is not to be underestimated. It is by such step-by-step mastery that Ben begins to talk about his environment.

Point-and-say books give Ben hours of opportunity to increase his naming skill and later his narrating, conversing skill. He, after all, needs to know what things are called if he wishes to share with his caregivers his feelings and ideas about them.

The following titles provide Ben with opportunities for recognizing and rehearsing labels.

Bang, Molly. (1983). *Ten, Nine, Eight*. Illustrated by author. New York: Greenwillow Books. In a clear, rhythmic counting-backwards book, this tale breathes tenderness and "familyness." It is suitable at any time but especially at naptime or bedtime.

Barton, Byron. (1986). *Boats*. Illustrated by author. New York: Thomas Y. Crowell. Also, *Trains, Airplanes,* and *Trucks*. These contain simple colorful, heavily outlined drawings with one sentence per every two pages illustrating different types of boats, trains, trucks, and airplanes. Despite the simplicity of the drawings, there are a number of things to be pointed out and identified.

Gibbons, Gail. (1987). *Farming*. Illustrated by author. New York: Holiday House. Filled with simple, seasonal farm scenes, this is one of many such wordless and almost-wordless books by this author for the young child with much to talk about and point to.

Hoban, Tana. (1986). *Shapes, Shapes, Shapes*. Photographs by author. New York: Greenwillow Books. These clear, colorful photographs show everyday things and scenes for toddlers to relate to, identify, and discuss. Although not as simple in composition as some of the author's other books, this book has much to interest the young child.

Lobel, Arnold. (1981). *On Market Street*. Illustrated by Anita Lobel. New York: Greenwillow Books. This is a colorful and exciting rhyming alphabet book with one letter per page. The letters are less interesting for the toddler than the marvelous figures they stand for such as the lollipop lady and the wig lady and the zipper man and. . . .

Tafuri, Nancy. (1984). *All Year Long*. Illustrated by author. New York: Greenwillow Books. A simple, sequential seasonal book illustrating days of the week and months of the year that will generate talk for the toddler.

Ben's practice play should be full of movement and action words. Concomitant with the labeling of things, Ben moves easily into naming actions. By demonstration, he gets to know what march, hop, jump, run, bend, swing, rock, skip, and twirl mean. Ben is finding words quite useful and is eager to increase his store of them.

Picture Book Probes and Prompts

Ben looks at Pat Hutchins' *I Hunter*, an almost wordless picture book. He points to things he recognizes in the picture. He listens as his mother shares the text with him. On each two-page spread, the text consists of a number and the names of an animal, bird, or reptile, as in "7 crocodiles."

Ben's mother runs her fingers under the number-word combination from left to right as she turns the pages waiting for Ben to identify what he knows and to offer his interpretations of what is happening in the picture. Ben chuckles at the elephants as they emerge from behind the tree trunks and swing their own trunks at the determined, unseeing hunter, seeming to speed him on his way. Ben listens to the word, "giraffe" and says "giraffe 1, 2, 3" pointing as he counts the giraffes in the picture. His mother says, "Yes and what is the hunter passing now?" Ben looks at the clump of strange feathers on the ground and is mystified. As his mother turns the page, she points to the unfolding, rising clump of feathers and says, "Ostriches." She adds, "Ostriches are very large birds." "Ostriches, " says Ben and observes that "they look mad."

Ben's mother provides time for him to think about that and then asks "What's happening now?"

"The hunter," points out Ben, "is still walking fast and he's looking."

"What do you think this is?" asks Ben's mother as she runs her fingers across brown, wavy spears that protrude above the brush in the background. Ben replies, "Big, wiggly plants." "Let's see," says his mother.

When the big, wiggly plants turn out to be the antlers of five antelopes, Ben giggles and says, "Deers." Ben's mother says, "Yes, they look like deer, but they are called antelopes." Ben repeats "Antelopes" and counts "1, 2, 3, 4, 5."

"Let's look at this picture," says mother. "What do you see?" "The hunter and . . . eyes," says Ben.

"Hmm, hmm," says mother. "Whose eyes?"

"Tigers," says Ben excitedly. Ben has seen pictures of tigers in some of Brian's books; he has also been to the zoo.

"Right," says mother, running her fingers under the word "tigers." Ben smiles and says "tigers" again and begins to count to six.

Ben continues to enjoy the pictures and to guess the upcoming animals. He now understands the pattern and he identifies the monkeys before they fully appear. Mother and Ben chuckle long and loudly when the hunter turns and finally sees the animals, reptiles, and birds that have been following him and takes off at great speed.

As his caregiver and he have shared *I Hunter*, Ben has participated in many types of literacy activities. He has identified things he knows and has learned the labels of things he does not know. He made some predictions based on prior book knowledge about creatures that might appear on the following pages. Predicting facilitates comprehension of story. He is beginning to learn that he cannot always make accurate judgments when only a partial picture is visible. He has confirmed for himself his suspicion of the pattern—feature on one page, creature on the next. The left-to-right pattern for reading has been reconfirmed. He checked on the number of creatures mentioned and the numeral at the bottom of the page as he counted the creatures. He hugely enjoyed the hunter's surprise and retreat. Ben does not doubt that books can entertain!

Other books that challenge toddlers to make predictions follow.

Carle, Eric. (1971). *Do You Want to Be My Friend?* Illustrated by author. New York: Thomas Y. Crowell. This is a wordless picture book which will lead children to make several guesses as the little mouse seeks a friend among many creatures. It is the tail of the animal on one page that gives the toddler the clue to the animal's identity and the likelihood that the mouse has indeed found a friend.

Eastman, P. D. (1960). *Are You My Mother?* New York: Random House. A bird keeps searching for his mother. The toddler has to decide whether the creature being questioned is a likely mother. This is a long-time favorite.

Kuskin, Karla. (1956). *Roar and More*. Illustrated by author. New York: Harper & Row. Simple drawings and catchy poems about various animals visualize the sounds they make as clues to their identities. Fun to hear and see, toddlers will want to come back to look at the pictures and listen to and even mimic the sound.

Piper, W. (1954). *The Little Engine That Could*. Illustrated by George and Doris Hauman. New York: Platt & Munk. This book is predictable and participatory. Every toddler must at some time urge the little engine on, predict its success and chant it up the hill.

Seuss, Dr. (Geisel, T.) (1957). *The Cat in the Hat*. Boston: Houghton Mifflin. This rote-able and chantable, silly, rhyming story will tickle the eardrums while clearly suggesting to the toddler the next rhyming word and phrase.

Chant Reading
Ben's caregiver takes from the bookshelf *Bears in Pairs* (Yektai) and shares this with Ben and his friend Sarah. The caregiver says, as she runs her fingers under the words from top to bottom of the page,

"Black bear
Brown bear
Up Bear
Down Bear."*
She returns to the left page of the double-spread and repeats
"Black bear
Brown bear"
then goes on to the right page of the double spread and says
"Up Bear
Down Bear."

Ben and Sarah are quietly giggling at the small bear who is piggy-backing on the balloon-holding big bear. As the caregiver returns to the left page, Ben and Sarah join her in "Black bear, brown bear" and then continue to the right page "Up Bear, Down Bear." Liking the cadence, the sound, the rhyme, they chant it again.

As the pages are turned and shared, Ben and Sarah easily identify the next quartet of bears and they chant along smiling at the royal bear pair, the theatrics of the orange bear, and the glorious collection of bears who attend Mary's tea party at the end.

Ben and Sarah talk bears for a long time. "Hug-a-bear, jug-a-bear," says Ben. Sarah follows with "Love-a-bear, love-a-bear." They ask for paper and crayon to draw a bear—several bears. The caregiver suggests perhaps they might like to tell a story about the bear they would most like to have for a particular friend. She leaves Ben and Sarah to think about it. Holdaway's imaginative or "let's pretend" function of language is strongly evident here. Sarah and Ben have entered wholeheartedly and expressively into the tale of a parade of bears. They repeat the story, extend the story, and draw the characters. In short, they live the story.

Ben and Sarah have been provided with an appealing story experience. They discover that they can join in chanting it; they like to hear and to participate in the sound and the beat. They discover all sorts of details in the illustrations and they discuss the tea party at some length.

They then explore all sorts of phrases, patterning their syntax after the text; they develop phrases like "hug-a-bear, love-a-bear, jug-a-bear."

Independently, they then seek the book again and ask to have it reread. As they listen, they join in more confidently, utilizing picture clues, rhyming patterns, and their prior experience. After several rehearsings, echoic readings, and personal decoding, they are ready to invent a brief bear story of their own, and they keep their crayons handy to illustrate it. At this time, Ben is ready to, and indeed does, begin to create his own stories.

---

* Reprinted with the permission of Bradbury Press, an Affiliate of Macmillan, Inc. from *BEARS IN PAIRS* by Niki Yektai, illustrated by Diane deGroat. Text, Copyright © 1987 by Niki Yektai.

Story Creations

The young child immersed in print that is functional and entertaining is going to want to create his or her own stories. Ben knows that his squiggles are like the squiggles in books. He is learning that he too can create books like an author. Crayons in hand and more dexterous at three, Ben scribbles his squiggles and tells what they mean. He knows that they should mean something. It will be a while before the squiggles become recognizable letters and Ben's invented spelling readable. For now, Ben knows stories can be written down and that what is written can be read; he sees it happen at home and in nursery school all the time.

The young child's involvement with print should be a pleasurable immersion and should range from the satisfaction of labeling more and more of his or her environment to the delight of probing pictures, chanting, and creating stories. Combined with fantasy play and building upon a growing repertoire of tales, these excursions into the world of print can assure a happy literacy.

What Is the Role of the Caregiver in Nurturing the Child's Growth Toward Literacy?

The behavior of the caregiver of the two- to three-year-old child ranges from nondirective to directive, from observing to telling and showing. The role of the teacher or mother may be to facilitate, alter, or broaden the play of the young child. Decisions concerning which behaviors the occasion demands are sometimes difficult. Too much direction and the child's reach for independence is thwarted; too little direction and the child may not complete the task successfully and therefore be unhappy with himself.

If literacy nurturance is a goal, the caregiver of the two- to three-year-old needs to exhibit the following behaviors:

- be aware of the importance of his or her own modeling. The observers of young children easily identify young children's use of models. Such use is obvious in their fleeting role-plays and in their desires to help. "I'll help you," says Ben following after his father with his own armful of leaves toward the mulch pile. The effects of such modeling are easily and quickly heard when the words and phrases common to the caregiver pop from the young child's tongue. Modeling, too, is evident in children's knowledge of story structure. They begin a story, for example, with "once upon a time" and end it with "happily ever after." Caregivers are far greater and more persistent models than they themselves know.

- encourage the young child's involvement in daily routine tasks. As has been noted, deciding how much help to provide is a difficult matter. When safety is an issue, there is no question. In all other instances, it is best to observe and provide help to prevent frustration. The inherent reach to explore, to push toward independence, and to imitate parts of the behavior they see—all these fuse in the young child's wish to help. Because motor coordination is not yet completely honed, attempts are clumsy; efforts, however, are important. Safety must be assured, but dusting, baking under supervision, sweeping, or cleaning, insofar as the child can manage, should continue.

  Material-filled environments invite much experimentation—a healthy testing. Toddlers have preferences and to assure that such preferences are as wide-ranging as possible, caregivers may need to demonstrate how materials can be used. A toy telephone conversation starts with the caregiver picking up the receiver and saying "Good morning, Ben." When Ben replies, she asks him what he did after he left nursery school yesterday. Ben says, "Me and daddy go to the park and play and . . . "

- make educated observations. In effect, caregivers should be as curious about the child as the child is curious about the caregiver and his or her environment. The observant caregiver not only notes language, social, physical, and cognitive development but does it based upon a background of knowledge and experience with Ben and his agemates. Such notes over time reflect patterns most helpful in guiding Ben. The portfolio of observational notes and of checklists yields more and more information about Ben, enabling better and better nurturance. This text includes many aids to caregivers in charting Ben's development, particularly his growth toward literacy.

- support fantasy play. This pretend play, a movement toward decentered thinking, is the beginning of the lifelong need to fantasize, sympathize, empathize—to "walk in another's moccasins." As Ben participates, over time, he exhibits a pattern of development. According to Rogers and Sawyers (1988) who refer to Piaget's framework of stages, Ben will grow through different types of symbolic/fantasy play. During this period of growth, the caregiver may need to provide play props, may need to model, and may even need to work with the young child in a one-to-one fashion toward what may be for Ben the most beneficial form of play, namely, sociodramatic and constructive play. It is during play that the first attempts by young children who read early reveal that the play most likely to lead to better reading and writing skills is dramatic play (Rogers and Sawyers 1988).

- facilitate friendships. The two- to almost three-year-old child is very young for friendship formation; he or she may, in fact, still be parallel playing. Opportunities, however, for Ben and Sarah to play together and with others, no matter how briefly, must be present and planned. Such opportunities nurture the social skills children must develop. Ben may have a slight advantage in achieving new friendships because he, Brian, and Mary Kay interact daily (Rubin 1980). Not only does Ben's social development require that his caregivers provide opportunity for two-somes and small groups to work together, but his language development depends upon such planning.

All the prop box activities that require group planning or scripting serve Ben well. The choral chants that require Ben and his friend to say certain lines together and certain lines separately reinforce the your-turn, my-turn format of conversation.

Without the opportunity to interact with others, not only is Ben's language development thwarted, but he may also find himself without a friend, without a chum—a situation that psychologists and profession-als in mental health fields deplore. Over time, the long-range effect of such deprivation can lead the child down the path from lonely to loner. Rubin (1980) recalls the word of the psychiatrist Harry Stack Sullivan who was convinced that the failure to have a childhood chum created irremediable problems later in life. It appears that although early rela-tionships are fleeting—as beautifully illustrated in Janet Udry's *Let's Be Enemies*—they are vital in guiding the child toward lasting friendships.

Ben and his agemates at three are within the age range of Parten's (1932) six types of peer play—from the simplest to the most advanced. At different times, Ben exhibits the last three stages (parallel, associative, and cooperative). While he still parallel plays, he can be seen engaging in associative play when he briefly exchanges toys with his agemates and once, in a rare while, when he and his friends invade the prop box, Ben engages in cooperative play to enact a tale. Ben is advancing toward more and more collaboration.

- share Stories, Poems, and Songs. The caregiver's ideabook should be replete with ditties and tales and songs, with clap games, and with "stamp" games and dance games. Musical "naturals" like "Row, Row, Row Your Boat," "Are You Sleeping," "Looby, Loo," and "London Bridge" should ring out in homes and classrooms.

   This is the time for introducing or retelling the delightful three-somes—"The Three Little Pigs," "The Three Billy Goats Gruff," and "The Three Bears,"—and other early tales, such as "The Owl and the Pussy Cat" and "The Little Red Hen." If simple props or prop kits are available following the sharing, literature can be transformed into real life via fantasy play.

   Important to the sharing of tales is the child's wish to share back. Ben tells the story he has heard to an attentive audience. He relates a recognizable plot in his own words and his own syntax with his own twist. This is the time to encourage Ben to retell the story he has heard on his own. This retelling is referred to as an unguided recollection of story. (Guided and unguided retelling as a vehicle for developing and assessing comprehension are discussed in chapters 9 and 10.)

Peek-a-boo has been extended. Turn-taking is again in evidence. Ben listened to a story; Ben tells the story. He may also scribble and draw the story. He may "script it" (i.e., think of actions and words and then act it out). If he likes it, he will retell it many times. Sometimes Ben will retell the story on his own. "This is what happened," he says and continues to demonstrate what he recalls from the reading.

Often retellings occur immediately following a story reading. When they do, the caregiver must listen attentively, without interruption. Ben needs to retell the story in his own words, without questions, comments, or additions to his talk about the story. Retelling, spontaneously, to the caregiver provides a vehicle for Ben to rehearse the story setting, theme, plot and episodes, the story's problem, and the resolution to the problem.

Listening to stories with well-formed story structure teaches Ben the language of story. Retelling reinforces that knowledge and confirms Ben's notion that he, in fact, knows how to tell stories like his caregiver. Unguided retellings of stories that happen in a literacy-rich environment encourage growth in the language of stories. The vocabulary of stories becomes Ben's language, and he is able to demonstrate ownership in these unguided retelling sessions. Ben, when retelling, is learning the language of story. This knowledge is necessary for successful reading and writing at a later time. This activity is a self-teaching precursor for more formal types of reading behaviors.

Listening to Ben retell stories helps his caregiver assess what he has learned about how stories are structured. It also permits Mom and Dad to beam when he uses words like, "terrible," "screeching," or "moustache" because he has heard them in James Stevenson's *That Terrible Halloween Night*. Ben's nursery school teacher is delighted when she observes Ben illustrating his ability to recall the story in the order in which it was presented. Assessing Ben's recall helps his caregiver to determine the kinds of storybook experiences Ben needs in order to recall even more effectively. Books with well-structured plots and enticing words read in inviting settings guide Ben to increase his memory as well as his understanding of texts. Retelling is talking through the story in his own words and thereby demonstrating his ability to make the book part of himself.

The following books are appropriate for reading to Ben because the story structure is definitive and clear.

Books with Clear Story Structure

Aruego, Jose. (1971). *Look What I Can Do!* Illustrated by author. New York: Charles Scribner's Sons. Children will chuckle over this funny sequence in which one carabao keeps calling attention to himself and challenging the other.

Galdone, Paul, reteller and illustrator. (1968). *Henny Penny.* Boston: Houghton Mifflin. The collection of animals who follow Henny Penny as she cries that the sky is falling down is comical. Alas, they are also far too gullible. Toddlers will love the names of the animals and remember them easily as they chuckle about the lengthening line parading behind Henny Penny.

Galdone, Paul, reteller. (1974). *The Little Red Hen.* Illustrated by reteller. New York: Clarion Books. Also Zemach, M. (1983). *The Little Red Hen.* New York: Farrar, Straus and Giroux. The Little Red Hen is the only productive member of her household. After seeking help many times, she decides quite firmly that if you do not labor you should not enjoy the fruits of labor: enough is enough. This is a lesson neatly told.

Galdone, Paul. (1985). *The Three Bears.* New York: Clarion Books.

Galdone, Paul. (1981). *The Three Billy Goats Gruff.* New York: Clarion Books.

Galdone, Paul. (1979). *The Three Little Pigs.* New York: Clarion Books. Here are three beast tales illustrated by the reteller that represent the best in nursery-folktale heritage for young children.

Stevens, Janet, adaptor. (1984). *The Tortoise and the Hare: An Aesop Fable.* Illustrated by adaptor. The well-known fable is perfect for nudging a prediction from toddlers and watching and guiding as they see they must revise their prediction.

Zemach, M. (1965). *Teeny-Tiny Woman.* New York: Scholastic. This tale invites toddlers to air their own frustrations as they join in continuously louder shouts to the mysterious bone.

Summary

From two to three, children develop dramatically with greater muscle control, greatly increased language skills and range of language functions, expanded perceptual and emotional experiences—all of which shape personality.

Children delight in their greater dexterity and coordination. Given environments that invite them to test their own perceptions of things around them and exploring their ability to carry out tasks, children begin to feel successful and confident enough to continue their explorations and experimentations with new materials. They are also eager and confident about listening to stories and retelling them or inventing, with heavy doses of fantasy, their own tales. They giggle at some of the wordplay they hear and form new word combinations and nonsense rhymes of their own. They identify happily with words that depict actions and repeat them.

A child likes to make things happen—bells ring; trains move; wheels turn. The ability to integrate intersensory perceptions has improved.

Children can now handle clay, blunt scissors, and paints, and they are proud of the products they create. As their experiences increase, language expands and they will talk about the things they make.

Socialization does not come easily to children. When annoyed, they will push or shove. It will be some time before they use words, not hands, to vent frustrations.

In addition to a loving caregiver, children's nurturance toward literacy requires space, activity, talk, materials, play, stories, poems, songs, and friends who model functional literacy actions. They need to be part of designing their own environment. They need to be heard, to have their questions answered, feelings respected, and choices honored. Children's advancement toward cooperative play needs guidance. Their development toward sharing needs easing.

A print-filled environment to note and label, a materials-filled environment to handle and investigate, books to hear and see and chant about, and a caregiver to love and to be loved by—given these, a child flourishes.

7

The Fourth Year of Life

This chapter addresses the following questions:

- What growth patterns characterize the fourth year of life?
- What is the role of caregivers in nurturing the child's growth toward literacy?
- What activities and materials foster literacy?

What Growth Patterns Characterize the Fourth Year of Life?

Sarah between three and four is a happy child, pleased with her independence and eager to display her self-reliance. "Look what I can do!" is often implied and, more often, said.

Physical Development

Sarah's physical development is reflected in her taller and somewhat slimmer appearance. At four, her legs are beginning to lengthen in comparison to her body. Now Sarah pedals her tricycle with great vim, vigor, and assurance. She can toss a fairly large ball with one hand. By the time Sarah is four, she will be able to catch a bounced ball easily with her hands. This skill will permit her to enjoy, even more, the social fun.

Sarah loves to dance and twist and bend. She smiles as she twists her body while keeping her feet firmly in one place. She and Ben gleefully scamper up and down the jungle gym with ease. Between her third and fourth birthday, Sarah learns to hop on one foot. At three, Sarah can get in and out of her coat by herself. She is toilet trained, is able to dress and feed herself, and is able to communicate her needs and separate from her home without great problems. Sarah is ready for the physical, social, and emotional challenges expected in day-care centers for three- and four-year-old children. In general, even clothes with buttons rather than zippers can be managed by Sarah whose face shows her determination and pride as she works a small button through its buttonhole.

Sarah sometimes chants to herself as she plays—much like Frances, the character in Russell Hoban's series about the friendly badger. Such chants and monologues of solitary play become the basis, at four to five years of age, for sociodramatic play.

Sarah is learning how to use a scissors so that she can cut straight lines. She is more adept now at handling drawing and writing tools. Sarah can copy a circle, knows it is a circle, and will parade her paper about showing everyone her drawing.

The jigsaw puzzles, some of which confused Sarah earlier, now are fun; she sees how the pieces fit together and easily places them in their appropriate spaces. Then she sits back and enjoys her accomplishments and seeks a friend in order to share the completed picture, using language that implies "Look what I did!"

Caregivers delight in Sarah's tidier eating. Food stays on the spoon until it reaches her mouth. She spills and wastes food less often than she used to. Other eating habits, however, are somewhat unpredictable. Clearly these are not so delightful for caregivers who tolerate reluctantly Sarah's "I want it in *my* bowl," as she bangs on the table, or "I don't want anymore," when she has barely sampled her food, or "I don't like it," when she has not tasted a new food at all. So unpredictable are Sarah's eating habits that caregivers need to provide healthful, nutritious snacks.

One way of dealing with Sarah's seeming disinterest in food is to involve her in its preparation. Her fine and gross motor skill development enables her to help assemble ingredients, pour the liquid and dry ingredients, stir the mixture, and set the table. The apron the caregiver ties around Sarah's waist makes the whole involvement "serious fun" and, of course, the final tasting makes it delectable. Dialogue between her caregiver and her characterizes activities. Sarah's caregiver engages primarily in regulatory and informative language while Sarah engages in instrumental speech. Both savor the interactional function of language and both find that cooking lessons bind them closer together.

Emotional and Social Development

It is largely through play that Sarah develops in all areas, but her emotional and social development are, as has been noted in earlier chapters, particularly dependent on her play activities. At three, Sarah beams as she works with simple construction sets and puzzles. As she masters these manipulations, she is "in control." Success in such activities supports Sarah's self-esteem and nourishes a determination to try some more.

If at three Sarah attends preschool, she is coping for the first time with separation from her major caregiver. For Sarah, who is generally an independent child, stress because of separation is eased by the expectation of being, each day, reunited with her caregiver. Coping well with this separation from her chief caregiver strengthens Sarah's independence and enables her to expand her learning environments. It increases her social contacts and her ability to engage in more diversified play and intensifies her thirst for interactions with language.

Sarah's caregiver helps her to exercise self-discipline by providing "think" times when Sarah considers what she has done, how to change her behavior, and then actually does it. Putting her toys away has no appeal for

Sarah. "I don't want to," she says, so her caregiver remembers to praise Sarah when she does store her toys. When she does not, her caregiver firmly says, "Sarah, you need time to think about your toys and what you should do with them. After five minutes, I'm going to ask what you have decided to do." The caregiver's primary task is to use consistent language and actions to reinforce Sarah's strengths and lessen her weaknesses. Sarah's desire for more independence and self-reliance contributes to some stubbornness in acceding to the directions of the caregiver.

Sarah is fearful and troubled at times. Caregivers are advised to treat children's fears with care and caution. The following guidelines are adapted from Ilg, Ames, and Bates (1955):

- do not make fun of the child's fears
- do not humiliate the child because of his or her fears
- do not force the child to confront the fear when he or she clearly is not ready
- realize that the child will, with time, outgrow his or her main fears
- allow the child to withdraw from whatever excites fears. Then gradually attempt to work with him or her through the fear
- avoid situations that frighten the child beyond his or her ability to cope

Books About First Experiences

Among the many fears of children like Sarah are fears of "firsts." Books helpful to children dealing with first times follow.

Ahlberg, Janet, and Ahlberg, Allan. (1988). *Starting School*. Illustrated by authors. New York: Viking Kestrel. This is a very detailed, happily illustrated account of what to expect on the first day of nursery school.

Keats, Ezra. (1964). *Whistle for Willie*. Illustrated by author. New York: Viking. It is not easy, but after many tries, Willie is finally able to whistle.

Krauss, Ruth. (1945). *The Carrot Seed*. Illustrated by Crockett Johnson. New York: Harper & Row. It takes not only care but patience to nurture a carrot seed into a carrot.

McPhail, David. (1987). *First Flight*. Boston: Little, Brown. Anxiety about a first airplane flight is eased by this illustrated, factual story.

Rockwell, Harlow. (1975). *My Dentist*. Illustrated by author. New York: Greenwillow Books. Pictures and words help to inform the young child about what to expect at the dentist's office.

Rockwell, Harlow. (1973). *My Doctor*. Illustrated by author. New York: Macmillan. Clear and simple illustrations help prepare the young child for a visit to a doctor.

Viorst, Judith. (1970). *Try it Again Sam*. Illustrated by Paul Galdone. New York: Lothrop, Lee, & Shepard Books. Sam has difficulty but finally succeeds in finding his way to David's house.

Wells, Rosemary. (1981). *Timothy Goes to School*. Illustrated by author. New York: Dial Press. Timothy is overcome by Claude's perfection in school; Claude does everything right. Timothy is dispirited until he meets Violet who has difficulty coping with Grace's perfection.

Sarah's emotional development is greatly dependent upon the strength of her relationships with her caregivers and her success and joy with her peers. Sarah's caregivers, who now may be parents <u>and</u> teachers, provide her with much behavior to model. Since Sarah does not see her parents "glued" to television, Sarah is not developing into a television addict. Rather she engages in and thoroughly enjoys active play and physical activities; these afford her great opportunities for social development. Sarah's parents limit her television time and see to it that it does not compete with family talk times—meal times and other literacy-rich interactions.

Rubin (1980) comments on social relationships of three-year-old children as providing the content within which they can realistically compare themselves to others. Read (1976) finds this necessary if young children like Sarah and Ben and their peers are to grow in finding their own strengths and in facing their own weaknesses.

We know Sarah enjoys solitary and parallel play but she, like her peers, is increasingly interested in associative and cooperative play. By five, Sarah will be adept at planning and enacting different family and other social roles. At three, Sarah has some developing to do before she is ready for subtle and careful cooperative planning. Her early announcements of "I'm the mommy" and her friend Melissa's "I'm the baby," suggest that both girls understand what a "play frame" is (Goncu and Kessel 1984). Clearly the family "frame" is the predominant one for Sarah and her peers. In her imitation of family roles, Sarah, cries, shouts, and stamps her feet. She is sad; she sings; she dances; she displays a gamut of emotions. Each emotion may be accompanied by appropriate words and Sarah begins to develop an angry vocabulary, a sad vocabulary, a directive vocabulary—one for each environment in her life. Important, too, is role-switching. Sarah's conversation gives evidence of her awareness of different social roles demanding different tones and words. Her "baby" speech is markedly different from her "mommy" speech. Her Papa Bear's "Who's sitting in my chair?" is loud and angry; her "Chicken soup with rice" (Sendak 1962) is merry and cheery.

The thorough and subtle analysis of roles and the consideration of appropriate dialogue are well beyond Sarah. She reacts, however, to the modeling she sees and hears, giving it her own creative twists.

All types of play help Sarah to develop holistically. Caregivers need to provide an environment with more than enough space, toys, and props for Sarah to engage in solitary, social, and imaginative activities. When Sarah exhibits frustrations with play materials, caregivers need to suggest that she try others for now.

The primary need caregivers must address is securing available playmates for Sarah. Interactions with her agemates are vital for Sarah's healthy holistic development.

Cognitive Development

The countless activities in which Sarah engages increase and confirm the concepts she is forming about people and things around her. It is from these experiences that mental representations (concepts) are shaped paving the way for more and more labeling (Genishi 1988). Sarah often asks "What is that?" Her active growing involvement in all sorts of object and social play greatly expands her concept formation and her vocabulary development.

In addition, Sarah loves stories and absorbs more and more book behavior. She watches her caregivers as they read with her. She is learning to think about and look at parts of the book; she independently makes predictions about what will happen next. She delightedly identifies more and more things in pictures that she knows and asks about things that are new to her. Sarah's awareness of books and elements of print is a precursor for successful reading. The checklist in Table 7–1 can help the caregiver assess a child's print awareness.

Sarah's caregivers supply her with "high realism" toys—small brooms, brushes, telephones, and garden tools (McLoyd 1985). Sarah delights in using, placing, and replacing these, and positioning the furniture in the doll house and the miniature toys in the toy box.

High realism toys increase noninteractive play (i.e., solitary or parallel play) (McLoyd 1983). Sarah is quite content spending hours arranging and rearranging "family members" and doll house furniture, chatting to herself as she does.

Caregivers invite Sarah to talk as she changes doll house furniture, confirming her behavior through words. "Where do you think the lamp looks best?" "I see you like the sofa in the corner near the serving table." Sarah stops and thinks and then says, as she moves the sofa, "No, I think the sofa should be here (near the lamp) so the daddy can read." Increasing the numbers of objects over time helps Sarah to clarify concepts and adds to her word supply.

As she grows, Sarah will become less dependent upon high realism toys to initiate pretend talk and play. However, at three and one-half years, Sarah needs many objects with smooth edges that are well-constructed, nonflammable, and nontoxic to stimulate thought and talk.

TABLE 7–1   Print Awareness Checklist

Responses to Stories	Yes	No	Not Sure
Knows what the title is			
Can find the title			
Knows who the author is			
Can find the author's name			
Knows where the story begins			
Knows where the story ends			
Knows that print and pictures match; points to the pictures and the word that represents that concept			
Pretends to read			
Shows how to read by using finger under the words			
Knows which page to turn and how print moves (from left to right)			
Retells story voluntarily after listening to it read			
Retells story when prompted			
Requests stories, books, poems, etc. to be read to him or her			

Language Development

Sarah's vocabulary grows by leaps and bounds between her third and fourth year of life. Her sentences at three are generally four or more words long. Sarah's insatiable curiosity is reflected in her endless questions about everything—print, pictures, objects, and people. As she reaches her fourth birthday, she may invent an imaginary playmate. Given Sarah's highly imaginative behavior, the invention of a playmate is certainly in keeping with her pattern of development. Generally, within a number of months, her imaginary companion will be overshadowed by other interests and other friends. Some caregivers make use of imaginary companions, involving them in the child's activities and citing them as models. Others just let their normal development run its course.

Between three and four, Sarah's speech reflects many of the regular rules of language; unusual plurals and irregular verb forms have yet to be achieved. At age three and one-half, Sarah, recounting her trip to the zoo, overgeneralizes a verb form when she reports that "The monkeys swinged up and down."

Sarah absorbs the speech of her caregivers and agemates. She listens more and she speaks more at home and at nursery school.

Sarah has had trouble with her mittens and is tearful as she says she cannot find them. Her caregiver, noting the tears, says, "We'll have to look for them together."

Sarah brightens. They search and, as they do, the caregiver says, "You're like the three little kittens who . . . " and Sarah finishes "lost their mittens." "Remember the song," asks the caregiver, and begins to sing "Three little kittens, they lost their mittens and they began to cry. . . . " Sarah and her caregiver proceed to the final meows while they search. Realizing that this is the fourth or fifth pair of mittens she has misplaced, Sarah is beginning to feel and look very anxious. The caregiver detects this and says "Why don't we put Sarah in the song?" Sarah looks puzzled and the caregiver begins to sing "Sad little Sarah, she lost her mittens and she begins to cry, Oh Mother dear. . . . " The teacher beckons Sarah to sing and Sarah indeed puts herself in the song distancing herself somewhat from the reprimand she thinks she deserves. As they sing, they locate the mittens.

Later, the caregiver hears Sarah singing "Bad Sarah, bad Sarah. She lost her mittens; Good Sarah, good little Sarah. She found her mittens, she found her mittens."

The caregiver associated Sarah's predicament with an appropriate nursery song and put Sarah into the song. Sarah later took the next step and created several new verses herself. Numerous language experiences grow out of everyday events such as losing mittens. The astute caregiver, assessing readiness to learn and the opportune time, takes advantage of such daily occurrences.

What Is the Role of the Caregiver in Nurturing the Child's Growth toward Literacy?

Behaviors nurturant of literacy are those that provide materials, time and space, encouragements, and praise for all leaps into literacy. In the settings these behaviors create, materials full of print and illustrations, information, and entertainment abound. Stories and poems seen in books and heard on cassettes are sung and sometimes danced to. Space for object, solitary, and social play is provided as are varieties of props and toys. Time in home and in nursery school is arranged for book sharing, book browsing, book talking, book enacting, and picture and print creating.

These settings are also rich in verbal and nonverbal encouragement and praise. When Sarah retells stories, acts them out, and exhibits energetic singing, dancing, and rhyming, caregivers are excited, too. Teachers and parents best serve children's climb to literacy when they are excited about words and stories, creating and sustaining strong story involvement. Such caregivers ensure Ben and Sarah's access to books. They provide children with book and story collections not only in the home, but they introduce Ben and Sarah to the children's room in the nearest library. They plan for browsing time, sharing time, and extending time.

For browsing, they provide the books and quiet time needed to thumb through and look through them. When Sarah picks up *Baby Dinosaurs* (Sattler 1984) and begins to ask questions about the names of these animals, her caregiver answers and helps Sarah when she tries to imitate the name.

Caregivers incorporate into their sharing sessions not only stories but poems, riddles, word games, and finger rhymes. Variety is the spice of sharing time and Sarah enjoys the change from prose to poetry. She enjoys the invitation to match words with motion in Merriam's

> *Hop on one foot,*
> *jump with two,*
> *skip, skip,*
> *Where's my shoe?*
> *Skip in a circle,*
> *skip in a square,*
> *lost my shoe,*
> *don't know where.*
> *Jump on the bed,*
> *lump inside:*
> *here's my shoe*
> *trying to hide.**

The self-monitoring tool that appears in Table 7–2 can serve as a checklist guide for caregivers of three-year-olds and older children. Questions asked help mother or father, grandparents, or teachers to assess their own behavior for more effective modeling for children.

---

* From *You Be Good & I'll Be Night* by Eve Merriam. Copyright © 1988 by Eve Merriam. (Morrow Junior Books) Reprinted by permission of Marian Reiner.

TABLE 7–2 Caregiver's Self-Monitoring of Behavior

Caregiver's Facilitating Behaviors	Comments
When I carry out an activity, I encourage the child to follow and role-play the action. (When setting the dinner table, the child says, "I'll help." Let him.)	
I can hear my words from activities used by the child.	
I use the same story markers when telling a story ("Once upon a time" or "happily ever after").	
I take notes about language use and behaviors —physical, emotional, social, and cognitive— to determine what I need to do to further encourage development.	
I look for behavioral patterns in the notes over a specified time period. The patterns that are productive are preserved and are used as data for changing environments, materials, and activities.	
I model role-play with the child. I put on, for example, a policeman's cap and badge and act out the role.	
I keep a record of the songs, chants, poems, and ditties used with the child. I use these again and again and add one new one at a time to the repertoire.	
I provide time, when the child is ready, to listen to retellings of stories.	
I begin to use prompts to guide retellings. (See chapters 9 and 10 for guided and unguided retelling activities.)	
I arrange to have the child engage in parallel, associative, and cooperative play activities.	
When I read a story, I move my hand under the line, point to pictures that match words, and name objects when using object books.	
I talk about stories and personal experiences that match those of characters in stories.	
I draw and talk about what I draw when the child begins to do this. This helps the child associate oral language with what is being drawn.	

Sarah loves wordplay, especially alliterative verse. When her caregiver shares Prelutsky's "The Giggling Gaggling Gaggle of Geese" (1983), Sarah does not understand all the words. She does know about giggling and, before she realizes it, joins in on the first and last line of each stanza. This action and other similar ones, mentioned earlier in this text, may be considered a formal activity for the beginning reader and writer.

Sarah is aware of space that is hers—her own cubby, her room, and her chair. She is becoming aware of shared space and group space. Since Sarah has no siblings, she has had limited experiences in sharing space. When her cousins play with her or her friends, it is often in her own home where space is hers. As she leaves home and begins to meet other groups where all spaces are shared, Sarah learns about the need to share. Sarah's caregiver may need to guide and model space-sharing behavior for Sarah. "Thank you Sarah for sharing this bench with David." "I like the way you recognized your name on the play floor and found your space, right away." "Jimmy seems to have very little room. I'm glad you shared your space with him."

Sarah's caregivers nurture prosocial behavior and in nursery school plan activities in which Sarah and her peers must work cooperatively to succeed. Preparing for snack time or setting up for a skit requires that Sarah work with others.

Books About Friends and Sharing

Some helpful books about sharing follow. These include fictional characters that provide the fun side of cooperative and collaborative play.

Flack, Marjorie. (1932). *Ask Mr. Bear.* Illustrated by author. New York: Macmillan. Danny is anxious about choosing the best present for his mother's birthday. He seeks advice from many animals but it is Mr. Bear who seems to know best.

Lobel, Arnold. (1979). *Frog and Toad Are Friends.* Illustrated by author. New York: Harper & Row. The several adventures of frog and toad in this volume celebrate the warm and gentle feelings of true friendship. There are also *Frog and Toad Together* (1972), *Frog and Toad All Year* (1976), and *Days With Frog and Toad* (1979).

Marshall, James. (1972). *George and Martha.* Illustrated by author. Boston: Houghton Mifflin. Here are brief stories relating the friendship of two hippos who enjoy each other's weaknesses as well as strengths.

Pomerantz, Charlotte. (1984). *The Half-Birthday Party.* Illustrated by DyAnne DiSalvo-Ryan. New York: Clarion Books. Danny wants to celebrate his sister's half-birthday at six months. When he forgets to bring a gift, after arranging the party, he is embarrassed but creative.

Williams, Vera B. (1982). *A Chair for My Mother.* Illustrated by author. New York: Greenwillow Books. When everything they own is destroyed in a fire, a young girl wants more than anything else to buy her mother a chair. How the pennies add up in a big jar and the chair is carefully and lovingly selected are the bases for this warm, happy story.

At home, Sarah's parents have encouraged her to care for her kitten and to assume responsibility for some family tasks such as helping to keep her clothes and toys in order, setting the table, and helping her daddy in the garden. Young children who are consistently encouraged to accept responsibility for certain home tasks are more likely to exhibit prosocial or cooperative behavior (Staub 1975).

Sarah is also learning that she can help to make her bedroom or classroom prettier. When her caregiver asks Sarah's opinion about where to place the flowers, posters, murals, pictures, books, Sarah thinks and reflects, finally offering an opinion.

Aesthetic understanding and the social and language development of young children are nurtured by:

- involving young children in decisions about enhancing their space. "Where shall we put the pictures that Johnny brought to us today?"
- demonstrating alternatives in placing things in the classroom or at home in the bedroom; i.e., showing how different posters look set against different backgrounds. "Sarah, let's decide where we should hang this poster. Should we put it near the window? What do you think?"
- helping children to seek beauty in everyday activities such as setting up the snack table so that the snacks look good as well as taste good. "How might we make the table prettier?"
- involving children in discussion on where to place the chairs or the props for easy use by everyone. "Think about where we should put our scenery so everyone can see it."

Participation in decision making about space and settings generates a greater awareness by young children of their environment, their use of it, and the possibility of making it more pleasing.

The caregiver is sharer and observer-teacher and learner. Sarah's caregiver fills her room with picture books and her ears with stories. Sarah asks for the stories again and again and returns to her picture books many times.

In her role as observer-learner, Sarah's caregiver has studied Sarah and her interests. She knows Sarah loves pancakes and she knows Sarah loves poems—short, bouncy ones and long story ones. She introduces Sarah to "Mix a Pancake":

Mix a pancake
Stir a pancake
Pop it in the pan.

> *Fry the pancake*
> *Toss the pancake*
>   *Catch it if you can*   *(Christina Rossetti)*

Sarah listens and follows along. She mixes and she stirs and then she pops herself up. She "fries" and tosses and shouts the final line with a strong intention to "catch it." In no time at all, Sarah knows the whole poem. She carefully observes the different gestures for mixing and stirring and finds in the "house" corner of the nursery classroom a large spoon with which she demonstrates some hearty movements. She comes to a halt when she realizes that she really cannot "pop it" or "toss it" from a spoon. She asks her caregiver for that "thing" to get the pancake up. After frowning in puzzlement over the question, the caregiver smiles and says, "Oh, you mean a spatula" and she finds one in the "kitchen." Sarah beams and enacts the tossing of the pancake. Throughout the day, Sarah repeats the poem sometimes returning to the real prop, sometimes doing without it. One or two of Sarah's friends are curious and start to mouth "Catch it if you can."

After a while, Sarah picks up her crayons, places her paper carefully in front of her, and draws pancakes and more pancakes—big circles and little circles and some uneven circles. After a while, Sarah sits back and looks at her drawing; she decides she wants to label it. She asks her caregiver to write "Pancakes" under her drawing. When Sarah sees the big P, she takes a fresh sheet of paper and fills it with a big wobbly, "P." Then she imitates the other letters. When she finishes, she proudly points to her uncertain printing and says, "That's Pancakes, see?" and proceeds to draw small pancakes all over the sheet and around the print, chanting "I love pancakes."

Her caregiver, sensitive to Sarah's interest in pancakes, shares Tomie dePaola's *Pancakes for Breakfast.* Together, Sarah and her caregiver create the tale from this humorous, wordless story of a woman who is determined to have pancakes for breakfast but encounters all sorts of difficulties in the process.

In her role as teacher, Sarah's caregiver needs to provide the conditions in Table 7–3 to guide her through this fourth year of life.

In the role of observer or learner, Sarah's caregiver supplies her with high realism toys and a prop box. She watches as Sarah arranges and rearranges furniture, nodding quietly from time to time. She observes that Sarah, when tired of furniture arranging takes a small pail of water and liquid detergent and starts to wash her doll's clothes, murmuring that her doll has pretty clothes like Annabelle in *A is for Annabelle.*

Ben, meanwhile shuffling through the prop box comes upon a fireman's hat, dons it, and swings into action—pulling hoses, running, gesturing, and sending his voice forth in fire bell fashion. The caregiver, noticing Ben's intense interest in firemen, decides to share *Owliver* with Ben who would

TABLE 7–3   Caregiver's Provisions for Literacy

Provisions for Literacy	Comments
The child's room is stocked with books.	
The caregiver shares stories, poems, word puzzles, and other activities that include pictures and print.	
The caregiver encourages the child to retell stories after being read to. He or she might say, "Tell me the story." "What happened in the story?" "Make believe that I never heard the story before and tell it to me."	
Observes the child and identifies interests with the purposes of selecting books, selecting poems, selecting songs, or selecting day trips.	

appreciate the story of the little owl who, subjected to all kinds of pressure to become a doctor or lawyer, makes his own career decision. He becomes a fireman. Table 7–4 can be used by the caregiver to self-monitor behaviors when observing children's interactive play behavior.

Observations reveal Sarah's interests, her understanding of various roles, and the behavior relevant to them. Caregivers see the depth of her feelings regarding these roles, the length of her attention span, her preference, at any given moment, for solitary rather than social play. These observations serve to create changes in the caregiver's actions and environmental preparations.

If Sarah chants or murmurs to herself as she pursues her play, the caregiver listens carefully and judges whether it is appropriate to comment. When Sarah picks up her doll and cradles it and hums, the caregiver quietly says, "Maybe your doll needs a lullaby" and begins to hum "Hush little baby, don't you cry. . . . " The caregiver "flip-flops" between assessing Sarah's needs, and providing for them as she listens to and looks at behaviors. Sarah remembers listening and smiling at all the verses as the caregiver introduced the song days before. She hums along very softly and joins in on "Hush, little baby, don't you cry." Later, she puts her doll down and asks, unexpectedly, if her doll is a "china" doll.

Play choices and play behavior—solitary and social—reveal much about Sarah and her development. The observant caregiver uses such information in creating play settings nurturant of activities, discussions, and drawings basic to literacy development.

Real-life books are much appreciated by Sarah. Stories such as *The Little Puppy,* full of pictures of a puppy-to-dog life, generate Sarah's interest and

TABLE 7–4   Caregiver's Self-Monitoring Checklist

Caregiver's Behavior	Comments
When and in what activity is the child able to play successfully with others? How have I adjusted time for such interactions?	
How much time does the child spend in a particular type of play? How have I provided the time for each type of play for each child?	
Where and when does the child play alone (solitary play)? How much time and space are sufficient for this play frame?	
How does the child make decisions about roles in social play (i.e., who is the mother, the baby, the doctor, etc.)? This is important for decision-making ability in academic/interactive activities in later grades in school.	
How intensely does the child play each role?	

urge to create her own story. She cannot wait to tell about her kitten's antics and she does so quickly and delightedly.

Sarah shortly finds that she has much more to share about her kitten so she takes a crayon in hand and begins to draw her story. First there is her kitten and then all sorts of things on the page which Sarah says are balls—paper balls, wool balls, and plain small balls—that her kitten pushes and tosses about. Sarah loves thinking and talking about her pet and mumbles as she fills the page with the kitten's playthings. Then she wants a title and asks her caregiver to write, "My Kitten, Star" on a word card, a 4 × 7 inch piece of paper. This is the very beginning of Sarah's Word Bank. She will collect words that represent concepts and objects. Now she may be ready to recognize them. "Here," says she, thrusting forth the piece of paper on which her caregiver prints. Sarah then, using the print as a model, proceeds to "print" on her drawing.

Books About Pets

Books about pets provide a frame for recalling past and present personal experiences and they provoke an urge to share them.

Bridwell, Norman. (1969). *Clifford, the Big Red Dog*. Illustrated by author. New York: Scholastic. Clifford is lovable but clumsy; anxious to please but awkward at achieving it. He has many adventures so that a young child who grows fond of him can experience many more of his adventures in *Clifford's Good Deeds* (1976), *Clifford Takes a Trip* (1969), *Clifford's Tricks* (1971), and others.

Flack, Marjorie. (1931). *Angus and the Cat.* Illustrated by author. New York: Doubleday. Unlike Clifford, Angus, a Scotch terrier, is a wiry and quick investigator. In addition to his adventure with the Cat, he and the ducks experience some frustrating and amusing times (*Angus and the Ducks*, 1939), and he manages to get himself lost (*Angus Lost*, 1941).

Gackenbach, Dick. (1975). *Do You Love Me?* Boston: Houghton Mifflin. After much searching, Walter is given a puppy he can love and fondle and who can love him back.

Provensen, Alice, and Provensen, Martin. (1978). *The Year at Maple Hill Farm.* New York: Atheneum. Farm life and the animals living on the farm are shown in many seasonal activities. This is one of a number of Maple Hill Farm stories.

Sarah's caregiver in his roles as teacher and learner finds himself adjusting his roles as Sarah's behaviors warrant.

What Activities and Materials Foster Literacy?

Two types of activities especially facilitate literacy at this stage: picture talk and story talk.

Picture Talk

Sarah is learning more and more from picture books; her visual literacy is developing. Her grandmother has given her Tasha Tudor's *A is for Annabelle*. After listening to her caregiver and watching him run his fingers under the words as he says them, Sarah repeats "A is for Annabelle." Sarah looks closely at the book. She wants to know what flowers are "all around Annabelle." Then she points to Annabelle's checked dress and hat and observes that the doll on the opposite page cannot be Annabelle because "She looks different."

When her caregiver asks her to talk about the difference, Sarah says, "The colors are different and the hat is different." She notes too that the girls are talking to Annabelle "in the other picture."

Sarah wonders why the next two pages are not "colored." She likes flowers "colored." She points to the mouse sniffing at Annabelle's box. "What's the mouse doing?" "Why does Annabelle have a box?" Sarah never heard of a "cloak." "What's that?" she asks.

On the "E" page, Sarah sees earrings and talks at some length about the earrings her mother has that she likes best. She uses words like "sparkly, hanging, jingling" and even says "Some are like buttons." When her caregiver smiles and says, "They're ear buttons." Sarah giggles and chants "Mommy wears ear buttons, ear buttons, ear buttons. Mommy wears. . . . " Sarah remarks that the jacket on the "J" page is "fancy." Sarah likes the sound of "frilly" on the "K" page. As soon as it is read to her, she finds a rhyme for it and sings "dilly, silly, Milly, Billy" and stops. She giggles. "That's my friend, Billy—silly Billy, silly dilly. . . . " The word "frilly" has generated so much wordplay that it will keep Sarah occupied for intermittent minutes throughout the day. At a later age, each of these will become a word card, added to Sarah's word bank. These word families will be used for creating rhymes and song.

When Sarah sees Annabelle's locket, she runs to get her own. "Now we both have lockets," she grins. "Mine's bigger."

Sarah's meandering through *A is for Annabelle* brings her many fresh visual experiences. Caregivers will observe Sarah's browsing and encourage her to describe what she sees. According to Stewig (1989), the first skill needed for visual/oral literacy is that of describing. Listening to Sarah and helping her to tell what she sees in the pictures, expanding her language informally and naturally as she studies a page or proceeds to the next one, helps her:

- to look carefully at pictures for all the information they convey
- to begin to describe pictures by size, by color, by numbers of people and/or things in them
- to begin to understand how pictures and words relate to each other
- to match new pictures or parts of a picture to words and new words to pictures
- to extend vocabulary by rhyming, by questioning
- to notice differences in pictures from one page to the next
- to associate pictures and words with her own past or present experiences

Caregivers need to provide activities to facilitate these actions.

As Sarah grows older and continues her walk through picture books, she will advance to the next steps in visual literacy—comparison and appreciation. Indeed, Sarah's observation about Annabelle's dresses and her own demonstrates that she is already doing some comparing and appreciating. Caregivers ensure such development when their sharing of picture books with young children is consistent and interactive.

Refer to Table 7–1 which may be used to record observations made as children interact with stories. Several other checklists which may also be used as tools to collect and assess strengths and needs are in chapter 3.

Story Talk

Sarah and Ben both enjoy *Friska: the Sheep That Was Too Small.* The teacher shares the tale of how the small sheep saves the flock and finally earns the respect of her large peers. It is a painful story of rejection because of size, but Friska, the small sheep, has both imagination and persistence.

Ben and Sarah talk extensively about Friska's efforts to impress the flock. Some of these efforts Ben calls "silly." "The snow will melt," says Ben reacting to Friska's attempt to make herself bigger by letting the snow mount on her back. Sure enough, the snow melts. Sarah thinks the blanket of cherry blossoms is silly too. "They will blow away." Sure enough, a brisk wind scatters all the blossoms from Friska's back. Friska, now desperate, steals a fleece in order to appear bigger than she is. Ben becomes judgmental at this point and says, "That's naughty." Sarah says of Friska, "She's sad." Sarah and Ben relax with Friska's victory over the wolf. They retell this, shouting together with great glee as the wolf speeds into the forest.

Children need story talks; they need opportunities to reflect and to talk about what they understand and how they feel about stories. When they empathize with characters, they may need help in expressing how they have personalized the happenings in the story. "She's sad," says Sarah, recognizing Friska's dilemma and sad expression. Both Sarah and Ben engaged in judging the worth of the various solutions to Friska's problem. Finally, in Friska's case, they learn that "small" can mean success. Small can "win out." For Sarah, who is petite, this is a particularly happy thought. Sarah likens herself to Friska and remarks that her cousin always calls her "midget." In a culture that prizes "big," it is an interesting new thought for small to succeed. Ben and Sarah talk about poor Friska and they reconfirm how important friends are.

Unlike *A is for Annabelle,* an alphabet book, *Friska* has a definite story structure. Friska, the main character, is born small and stays small. Because of her size, she encounters a problem—rejection. Several episodes carry out the story's plot. A resolution emerges. She makes three attempts to become bigger. None of these succeeds. Because of her size, she is able to hide from a wolf, creep up from behind, and give his tail a vicious bite which sends him scurrying back to the forest.

In their story talk, Sarah and Ben have clearly shown that they understand Friska's basic problem. They have identified her three noneffective solutions and they have rejoiced in Friska's outwitting the fox. Roy Lewis's wonderfully structured text helps these children to know how to structure stories for themselves.

Sarah and Ben's developing awareness of story structure can be quickly recorded via the checklist (Table 7–5) of story structure elements. This checklist can be used after each retelling. Keeping a running record of growth—those elements that are included each time the child retells a story—permits

TABLE 7–5 Sense of Story Structure

Child: _____ Age: ____ Date: _____

Story: _____

Comprehension after (check one) listening _____ , reading _____ ,

reading and listening to tape _____ , viewing video cassette _____ .

Check One: Oral retelling _____ Written retelling _____ .

Check One: Unguided retelling _____ Guided retelling _____ .

	Yes	No	Not Sure
Setting Begins story with an introduction (i.e., "Once upon a time," "It started when," etc.)			
Tells where the story happened (location)			
Tells when the story happened (time, day, date); names the main character			
Names other characters (include number named/total number in story)			
Theme Names story problem or goal			
Plot Episodes Number of episodes recalled			
Total number of episodes in the story			
Resolution Names the resolution to the problem, or attainment of goal			
Ends story appropriately.			
Sequence Retells story in the order as written by the author			

Statement of Assessment (Strengths and Needs): _____

_____

_____

the teacher to report progress observed in classrooms. The retelling checklist and a transcript of that retelling are the raw data needed to confirm the teacher's notions about the child's strengths and needs. The data provide information that helps the teacher decide the sort of prompting the child needs to recall more story elements.

Prompting Sarah to retell elements of a story, after listening, helps to enhance her awareness of story structure. Awareness of story elements will help Sarah to recall and comprehend more effectively and will guide her to create her own stories. Sometimes Sarah recalls all elements of stories and other times does not. Her teacher notices that she begins story retellings with "Once upon a time." She has internalized this story element from listening to stories since the earliest years of her life. Her teacher notices that she usually retells the story without including the name of the main character. One day, immediately following a story reading time, Sarah said, "Let me tell the story." She began, "Once upon a time, there was this boy." Her teacher, immediately asked, "What was the boy's name?" This question was used, again and again, each time Sarah referred to the main character in a story generically or with a pronoun. Sarah, after several retellings said, "This time I'll tell you the name of the boy in the story." Questions prompt story sharing. They help three- and four-year-old children to focus attention when retelling. Asking a question using the same language again and again helps the child internalize the questions. When retelling, the child will, eventually, ask himself questions to guide recall. The prompts in Table 7–6 may be used

TABLE 7–6   Guides to Aid Children in Retelling Stories

Story Element	Prompts/Questions
Introduction	Did you begin your story with an introduction? Suggestions: Once upon a time . . . It began . . . (Children may need one of these suggestions to begin.)
Setting (place) (time)	Where did the story take place? When did the story take place?
Theme (main character) (other characters)	Who is the story about? Who else is in the story?
Plot (problem or goal)	What is the (main character's) problem?
Episodes (events)	What happened first? What happened next? (Use this prompt for each episode in the story, if necessary. Some children will need only one prompt in order to recall events; others may need several.)
Resolution (problem solved)	How was the problem solved? How did (mention the main character) solve his/her problem?

Modified from Glazer (1992).

to guide youngsters to recall a story. This strategy will be referred to as guided retelling throughout the text.

Sarah's literacy development is greatly accelerated by access to many well-structured picture books, storybooks, and picture-storybooks. The continuous sharing of these and talking about them are the solid bases upon which literacy grows.

Summary

The fourth year of life marks many changes—body length, improved coordination in both gross and fine muscles, possible first-time management of separation from the primary caregiver, increase in social contacts and, with the caregiver's guidance, the beginnings by the young child of a monitoring of his or her own behavior. The child this year may experience many first-time situations, some of which may generate fear. Caregiver behavior is critical at these times. Appropriate sharing of books and attendant book-talk accompanied by sensitive care, and caution will help to ease all kinds of fears including those incurred when the young child encounters a "first."

Children participate in many types of play in which they vent a variety of emotions while assuming different roles. They increase and intensify their social contacts, extend their vocabulary, and broaden and deepen their conceptual knowledge. Both object play and social play catalyze a child's growth. The availability of playmates and playthings are crucial not only to social development but also to language and emotional development. A growing awareness of print, enjoyment of picture books, book sharing, book talk, and story retellings signal acceleration toward literacy.

Encouragement, praise, gentle consistent guidance, provision of materials, time, and space nurture the child's literacy. Caregivers in their role of learner-observers facilitate growth by recording behavior as the child browses, choruses, and enacts songs, poems, and stories. By examining their own professional response behavior as well as the child's actions, they can construct a solid profile of development and identify the settings that will best facilitate further development. This chapter contains many formats for such recordings.

The child's participation in activities such as meal preparation and room decoration identifies him or her as a decision-maker—as a person whose opinions and actions do matter. When children's interests and preferences are seriously recognized, children themselves take them more seriously and give them more thought. Such reflection immeasurably aids intellectual development.

High realism toys and prop boxes, picture books and environmental print, writing tools, stories, poems, and song sharing, built-in talk as well as listening times mark optimal settings for literacy development.

Children are participating in more and more activities so they have many experiences to share. They need time and encouragement to talk. In such dialogues, children not only link their varied experiences together, but they also apply them to the stories, poems, and songs they hear and create— growing rapidly in connecting life with print. In fact, the child is growing quickly in meaning-making.

8

The Fifth Year of Life

This chapter addresses the following questions:

- What growth patterns characterize the fifth year of life?
- What is the role of the caregiver in nurturing the child's growth toward literacy?
- What activities and materials foster literacy?

What Growth Patterns Characterize the Fifth Year of Life?

Physical Characteristics

Ben at four is still outgrowing his earlier top-heavy appearance. In keeping with general development, Ben grows from the top down and from the center out. His body, arms, and legs continue to lengthen.

Ben delights in trying to throw his play balls as far as possible and needs his caregiver to admire his skill. Ben is particularly delighted when Brian, his older brother, plays with him and says, "Good, Ben" after a successful throw. Ben's stance, arm action, and even speed are improving. Fortunately, Ben has a large area both in preschool and at home to flex his muscles and continue to test and improve his skill. Ben is quite successful at jumping and as he nears five, he can succeed in spanning a yard or so in a broad jump. Tying his shoelaces is a bit of a challenge. Ben really prefers the Velcro-grip shoes he can tape together quickly to the shoelaces with which he continues to fumble. Ben at five has been given a bicycle, and he is trying to master the pedals and balancing; he has a way to go but is making progress. Physically, Ben's small motor development permits him to create designs described by Kellogg (1970). Ben creates "designs" as he engages in bridging from drawings full of recognizable shapes to some combining of these shapes. Ben, delighted about his work, wants it displayed and signed.

Cognitive Development

The ability to focus on the most essential facets of any stimulus (print, for example) apparently improves as one grows. Ben's ability to view quickly, to scan, is just developing. The visual discrimination required for reading necessitates a quick look at words and letters and quick differentiation of them. According to Nodine and Simmons (1974) honing in on the most critical features of such visual stimuli depends on age.

Ben demonstrates his ability to coordinate stimuli from many senses when he plays the "blindfold" game and feels small familiar objects while blindfolded and then is asked to name them. He sometimes has a good deal of difficulty labeling the objects from touch rather than sight and sings his own praises when he succeeds. According to Abravanel (1968) and Blank and Bridges (1964), Ben is now well into the age range where such intersensory communication is at its greatest growth. This integration of information from various senses is vital for learning (see chapter 6). Inability to accomplish such integration may lead to learning disabilities (Sarafino and Armstrong 1986). According to Gibson (1969), both the awareness of the distinctive features of any stimuli as well as the invariant (the constant) properties of the stimuli must be known as a basis for the perceptual and interpretive skills vital to reading. Ben's perceptual and interpretive abilities have matured sufficiently so that he can recognize many letters, saying them as he writes them. He recognizes many words from the print-rich environments in which he lives and learns.

Confronting many daily tasks in and out of school results in Ben's becoming more efficient. He categorizes better, grouping his toys and books by size for return to the play box or book shelf and stacking his counters by colors.

Books About Success and Achievement

Stories of success and achievement are helpful to Ben at this point. A list of such stories follow.

Lionni, Leo. (1987). *Swimmy*. Illustrated by author. New York: Alfred A. Knopf. Swimmy, a small fish, survives the hazards of the ocean by joining a large group of fish that swim together.

Magorian, Michelle. (1990). *Who's Going to Take Care of Me?* Illustrated by James Graham Hale. New York: Harper Collins. Young children will appreciate how Eric feels when his older sister goes off to kindergarten. Eric is not happy until he finds he can help a frightened new boy in his own day-care class.

McDonald, Megan. (1990) *Is This a House for Hermit Crab?* Illustrated by S. D. Schindler. New York: Orchard Books. Hermit crab scritch-scratches his way along the shore and finally finds a home for himself that is just right. If at first you don't succeed, try, try again and he does.

Rathmann, Peggy. (1991). *Ruby the Copycat*. Illustrated by author. New York: Scholastic. Ruby copies Angela's hair style, clothes, poem and. . . . An alert teacher helps Ruby to see that she need copy no one; she has special gifts of her own.

Smith, Maggie. (1991). *There's a Witch under the Stairs*. Illustrated by author. New York: Lothrop, Lee & Shepard. Frances finally cures herself of the notion that there is a witch in her basement constantly trying to catch her on the stairway.

Ben is learning to use his senses more effectively. He watches his father get ready to paint a room. He sees the roller and the paint brushes for trim; he watches his father collect the ladder, some cloths, and a big cloth his father calls a "drop cloth." He sees his father open the paint can, reach for the paddle stirrer, and very carefully begin to circle the thick mixture. He continually asks "What is that?" as his father assembles his tools. His father patiently explains, using the words—paint, roller, brush, trim, paint tray, ladder, drop cloth, stirrer, thick, and others. Ben associates these with their referents.

In addition to the words Ben hears, he notices the care his father takes in assembling his tools and how slowly and carefully he begins tasks. Impatiently, Ben reaches out to smooth the drop cloth. His father, realizing that Ben has to be active, suggests that Ben spread his large drawing sheet papers on a far corner of the drop cloth and fingerpaint a picture while his father paints the wall. Ben does not consider this "helping," and his father quickly adds that Ben can also watch for any "drops" that may miss the drop cloth and mop them up quickly with the cloths to which he points. Ben smiles, moves the cloths closer to himself, and runs to get his fingerpaints and paper. Ben appreciates the time he is alone with his father; Brian and Mary Kay are always vying for their father's time. The opportunity to have Father to himself is to Ben a golden one.

Ben proudly announces to his mother that he is helping Daddy paint and, before he returns to his father, excitedly tells his mother about his father's preparation and how he plans to help his father; he uses words like drop cloth, ladder, cloths, mop up, roller tray, brush, and trim. She smiles as Ben rambles on, puts one of his father's old shirts on Ben, and sends him off to fingerpaint.

Ben carefully spreads out his drawing sheet, places his fingerpaints around the sheet, tucks his cuffs up, glancing about to see whether any drops have accumulated in his absence. Satisfied that they have not, he begins to paint, subconsciously mimicking his father's movement. His palm and fingers begin to move back and forth across the paper much as his father moves the roller back and forth, up and down on the wall. Ben creates designs he has not seen before and looks up excitedly to share.

Ben is learning many things—a cluster vocabulary, i.e., many words involving one task, painting. He also observes the care one takes in preparing to do a job; he notes that specific tools are necessary for some tasks and that assembling them before one starts is helpful. His father uses the "paint" words many times as he continues his task and Ben, seeing the referents, has formed very solid concepts of what the labels mean. Much later, Ben sees the care with which his father puts away his tools, discarding the roller but treating his brushes very carefully, folding up the ladder, making sure the drop cloth is dry, and folding it up. Ben watches everything.

Many aids to learning have been operative here. Motivation is strong; his father is important in Ben's life and helping him is something Ben wants very much to do. The place of motivation in all learning has been well established. Repetition of the "painting" words helps Ben remember them.

His father's modeling has left an impression on Ben. Ben's father has carried out activities so that his child moves through Holdaway's stages of learning. Ben has observed much, has partially participated, has rehearsed, and is performing. He puts the lids on his fingerpaint jars, wipes his hands carefully, moves his paper too fast and upsets his design, groans, and waits for it to dry before picking it up to show his mother and father.

Motivation, repetition, modeling, time to rehearse, participate, and perform all conspire to help Ben's learning. Ben's father has helped Ben to begin to move more slowly and to reflect, to think before he approaches a task, to consider what tools he needs, and to proceed carefully. It will be a long time before Ben learns to pause before he acts, but his father has modeled well the preparation involved here and he has set the stage for Ben's becoming more reflective. According to Kogan (1983), children become more reflective as they grow, and reflective children are more likely to consider a problem before they act and to generate solutions that are apt and efficient. Ben's father's behavior has served Ben well.

Ben wants his painting signed and his mother helps; she models the letters in his first name and praises Ben as he writes, even though letters may not be clear or correctly formed. Ben is pleased with his efforts and his mother is too. They hang the painting in his room for all to see and admire (Figure 8–1). In general, Ben is still limited in his cognitive development by the strictures of preoperational thought detailed in previous chapters. He tends to view one facet of a situation at a time, cannot imagine that a sequence can be reversed, has difficulty understanding classes and subclasses, and thinks that anything that moves is alive. The painting scenario helps him to move away from some of these strictures; he sees that drops

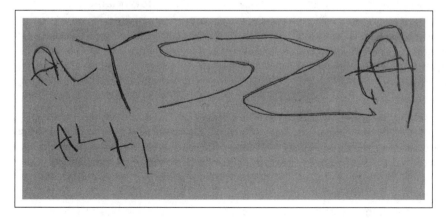

FIGURE 8–1 Deliberate Scribbles by Four Years and Six-Month-Old Ben

can be mopped up and a sequence reversed; he sees that father prepared not only tools to paint but also tools to undo mistakes. Apparently there are several facets to painting—he begins to understand that painting involves a subclass called tools and he has learned some of the members of this set. The painting experience has been rich in learning for Ben.

Emotional and Social Development

Ben has a growing sense of his parent's and teacher's roles in cooperating to keep him comfortable and clean and his classroom neat and functional. There are not only places but times in Ben's day that playthings are sorted and stored and play space is cleaned up.

In the apportioning of tasks, Ben's teachers see that everyone has a role and task for which he or she is held responsible. Sarah's task this week is exhibiting the present day on the calendar; Ben's getting the gerbil's food. Stories stream through each day, but the official set story hour is heralded by the quiet time that confirms the completion of classroom tasks cooperatively achieved.

Ben is liked by his schoolmates. Although less gregarious than Sarah, Ben is a good friend. He has observed his parent's response to each other and his teacher's response to him and his peers. He is learning that helping is pleasant and is rewarded. He also shares his ideas for play, and he is regarded as a helpful cooperative playmate with sometimes original ideas that delight his friends.

Although it is unclear what part biological factors play in social development, it is clear that they are operative (Sarafino and Armstrong 1986). It is also clear that what children observe at home is important. Because Ben sees a great many prosocial behaviors at home, he is inclined to behave that way himself. He presents a "let's-get-it-done-together" behavior to his peers. "Come on, George. Let's pick up the large pieces," or "Maybe if you do this part," pointing to one end of the mural paper, "and I paint here, we can put it up today."

Exhibitions of hostile behavior by other four-year-old children in the classroom confuse Ben because he sees little of it at home. He is used to being talked to by his parents about unacceptable behavior and his relations with his two siblings. Although the usual disagreements exist, they are not hostile and they serve to help Ben to view differences as problem-solving behavior. Ben listens as his teacher talks to children who exhibit hostile behavior. When thrust into a situation where a reaction to such behavior is called for, Ben withdraws and later becomes angry. He has much to learn about this behavior and how he should react to it.

Books About Social Behavior

Books about social behavior and social adjustment that relate to this developmental stage and will be of interest to Ben and his peers follow.

Cohen, Miriam. (1986). *Will I Have a Friend?* Illustrated by Lillian Hoban. New York: Macmillan. Jim worries about having a friend at school. Before his first day ends, Jim has found a friend and smiles happily at his father's question about how his day went.

Denslow, Sharon P. (1990). *At Taylor's Place.* Illustrated by Nancy Carpenter. New York: Bradbury. A gentle story for young children of a friendship between a young girl and an older neighbor who has a workshop in which the child and her neighbor create things together.

Hutchins, Pat. (1986). *The Doorbell Rang.* Illustrated by author. New York: Greenwillow Books. Friends gather where the cookies are. This is the tale of a home that always has room for one more.

Hutchins, Pat. (1990). *What Game Shall We Play?* Illustrated by author. New York: Greenwillow Books. Animal friends cannot settle the question of what game to play until owl settles it.

Udry, Janice. (1961). *Let's Be Enemies.* Illustrated by Maurice Sendak. New York: Harper & Row. The best of friendships have to survive rough weather. The young child appreciates this and the restored friendship when this text is shared.

Full cooperative play is much more characteristic of children older than Ben but Ben has observed much cooperation and is, at almost five, ready to join with others in simple tasks. Ben uses regulatory language in the negotiating children do as they specify roles each will play. He is likely to choose less domestic roles and continues to prefer dramatic and fantasy play (Fein and Schwartz 1986).

Ben's teacher has just shared the book *A Children's Zoo* by Tana Hoban, and Ben delighted in the action verbs. He thinks of some of his own— "squeaks" and "howls" and "wallops." He suggests a children's zoo in the classroom and gets his peers interested, and they practice squeaking, howling, galloping, and squawking as a mouse, a wolf, a zebra, and a parrot do. Ben agrees with the teacher that it is much better to perform in sequence, and together his friends and he decide on what that is to be. Ben is in his element and takes various parts as they fantasy play together.

It is, as has been noted for both Ben and Sarah previously, principally in his play, that Ben develops social skill and practices what he sees modeled at home. In setting the stage for the zoo, he gains experience in making friends, in making decisions, in sharing decision-making, and in testing the results of successful cooperation. The teacher suggests that they might want to look like the animals they are playing and Ben and his friends begin to talk about that—about colors and paper hats that might suggest a parrot, a lion. . . .

Popping up and down as the various animals talk or move intrigues Ben and his peers. They want to do it some more. Kevin thinks they should do it with the letters, "like in the alphabet song we sing." So they try it, bobbing up then down as they become the letters. They have learned some key words and they embellish the living alphabet with a—animals, b—boat, c. . . . The group has found another sequence to be dramatized. When the teacher adds a few slow but regular piano chords to the recitation, the dramatized alphabet takes on full performance status. Ben's interest in *A Children's Zoo* certainly set in process a good deal of activity, organization, coordination, decision making, thought, and fun. His friends are likely to remember Ben's part in creating and managing this activity.

Books About Animals

In the following books about animals, a sequence of actions is clear: such tales are easily retold or dramatized.

Brown, Margaret Wise. (1946). *Little Fur Family.* Illustrated by Garth Williams. New York: Harper Collins. This is the story of a small fur child who spends a day in the woods observing and playing; he seems happy to be back at home for dinner and bed: a comfortable story and an easily retold one.

Kellogg, Steven. (1979). *Pinkerton, Behave!* Illustrated by author. New York: Dial. One of the adventures—a particularly hilarious one—of Pinkerton, the Great Dane, who fails obedience school but happily, although accidentally, saves the family from a burglar.

Marshall, James. (1988). *Fox on the Job.* Illustrated by author. New York: Dial. Here are simple short chapters about a fox who wants to earn enough money to buy a bicycle but does not seem to have any marketable skills.

Mayer, Mercer. (1971). *A Boy, A Dog, A Frog and a Friend.* Illustrated by author. New York: Dial. Others are *Frog, Where Are You?* (1969); *Frog Goes to Dinner* (1974); *One Frog Too Many* (1975). These are wordless or almost-wordless picture books about a frog, his friends, and his adventures with actions readily repeated.

Mayer, Mercer. (1976). *Hiccup.* Illustrated by author. New York: Dial. Almost word-less humorous tale of two hippopotami who annoy each other when each gets the hiccups. They repeat each other's behavior.

Language Development

The painting chore shared with his father, his negotiations with his peers, his involvement with *A Children's Zoo*—all activities fuel Ben's vocabulary development. Indeed, if dramatic play leads to better reading and writing as suggested by Rogers and Sawyers (1988), Ben is solidifying a base for successful literacy.

Ben now interacts fully with his peers. Conversation helps to sharpen his listening and speaking skills, and so does negotiating with his friends. He takes part in many group activities and leads in some, as he did in the case of the zoo production; each of these encounters builds Ben's growing comfort in social situations and his ability to succeed in them.

He can supply rhymes for words when the teacher pauses in reading couplets or quatrains; he knows some word parts—grand and mother are in grandmother; he likes tongue twisters and may be able to add to the sequence if given a chance; and he can lengthen his sentences with conjunctions. He likes books, particularly books about animals. He is ready to go beyond the pet stories of a year or more ago to stories about animals he knows only vicariously.

Ben's word acquisition expands with every story read and told, with wordless books that he himself narrates; with print seen and print he writes, with talk and more talk. Ben knows the letters in sequence, can sing the alphabet song; can point to the letters and can approximate a number of them. Overgeneralized forms such as "runned" are much less frequent in Ben's speech. On the whole, Ben's language is healthy and developing rapidly. Activity, direct and vicarious, accelerates this development. The more diverse the activity, the more vocabulary is likely to assume new and greater dimensions.

What Is the Role of the Caregiver in Nurturing the Child's Growth toward Literacy?

Ben's home life—stable and wholesome—nurtures Ben's growth. For his full development, his preschool life must also be wholesome. A nurturant organizational climate in Ben's preschool is also vital to his development. Organizational climate is the "distinctive atmosphere that characterizes work settings" (Pace 1983; Steele and Jenks 1977). If the organizational climate in Ben's preschool is collegial, professional, supportive of staff, spacious enough to carry out a full program, and open to innovation, it has the qualities of a rich, nurturant organizational climate for staff (Jorde-Bloom 1986).

Ben notices that his teachers like and work well with each other and with him and his peers. He feels the stability and comfort of an environment in which people respect each other, and he benefits from these. He knows that he, too, will be supported in the things he tries to do.

Under Theme Centers and Story Ring later in this chapter, the human behaviors and physical settings nurturant of literacy are identifiable.

Space, time, and materials to book-browse, book-talk, book-enact, book-extend, and story-create continue to be critical parts of settings nurturant of early literacy. Ben still needs the prop boxes and the prompts to scripting (see chapter 6) but he is learning to use his environment more aptly and more efficiently to create new props and new scripts.

Space for cooperative play is essential for Ben and his peers. Ben's leadership in the enactment of *A Children's Zoo* exemplifies this need. (See the section in this chapter on activities and in chapters 6 and 7 on settings and environments.)

Lindfors' (1987) taxonomy for the roles of the teacher in language development include those of provider, demonstrator, learner, observer, and responder. These roles and others like them have been discussed and featured in this text. Lindfors' taxonomy helps us to review the overall role of the caregiver.

As provider, the caregiver assures that children have time, space, materials, encouragement, variety, know-how, and a no-risk environment in which to work. The nurturant environments described throughout this text incorporate these characteristics. These environments are much more likely to exist when the organizational climate of the staff is also nurturant.

Holdaway (1979) has convinced us to discuss the need to model, to demonstrate, throughout this text. Lindfors and others strongly urge that caregivers demonstrate a love for literacy themselves so that Ben and all children perceive the value placed upon reading and writing—upon language activities in our everyday lives. "Drop-everything-and-read"-type programs, where all school participants—from principal to the school's cook—read and share, demonstrate that school-wide reading and modeling are important. For four-year-old children, story rings, where everybody shares stories and everyone is completely attentive to the tales told, function as model structures; teachers listen as attentively as children to the tellers.

Teachers intent upon guiding children cannot ignore the role of learner. As they observe and note, they modify their pedagogy, their views of individual children. Ben needs freedom to explore and engage in the kinds of leadership apparent in the classroom zoo production; his friend Kevin needs more structure to succeed. The caregiver-learner notes this and helps Kevin to structure his collage work, for example, so that his materials are ready before he starts and success is more likely assured.

It may be that the teacher as learner is most effective in instilling an excitement about learning. When questions arise such as those generated about the porcupine in the next section of this chapter, the teacher models an interest in the answer and delights, with children, in finding the information and in raising more questions. The search for information and locating it is exciting to children and teachers: the road to scholarship wends this way.

The role of teacher/observer has been strongly highlighted throughout this text. It is in the honing of the teacher's observational skills, the recording of such observations, and the reflections on such records that guarantee a relevant pedagogy for each child. The caregiver's note of Ben's interest in Karla Kuskin's poem (next section) led to its introduction to the group and much discussion about the strange characteristics of this animal. Plans were modified here. Kevin's need for help in organizing his work was clear to the caregiver and she helped him to adjust his habits so that he could finish in a reasonable amount of time.

The checklists provided in all chapters of this text help the caregiver stay alert to changes in children's needs and behaviors and so provide the base for considering changes in plans and the use of time, space, and materials. It is not too great a claim to state that the teacher's observational skill and the implementation of observational records in daily planning may make the difference between the adequate and the master teacher.

The teacher as responder is another critical role. Not only the presence of a response, but also the way in which the teacher responds can facilitate or retard language development. Ben himself grows in his roles of spectator and participant; his role assumptions operate only if his caregivers respond. They need to listen to him; they need to engaged him in life-related language activities by responding to his asked and unasked questions.

Care in the role of observer is necessary to judge the right response to Ben. Although he is not an aggressive leader, he can interest other children in activities and engage them in working cooperatively together. His caregiver notes this about Ben and sees that he has the opportunity to exercise his quiet leadership. Only consistent study of Ben's behavior yields such knowledge about him.

The roles of provider, demonstrator, learner, observer, and responder interrelate strongly; one cannot exist without the exercise of the others. If we have not observed, we do not know what to provide nor demonstrate. If we have not learned, we cannot respond relevantly.

What Activities and Materials Foster Literacy?

Many of the literacy-nurturant activities have been detailed in the earlier chapters. For Ben and his four- going on five-year-old agemates, activities that confirm what he knows are as important as activities that introduce new, fresh skills and knowledge.

Ben now knows that stories tell about a sequence of events; activities which engage him in specifying these in new tales reinforce his sense of story, help him when he is rehearsing to share stories, and help him in thinking through his own story inventions.

Ben now realizes that reading for entertainment is only one purpose for reading, and Ben has become busily engaged in reading for specific purposes. He can find the picture that answers his questions about what the zebra looks like; he knows the book that contains that picture; he has seen his teacher refer to it many times.

He knows that when you want to share a story, you need to know what happens next. He needs activities that help him to concentrate on the sequences in stories. Simply-structured stories enable Ben to proceed easily from one event to the next.

Among the many activities Ben enjoys in his preschool are those involving the theme centers and the story ring. These are much like centers described more completely in chapter 9.

Theme Centers

One of the theme centers in Ben's preschool is labeled "Animals"—information books like *A Children's Zoo* and fiction stories like *Chanticleer and the Fox* are available here. There are books in which animals talk like people and books in which they growl and grunt. Ben sees here posters of animals and huge pictures of specific animals and gets a feeling of size and color and special characteristics as he gazes at them. He has visited the zoo with his parents and can call some of the animals' names without being told. The Center has paper for him to draw and label the animals he knows, pictures to guide him in learning about the animals he does not know, and many poems and songs about animals.

Ben looks again and again at the beautiful illustrations in Eric Carle's *Animals, Animals* and wants to hear the poems on the pages. He marvels at the size of the whale which consumes two whole double pages. He sees in Carle's bright collage designs pictures of the seal, lion, elephant, hippo, and penguin quite different from the photographs of Hoban and asks questions about how Carle "did that." The teacher demonstrates to the class a simple collage technique and Ben comes away with the glimmer of appreciation and understanding of Carle's art.

Ben giggles as he listens to his teacher's tape of Karla Kuskin's poem about the porcupine and stimulated by the word "quilly" he word-plays "Billy quilly, quilly Billy, silly Billy quilly," He studies the way Carle makes the quills and decides that he could do that and begins to shred some of the paper that is at the Center. Ben spends a good deal of time at the Center savoring the art of Carle, trying collage himself, listening again and again to the poem, and playing with the word "quilly." He asks his teacher for the Hoban book and looks at the photograph of penguins and then at Carle's penguins, as well. Ben is making comparisons, a critical skill needed for reading and writing.

When his teacher shares Lucy Rhu's poem about penguins, Ben is entranced. He never thought of that. Now he does not know whether his penguins, all dressed up, are coming or going, and he is intrigued with the puzzle.

Materials about the theme centers change often so Ben is exposed to many stories, fables, poems, and songs about animals. Since children's literature is full of such tales, the Center is an endless source of interest leading to reading, writing, listening, speaking, and dramatizing possibilities.

Story Ring

The story ring, later referred to as the literacy center, is the name Ben's teacher has given to the area in which Ben and his peers gather for the more formal story-sharing activities. As we see, Ben has poems and stories at the theme center too, but at least once daily, the teacher gathers her group in a story ring to hear and tell stories. Ben loves this time.

Today, the teacher shares *Chanticleer and the Fox.* The strutting Chanticleer fascinates Ben: Chanticleer is a proud bird. Looking at Barbara Cooney's illustrations, Ben can believe that, for crowing, Chanticleer had no equal "in all the land."

The teacher has been careful not to show the picture of the fox on the cover and the first few pages so the children do not know of what Chanticleer might be afraid or what his dream might mean. The teacher invites Ben and his peers to consider what might make a rooster afraid and children venture their predictions—all kinds of guesses from wolves to lions to snakes—in response. When the fox comes on the scene with his smiling compliments, Ben and his group immediately distrust the fox and their emotions guide them to tell Chanticleer not to believe him and not to close his eyes and not to stand high on his toes and not to stretch his neck but Chanticleer does. Their emotions were confirmed. The fox grabs Chanticleer and makes off with him.

Again the teacher pauses and invites predictions about how Chanticleer might still outwit the fox. There are many. "He could crow loud and let everyone know exactly where he is so they can get him away from the fox." "He could flap his wings, if he could, and surprise the fox so he can't see and will let him go." The teacher listens to all the ideas and then shares the rest of the tale. Ben and Sarah comment on how smart Chanticleer was, but their peers think he was "dumb first" or "he wouldn't have got caught." The teacher asks about what they might learn from the story and Ben and others think about that, concluding that Chanticleer was "dumb" to be led by the silly compliments of the fox.

The teacher asks for words that describe Chanticleer and the fox and such words pour forth. This brainstorming activity (see chapters 9 and 10) results in children calling Chanticleer fine, proud, maybe too proud, colorful, handsome, good crower, merry. They describe the fox as sly, creepy, hungry, wicked, knows what he wants. . . . The fable continues to generate much talk and thought; the lesson was definitely learned.

Other fables for young children follow.

Fables

Brown, Marcia. (1961). *Once a Mouse*. Illustrated by author. New York: Charles Scribner's Sons. For young children just beginning to imagine another point of view, this fable of the greedy mouse turned tiger then returned to mouse shape makes the point. Caregivers should discuss this after the story is shared and woodcuts are noted.

Galdone, Paul, reteller. (1979). *The Monkey and the Crocodile*. Illustrated by reteller. New York: Clarion Books. The Indian fable about how the monkey outwitted the crocodile produces many chuckles about how very silly the monkey is. Young children are sure they are so much smarter.

Lionni, Leo. (1985). *Frederick's Fables*. Illustrated by author. New York: Pantheon. Leo Lionni's characters and their adventures congregate in this book. For young children who have met Swimmy, or Willy, or Cornelius, here are thirteen tales as "told" by Frederick the mouse representing many of this illustrator's major tales. Can be shared over the years.

Stevens, Janet, adaptor. (1984). *The Tortoise and the Hare: An Aesop Fable*. Illustrated by adaptor. New York: Holiday House. Large colorful pictures as well as the tale itself will spark much book talk from young children.

Stevens, Janet, reteller. (1987). *The Town Mouse and the Country Mouse*. Illustrated by reteller. New York: Scholastic. Aesop fable wherein a town mouse and a country mouse decide they are best suited to their own home settings. Also, see Lorinda Bryan Cauley's version (1984). New York: G. P. Putnam's Sons.

At the teacher's suggestion, children begin to reminisce about the stories they had shared over the last several weeks and someone said *"Owl at Home* is my favorite." Immediately, there is a buzz of voices about the silly owl who did not recognize that it was his own feet that caused the bumps in the covers at the end of the bed. "Chanticleer wasn't as silly as that," says someone else.

The story ring is called into session both when teachers and children have stories to share. Ben tells his teacher that he has a story to share today and he proceeds to relate the story of *A Treeful of Pigs*, one his father shared with him the night before. The sequence of the pigs blooming in the garden, growing in the trees, falling out of the sky, and finally disappearing like snow was difficult to remember and Ben fumbled a bit using the illustrations to help him. Ben successfully cast the characters of the lazy husband and the patient but ingenious wife very clearly, and the group laughed heartily at the tale. Ben brought the book with him and the teacher promised to read it to the class and show the pictures the next day.

The story ring is established as a prominent part of Ben's day. It offers Ben and his friends choice tales and much story talk; the ring becomes the basis for comparing story plots and story characters in much the way that Chanticleer and the owl were compared. It gives the group space and opportunities to roam back and forth to past and present stories, to recall the ones they liked, to rethink them in the light of the current tale, and to make fresh observations; it becomes the place for children to rehearse and practice their own telling, and also the place to sense the novelty of capturing an audience. Ben learns to enjoy both listener and speaker roles in a storytelling frame.

Around the edges of the story ring are all sorts of exhibits—ones that relate to the themes featured but ones also that change constantly and are dictated by any child's most current interest and or a world event. Early morning talk is often focused on the recent chance in exhibits surrounding the story ring and questions radiate about new book jackets, magazines, posters, and charted poems.

This morning a large chart displays Karla Kuskin's poem about porcupines; the teacher noted Ben's interest and giggles and decided that the entire group should hear it and also see Carle's art. Questions flow quickly—some related to the poem and some from children's previous knowledge as it relates to this experience.

"Can porcupines really send those quills at you?" "Who would want to play with them?" "Do they have any friends?" asks Sarah. "How big are they?" asks someone else. Nothing will satisfy the children's curiosity until the teacher with the group finds a book that tells about porcupines, their size, color, habits, location. . . . As the class discusses their need for information, Ben quietly goes off to a shelf housing books the teacher has referred to before. He tries to pick up *The Larousse Encyclopedia of Animal Life,* but it is much too heavy. Ben, unknowingly, is engaging in the research/report activities so needed for study skills later in school years. The teacher notes what he is doing, gets up, and helps him, smiling at his quick recognition of the need and the appropriate book. The teacher talks as she finds the right pages, mentioning the word "index" and carefully locating the pages. After the teacher shares the facts about porcupines and invites further questions, the group continues to remark about Carle's collage art.

As a conclusion to the day's story ring, the teacher shares again *The Adventures of Simple Simon.* Ben and his friends have all seen the book before and tried to find the hidden nursery characters in the fanciful detailed, remarkably imaginative illustrations by Chris Conover. The teacher today reads the many verses of the well-known rhyme and waits for the class to supply the rhyming word. Listeners are attentive, waiting for the time to join in, and partially participating by happily supplying the missing word, smiling knowingly as they do.

After they have supplied "whistle" to rhyme with "thistle," a voice says "That's the page 'Jack-Be-Nimble' is on."

So well has the book been collectively and individually shared and the pictures studied that the particular rhyme is now associated with some of the hidden nursery characters spaced throughout the book. The teacher recalls with the group the other hidden rhymes and suggests that Ben and his friends might want to draw pictures of the many nursery characters found in the book. They enumerate these together: Little Jack Horner, Humpty Dumpty, Peter, Peter Pumpkin Eater, and Wee Willie Winkie. Each child leaves the ring thinking of the character he or she most likes and comes to some decision about how to draw him. It is a fun time for all and ends in friends guessing (predicting) the characters each has drawn. Because of the detail of illustration and structure of the text, Conover's *Simple Simon* is a next step in nursery puzzle books to the Ahlbergs' *Each Peach Pear Plum* and gives Ben and his peers a visual challenge.

Story rings are nurturant areas:

- for the further confirmation of story structure
- for the expansion of information and knowledge of a variety of tales
- for the rich association and comparison among books and characters
- for the creative portrayal both verbal and visual of story characters
- for instigating research and report writing activities
- for the extensive additions to word banks, and
- for the continuing development of a lifelong love of story

The caregiver's help is needed in setting the stage so that recall of former stories is a part of each story session and talk that emphasizes comparisons is encouraged. In this way Ben's repertoire of tales is enlarged, reconfirmed, and rethought. Recalling other lazy characters after *A Treeful of Pigs* is shared and remembering other lovable but silly characters like owl in *Owl at Home* gives Ben and others the opportunity to bring tales together and to make actual friends of book characters. As they rethink the stories and the characters they begin to see them in the light of other characters and other tales. In a sense, this synthesizing of tales deepens the feelings and ideas about all tales and conjures up new words and new expressions to label the new ideas.

Ben at this point in time is print-aware. He:

- can point to many words
- can point to sentences in books
- knows that pages are read from left to right
- knows what a word is
- knows what a sentence is
- knows that letters make words
- knows that words make sentences
- knows that sentences make stories
- knows how to label work by approximating letters he knows (see Table 7–1)

He has learned that reading has different purposes. He needs activities that take advantage of his need to sign and label and write short messages. Modeling letters for him as he asks for them is one way caregivers help Ben; asking him to observe places and things that need labeling is another way to increase and reinforce his awareness of print, clarifying the notion that labels help us and we need them. Games that call Ben's attention to the same sequence of letters in different words help him to build an awareness of such patterns. The transition from the Conover book to the choice of a nursery character to be drawn leads to the label of each drawing. Ben and his friend wanted help in labeling Humpty Dumpty, Wee Willie, and others; caregivers model and guide the letter formation.

In arranging theme centers and in the consistent use of the story ring, caregivers provide structure and freedom in an already full day of language exchange among Ben and his peers. Utilizing space and time to invite children into vicarious experiencing as well as a continuous encouragement to experience directly and share direct experiences, caregivers provide the setting needed to ensure the social, intellectual, and literacy development of young children. Children's language blossoms when caregivers observe closely the interests of children and capitalize on these to stimulate literacy, when children are invited to share their experiences and their stories, when ready help is available in reading and writing, when a listening ear is always present, and when a telling, story-laden tongue is available.

Summary

Children during their fifth year of life demonstrate greater muscular and intersensory coordination, delighting in this new physical prowess. They are also experiencing greater intellectual control of their environment. They can categorize more effectively, recognize sequence more quickly, and can organize tasks more efficiently.

In relationships with siblings and peers, a child is developing a quiet leadership and is recognized for ideas and implementation of them. At home, children delight in participating in their parent's work and revel in the praise they receive. An understanding is developing that all family members have chores for which they are responsible.

Children blossom under the prosocial behavior they see at home and have yet to learn how to respond to antisocial actions. The home environment, where parents and siblings exhibit respect for each other, and school life where staff members treat each other professionally, nurture in a child comfortable success and ease in social situations. Such environments also contribute to the development of a child's emotional stability.

In filling their roles as providers, demonstrators, learners, observers, and responders, caregivers are highly effective in supplying the child with the positive modeling needed for strong holistic development.

Among the many literacy-productive activities in which children can engage are those emanating from theme centers and story rings.

In theme centers, children find literacy materials of all kinds—fiction and fact, illustrative and narrative, prose and poetry, print and nonprint—to stimulate listening, talking, reading, writing, drawing, and dramatizing. Children benefit from the center not only in terms of literacy development, but also the social and intellectual development attendant upon literacy.

The story ring, which is the name the teacher has given to the area in which children form a ring to hear stories, poems, or songs, represents "delight time" for children. They love the stories the teacher shares and the discussions that precede and follow them.

Predicting story happenings excites children; they cannot wait to find out whether their predictions are going to come true. In follow-up activities, children learned that they and their friends can enact stories. They learn too that their own ideas are valued.

Children are not only becoming more sophisticated in awareness of print and story structure, they are also learning that they can produce print and stories themselves and that their own stories can be shared and appreciated. Further, they find that print can serve many purposes and they get involved in more and more of these.

Children are now ready for greater literacy-learning adventures.

9

The Sixth Year of Life: Kindergarten

This chapter addresses the following questions:

- What growth patterns characterize the sixth year of life?
- What is the role of the caregiver in nurturing the child's growth toward literacy?
- What activities and materials foster literacy?

What Growth Patterns Characterize the Sixth Year of Life?

How wonderful for Sarah. She is finally five. This is the age for real school. Sarah loves feeling grown-up and, therefore, she wants to experience being trusted with responsibilities. She adores going on errands, doing household chores, shopping, and even trying to solve family problems. Sarah, at five, loves to learn new things. She has a difficult time attending to task, familiar or new, for long periods of time. Sarah seems to be grown-up, yet she needs lots of affection and support. She sometimes breaks down under stress and cries as she did in earlier years (Ames and Ilg 1979a).

Sarah is expected to make many adjustments as she enters kindergarten. Although excited, she feels apprehensive. Even though the school building is familiar, and older siblings have moved in this path previously, it is difficult for her to imagine the new and expansive world that she is about to enter. Sarah's mother has helped to relieve natural feelings of anxiety by taking her to visit the school before her first day. Sarah enjoyed the tour of the building. She decided, during her visit, that the room that will be her classroom and the library are the best rooms in the school. Her tour through the library helped her feel most comfortable for she came upon Margaret Wise Brown's *Good Night Moon* and other books that she has at home.

The first day of school came more easily for Sarah than for her parents. Mom and Dad seemed strained as the day passed. Sarah, however, began school with a great sense of anticipation for learning, particularly for learning to read. Sarah's rich heritage of literacy activities provided her with the necessary foundations for school. Sarah is able to

- look at pictures and tell a story
- read words that she recognizes in print
- create stories, for she knows how they are structured
- handle books appropriately; that is, she moves from left to right, pretending to read, or actually reading when she is able
- recognize differences between letters, words, and sentences

Sarah begins kindergarten with a confidence that will be enhanced by her teacher who is able to help her build pride in her literacy accomplishments.

Physical Development

In many ways, this is the end of Sarah's early childhood years. Her small and large muscle control is quite advanced. She is able to sit for longer periods of time. She laces shoes, zippers her coat, holds her pencil firmly, and finds writing and drawing pleasant experiences. The act of drawing is more important to Sarah than the final product. Sarah, unlike most of her peers, draws with much detail. She is aware of things around her. This is illustrated by the exaggerated mouth and teeth she includes in a portrait of herself visiting the dentist (Figure 9–1). Sarah enjoys cutting, for she can cut

FIGURE 9–1 Five-Year-Old Sarah at the Dentist's Office

on a line and copy figures, including triangles and circles. Sarah writes letters and words, often writing b for d and numbers from the top to the bottom of the page. Her teacher is not bothered by this, for it is natural. Reversing letters and moving in directions other than left to right are part of the natural development of writing. Sarah's small and large muscles permit her to ride a bicycle, and she has expressed a desire to learn to tap dance. Sarah's small motor abilities and her command of language make her ready for both reading and writing (Glazer 1980).

Language Development

Sarah's command of oral language has excited her about playing with words and letters. She makes up songs and rhymes, emulating the language of stories she heard in earlier years. When she draws, she often asks an adult to write down what she says about the picture. Sarah's desire to encode from oral to written language demonstrates her knowledge of the connection between speech and print. This connection is also demonstrated when Sarah carries out picture talk with ABC books, pointing and saying the names of letters and objects. Sarah has no difficulty in producing the appropriate sounds. She has repeated cat and hat in *The Cat in the Hat* and thought of fat, sat, and bat herself. As she writes, she says what her print represents. She speaks slowly as she writes, her oral language matching the marks she places on a page. Sarah's love for Dr. Seuss' books is reflected in her repeated word and sentence patterns, demonstrating her use of the recurring principle to create written language (Figure 9–2).

Sarah is able to recognize about thirty-five words. She points to them on posters, in books, and on food containers. Sarah's oral language often emulates the language in her favorite stories. "My brother's a pain," she says, again and again, referring to her younger brother. "He always gets to do the same stuff as me, and he's younger. That makes him a pain." One of Sarah's favorite stories is Judy Blume's *The Pain and the Great One*, a tale about sibling rivalry between an older sister and her younger brother. The text provided language for Sarah's feelings. Sarah's excitement and knowledge illustrate a formal readiness to read and write. When her teacher repeats sets of three or four words, Sarah can tell which word does not start with the same beginning letter sound.

Cognitive Development

Sarah's interests are continuing to widen. She persists at completing tasks in order to solve problems. She has notions about time and space. This she demonstrates when she speaks about things she did yesterday and the upcoming birthday party for her best friend, Ben. She knows which events

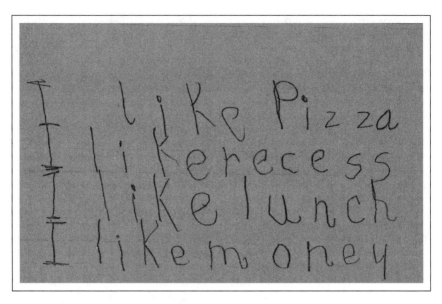

FIGURE 9–2 Recurring Writing Principle

come first, next, and last during the school day, but the specific details of time are still vague. Sarah is able to provide directions to the food market and to her dentist's office. Her ability to reason is demonstrated when she sorts objects according to specific properties—size, shape, or color. She is often seen putting crayons in order, according to one or more of these. She is also able to identify the smallest and largest circles and which comes first and last. This sorting ability helps Sarah to identify letters and words. Sarah is practical but curious. She asks often what things are for and what you do with them. Her practical side is demonstrated when she defines a car as "something you ride in to get to my grandma's house." Functional definitions are characteristic of Sarah's age. Her practicality permits her to enjoy fantasy stories as well as realistic and humorous fiction. Sarah's intellectual development seems to be a bit more advanced than that of most of her peers because she has a strong foundation in reading and writing activities.

Sarah's parents show an interest in literacy by reading themselves and borrowing books from the library regularly. She has lots of different kinds of reading materials around her home—magazines, newspapers, books, and reading related to work activities—and is taken to libraries and bookstores regularly. She can independently find activities during free times that involve writing or reading. Because she has probably been provided with structure in daily activities, she understands schedules. Schedules for eating, sleeping, and special activities (tap dancing lessons) are discussed; rules for activities are mentioned in daily conversations; and she has designated responsibilities at home—making her bed in the morning, and putting her clothing away before she goes to sleep (Briggs and Elkind 1973; Durkin 1966; Morrow 1983; Teale 1986).

Social and Emotional Behaviors

Sarah's affectionate manner and admiration for adults wins their hearts and ears. She plays well with her peers and older children. Her ability to play is enhanced by her poise, inner controls, and outgoing self-assuredness. Sarah can anticipate what is about to happen and knows what behaviors are acceptable. She has also learned to use regulatory language and accompanying behaviors to get her way. At age five, Sarah is often dogmatic. She is "right" most of the time and finds only one solution to a problem. Lack of success results in loss of patience. This means that she must get off to the right start in order to do well.

Sarah is quite self-sufficient, often acting like a miniature adult. Other times she cries spontaneously almost like a two-year-old. Going to school is a sign that Sarah is growing up, and Sarah is ready. Table 9–1 summarizes behaviors of five-year-old children that indicate a readiness for school.

What Is the Role of the Caregiver in Nurturing the Child's Growth toward Literacy?

Our role as teachers is to create environments and to guide children in ways similar to that of caregivers in earlier years. The environment created for Sarah and Ben at five and beyond is based on the following assumptions and expectations:

- a balance exists between teacher and student control
- some decisions are made by children and others by the teacher
- some activities are selected by children and some by their teacher
- self-monitoring growth and needs is an integral part of learning
- one-on-one conferences are held regularly between the teacher and each child, and together decisions are made
- achievements are reviewed daily
- parents are often part of classroom activities
- children are aware of purposes for instruction
- the development of literacy skills occurs when the children are engaged in a project, so an at-work tone permeates the classroom
- work begins and continues until there is a logical stopping place

TABLE 9–1   Developmental Trends for Five-Year-Old Children

Physically the five-year-old is able to:
  sit when interested in an activity
  enjoy drawing
  enjoy cutting and folding paper
  enjoy copying figures (triangles, circles, squares)
  enjoy coloring books
  write, but uses the entire piece of paper
  write, sometimes reversing letters
  write, at times, beginning at the left side of the page and moving right

At five, the child can:
  pronounce words correctly most of the time
  use complex sentences when speaking
  dictate stories
  label pictures he or she draws
  identify some printed words
  create stories that resemble the structures of favorite ones
  create rhymes
  create words and letters that are repeated again and again on the page
  delight in seeing his or her own name in print
  talk about pictures when drawing them
  demonstrate the connection of speech to print
  identify letters in the print environment

Intellectually, the five-year-old is able to:
  complete tasks
  solve problems
  remember and talk about past and future events
  locate places in and out of school
  understand the relationships of size, order, and space
  understand that letters make words
  identify letters in and out of words
  enjoy realistic stories as well as fantasy

Socially and emotionally, five-year-old children can:
  show affection
  admire adult behaviors
  protect and nurture younger children
  control inner feelings and emotions
  act mature, but also younger than their age
  engage in school activities for they want to be grown-up (Ames and Ilg
    1979a)

Teachers who create healthy naturalistic environments facilitate cooperative discourse between and among children. Preparing such environments has been found to affect the choices children make concerning activities (Morrow and Weinstein 1982; Weinstein 1977). Classrooms that accommodate individual and group needs include centers dedicated to specific activities or content areas (Morrow 1989). Paper and pencils, content-specific items such as dry leaves during fall season and living bugs in jars during spring provide food for thought that coerces children to create language. Centers need storage areas—shelving and cabinets—as well as work space—tables and chairs, rugs, and backflaps for sitting. We recommend that three centers be developed in the kindergarten classroom. These include a literacy center, a music and drama center, and a living-alive center (Figure 9–3).

Literacy Center

This is the focal location in the classroom. It includes a classroom library, places to be together with books, places to read alone, and places for writing.

Classroom Library

The classroom library is the focus of this center. It includes picture and joke books, arts and crafts books, science, math, and social studies books. Five books per child create a desirable classroom library. Arranging books by content makes it easy for small children to find what they want. Small round colored stickers can be used to designate content. Red, for example, might be put on books with holiday themes, and blue on those about dinosaurs. Shelves should be arranged at eye level so that children can reach books easily. Display racks for special books during special times encourage book selections. An attractive library corner placed in the focal point of the classroom invites children to read (Stauffer 1970; Morrow 1982). It encourages independence, for children will use the corner on their own (Coody 1982).

A variety of books and props are the core of the library. The following categories of books interest five-year-old children.

1. Wordless picture story and information books are designed so that children can look at the pictures and tell the story. Alphabet and number concept books are considered part of this category. Alphabet books that bring together the letter, keyword, and object are particularly helpful in building sound-symbol relationships and in inviting children to suggest additional keywords. When the alphabet books have a theme such as animals, the child's ability to categorize and to expand vocabulary and concepts is strengthened. Good additions to the kindergarten library include:

Alexander, Martha. (1968). *Out, Out, Out!* Illustrated by author. New York: Dial. This
    is the tale of the calm, bright child who succeeds in getting the pigeon out of the
    house while the adults indulge in all sorts of excited erratic behavior. Illustra-
    tions invite child-telling and can lead to discussion about problems and prob-
    lem-solving behavior.

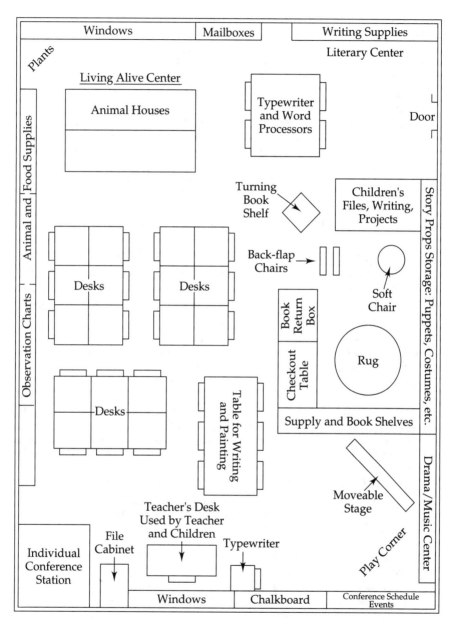

FIGURE 9–3 The Kindergarten Classroom

Briggs, Raymond. (1978). *The Snowman*. Illustrated by author. New York: Random House. This beautifully illustrated story recounts a young boy's creation of a snowman who comes alive and they enjoy each other for a day and night. The melting of the snowman is presented realistically.

Hayes, Sarah. (1990). *Nine Ducks Nine*. Illustrated by author. New York: Lothrop, Lee, & Shepard. Like *Ten, Nine, Eight* (Bang, 1983), this is a countdown book. Young children keep rooting for the ducks to outwit the wily fox.

Lobel, Arnold. (1981). *On Market Street*. Illustrated by Anita Lobel. New York: Greenwillow Books. A short verse and then street vendors wearing their wares as alphabet letters become the pages of this book. Key words label the pages and young children will love the lollipop lady and many others.

Ormerod, Jan. (1981 and 1986). *Sunshine and Moonlight*. Illustrated by author. New York: Lothrop, Lee, & Shepard. Daytime and nighttime are realistically presented in these two volumes. This is familiar content and can excite much talk about daytime work and play and the need for sleep at night.

2. Realistic fiction, which presents issues in life clearly and honestly, leads to much talk about the stories and a ready identification with the characters. Themes concerned with death and dying, illness, fear, jealousy, rejection, and human frailties are welcomed by children. Favorites for five-year-old children include:

Hill, Elizabeth. (1967). *Evan's Corner*. Illustrated by Nancy Grossman. New York: Holt. Sometimes living space is too small, and the young child needs a place that is his very own. Evan finds a corner just for himself.

Macdonald, Maryann. (1980). *Rosie Runs Away*. Illustrated by Melissa Sweet. New York: Atheneum. Like *Noisy Nora* (Wells) and *Baby Sister for Frances* (Hoban), Rosie feels neglected, if not rejected, by her mother. She runs away as far as a tree that is close by but thinks some of the family may need her and returns to find her mother waiting for her. Small hurts and their resolutions are what the book is all about.

Steig, William. (1988). *Spinky Sulks*. Illustrated by author. New York: Farrar Straus Giroux. Young children will understand Spinky's feelings of rejection, and while they wonder at his resistance to everyone's attempts to make him feel wanted, they will delight in the resolution of Spinky's temporary separation from his family.

Williams, Vera B. (1982). *A Chair for My Mother*. Illustrated by the author. New York: Greenwillow Books. Mother, daughter, and granddaughter have little of this world's goods and early in this tale lose, through fire, what little they have. But neighbors help and with a chair for mother as a goal, pennies are collected and slowly but surely equal enough to make the long anticipated purchase which everyone enjoys.

Zolotow, Charlotte. (1985). *My Grandson Lew*. Illustrated by William Pene du Bois. New York: Harper & Row. Grandfather is dead, and his daughter and his grandson miss him. Together mother and son recall grandfather and the time he and his grandson spent together. Love and fond memories help to ease the loss.

3. Information books, books that tell about planets, growing plants, cooking, holidays, and countries far away, help children with research projects, even in the kindergarten year. Five-year-old children love to explore ideas and also learn to investigate. Information books help to satisfy the child's need to know and can lead to a lifetime habit of using books for reference. Appropriate information books include:

Adler, David A. (1982). *A Picture Book of Hanukkah.* Illustrated by Linda Hiller. New York: Holiday House. Here are clear simple illustrations and explanations of the Feast of Hanukkah.

Crews, Donald. (1980). *Truck.* Illustrated by author. New York: Greenwillow Books. Large, clear shapes and signs provide the young child with information about trucks and roads. There is much to talk about and to label here.

Gibbons, Gail. (1987). *The Pottery Place.* Illustrated by author. San Diego, Calif.: Harcourt Brace Jovanovich. This is the colorfully illustrated story of a day in the life of a potter. Young children will note the details and the step-by-step procedure. Familiar with clay and Play-Doh, they will be fascinated with the procedures and the products the potter creates.

Gibbons, Gail. (1984). *Halloween.* Illustrated by author. New York: Holiday House. In her usual straightforward, clear fashion, Gail Gibbons narrates and visualizes the history and the customs of Halloween.

Mott, Evelyn Clarke. (1991). *Steam Train Ride.* Photographs by author. New York: Walker. A young boy takes his first steam train ride. Full color photographs mark each phase of the journey and the young boy's interest and excitement breathe through the book.

4. Traditional literature, fables, and folktales written as picture books are wonderful for reading aloud. *Cinderella* and other favorites ought to be part of the repertoire of all children. Fables and folktales help children learn about literature of other countries and provide information about other cultures. Reading these to children and children's reading them to their peers help to extend children's knowledge about the world beyond their own. Such books also help to confirm the young child's sense of story structure. Traditional literature for five-year-old children includes:

Grimm, Jakob, and Grimm, Wilhelm. (1975). *Hans in Luck.* Illustrated by Felix Hoffman. New York: Atheneum. Young children will love this noodlehead tale. They recognize the illogic quickly and are pleased with how smart they are.

Hague, Kathleen. (1981). *The Man Who Kept House.* Illustrated by Michael Hague. New York: Harcourt Brace Jovanovich. Brief text—it is the pictures that tell this funny folktale about the husband who contends he works much harder than his wife. They change places and household havoc reigns. The illustrations broadcast the chaos. Young children will delight in telling and acting out this tale.

Spier, Peter. (1977). *Noah's Ark.* Illustrated by author. New York: Doubleday and Co., Inc. This Caldecott medal book is practically wordless, but there is much to talk about. Young children will point to the delightful details in Spier's work and happily discuss them.

Turkle, Brinton. (1976). *Deep in the Forest.* Illustrated by author. New York: Dutton. It is not Goldilocks who tests the porridge, chair, and bed but a mischievous bear. Young children should hear the Goldilocks tale before presenting this variation. The wordless book is waiting for the young child to tell the tale.

Zelinsky, Paul O., reteller. (1986). *Rumpelstiltskin.* Illustrated by reteller. New York: E. P. Dutton. This version must be shared; the text is not brief, but the paintings can elicit much talk and the brief repetition within the tale as well as the suspense in the plot will generate attentiveness and appreciation.

5. Easy-to-read books are appropriate for some five-year-old children. A few will read, others will catch the cadence of the rhythm of repeated sentence patterns and the delight of rhyming words. Such books help to establish sound-symbol relationships (see also next section). Limited vocabulary; repeated words, phrases, and sentences; and pictures that match the text make these favorites for five-year-old children. Easy-to-read books loved by kindergarten children include:

Ets, Marie Hall. (1955). *Play with Me.* Illustrated by author. New York: Viking Penguin. A young girl seeks a playmate and asks many woodland animals to be her friend, but only when she sits quietly are they ready to come to her. The repeated question binds the satisfying tale.

Lindbergh, Reeve. (1990). *The Day the Goose Got Loose.* Illustrated by Steven Kellogg. New York: Dial. The silly, merry adventuresome goose creates all sorts of fun. Rhyme, humor, and rhythm are marked and are really appreciated by participating young children.

Pomerantz, Charlotte. (1984). *Where's the Bear?* Illustrated by Byron Barton. New York: Greenwillow Books. With only five words and a surprise number six, this rhythmic tale is told; it invites dramatization.

Williams, Sue. (1990). *I Went Walking.* Illustrated by Julie Vivas. San Diego, Calif.: Harcourt Brace Jovanovich. The repetitive lines weave together the child's walk in a farmyard where she meets a cat, cow, duck, pig, and dog. Colors are reinforced because each animal she meets is a definite and different color.

Zelinsky, Paul O., adapter. (1990). *The Wheels on the Bus.* Illustrated by adapter. New York: Dutton. The sixteen pages will fascinate the young child who quickly learns to sing the verses and repeated lines and who will love the foldouts and the many bits of paper that move—like the bus.

6. Books that build sound-symbol relationships help children see and say words. The stories are usually created with specific spelling patterns (ten, pen, wren, men). Following story sharing, children and teachers may build on specific sound-symbol patterns to create extended word families. These provide visual and auditory comfort, which builds confidence during the early stages of reading. Children are able to predict the next word or phrase and read on. These are usually categorized as easy-to-read books. Some to add to the classroom library include:

Degen, Bruce. (1983). *Jamberry.* Illustrated by author. New York: Harper & Row. A charming, rhythmic book-poem that establishes the "berry" pattern as basic to many words. Young children will create more "berry" words.

Geisel, Theodor (Dr. Seuss). (1968). *The Foot Book.* Illustrated by author. New York: Random House. Rhythm and rhyme abound; children will love the sound, will readily predict next words, and will march and clap to the entire narration.

Ginsburg, Mirra. (1982). *Across the Stream.* Illustrated by Nancy Tafuri. New York: Greenwillow Books. Dream and stream and other rhymed pairs of words makes this a wonderfully predictable book.

Oppenheim, Joanne. (1986). *Have You Seen Birds?* Illustrated by Barbara Reid. New York: Scholastic: TAB Publications Inc. This is a beautifully illustrated rhyming text, full of a variety of patterns to be heard and seen, all constructed around the oft-repeated question in the title.

Weiss, Nicki. (1989). *Where Does the Brown Bear Go?* Illustrated by author. New York: Viking. Repeated question and answers establish some sound-symbol relationships and tell a bedtime, comforting story.

Wildsmith, Brian. (1982). *Cat on the Mat.* Illustrated by author. New York: Oxford. Pictures tell the tale while the brief narrative repeats the cat-sat-mat sound-spelling patterns.

Using the library means taking out books. An easy take-out system helps books circulate. Simply place a library pocket in the back of each book. A card should be placed in each pocket with the book's name and author. To sign out a book, the borrower needs only to write his or her name on the card. That card is placed in a pocket chart made of book pockets, each with a child's name written on it. Adults who engage in classroom activities must have a check-out pocket, as well (Figure 9–4).

To return books, the borrower takes the book's card from the pocket chart, crosses off his or her name, and returns the card to the book's pocket. The book is then put into a book return box for reshelving.

Places to Be Together with Books

A place to be together with books encourages interactive, cooperative play. Children adore dressing-up and playing with roles in life. Some, like Ben, especially like to put on a postman's cap and deliver letters to friends in his classroom. A favorite book at five is the *Jolly Postman* or *Other People's Letters.* Janet and Allan Ahlberg have created an inventive, appealing group of missives—an invitation to a party, a postcard from a vacation spot, a birthday greeting, an advertisement, and other exciting things to receive in the mail. These are housed in individual envelopes that open easily. These entice Ben and other classmates into letter reading and writing, even though they

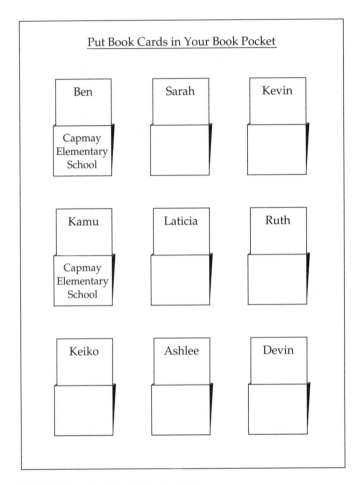

FIGURE 9–4 Book Pocket Chart

may not know how to read the words. Other costumes may invite children to play the roles of characters in books and in their lives. Being the man at the meat counter in the food market requires only an apron and a cap. Available paper from the writing center becomes a sign for selling the products. One kindergarten student wrote the quantity and name of the meat, the price, and the date designated as the final day of sale (one hamburger, $1.00, April 2) (Figure 9–5). The corner invites reluctant learners into cooperative activities. Stephanie, another kindergarten student, moved into the cooperative play area and shouted, "I'll buy your meat, Ryan, because I am going to have a barbecue picnic today."

The place must always change. Furniture can be rearranged and new and different props placed in a small chest of drawers. Storybooks and

FIGURE 9–5 Sign Written by a Five-Year-Old Child

matching props are placed together in large paper bags with the book's name written on each; sometimes a picture that represents the story draws children to books. Rug pieces and small chairs for sitting and a back wall dressed with a sheet with the word "Stage" written on it create the performance area necessary for building pride by displaying achievements.

Places to Read Alone
Several places to read quietly, to be alone with books, provide children with the chance to role-play using new knowledge about books and print. An empty carton, one used to ship a refrigerator, serves as one quiet area. A large pillow and blanket in a corner of the classroom and a study carrel—a desk with sides to create closure—create privacy. A bathtub lined with several blankets becomes a bed where Ben can curl up with his book. It is not often possible to know exactly what children are doing with books when they are alone, but privacy is important. One can surmise, by listening, however, that Sarah was probably reading chorally with Melissa acting the role of teacher. Private environments invite this peer teaching behavior. Signs to signify privacy encourage peer and private reading times. These might include

- Do not disturb
- Quiet
- Sh-sh-sh—we are reading

Children will choose one and display it in their private reading place.

Places for Writing

The place for writing must meet the compelling need that five-year-old children have to create written text. Pencils, crayons, colored felt-tipped pens and markers, and chalk should be placed in containers. Writing paper of various sizes with and without lines must be easily accessible. Typewriters and word processors are needed for those who find the physical writing by hand tedious. Posters and wall charts encourage small hands to create large print. Book-making materials must also be prepared ahead of time. Several pieces of paper stapled together become a storybook authored by a child. Orange construction paper cut into the shape of a pumpkin can serve as a cover for a Halloween story. Two red paper hearts assembled with staples and writing paper in between will encourage some to create a valentine for a friend. Favorite words should be posted for children to copy. Lists of words based on spelling patterns will entice some to write words, lists of words, and even rhymes and poems. Other posted charts should include songs with repeated language patterns. Copying songs and poems is a favorite writing activity. Such copies should then be used in singing and choral verse activities to confirm the writing-reading connection. Space, models, and time to copy must also be provided.

The writing center is the place for mailboxes. Each child must have one and the teacher too. These can simply be paper bags, each with a child's name written on it and thumb-tacked to the wall, or a shoebox.

A clothesline with clothespins might carry special objects to write about. Hanging a piece of the teacher's writing on the clothesline encourages children to display their writing and drawings. The writing center includes paints and easels so children can experiment with lines and curves used in making letters. These help children rehearse writing and also learn how to control paint.

Sarah had created a picture of herself playing outside. She drew a large, bright yellow sun. The paint was thin and watery. Sarah's sunny day became a rainy play day. As the paint dripped, she said,

> *This is me playing outside in my yard. It is summer. This is the ground, and it has flowers and bugs. This is my house, and this is my room, and it has red curtains. And this is the sunny—sunny—it is raining and Sarah likes to play in the rain.*

Sarah's ability to spontaneously change her story to match the paint illustrates her flexibility with both ideas and oral language. It illustrates her ability to take control of materials. The actions demonstrated her awareness of the relationship between written and oral language.

Music and Drama Center

Records and cassette tape recorders, drums, rhythm sticks, tambourines, empty plastic containers, and spoons are stored in this center. This is the place where recorded songs and stories are kept. Beating drums to language like "Row, row, row your boat" and hearing favorite story phrases on recordings are part of learning to read and write. Children especially like to listen to repeated patterns including Wanda Gag's (1928):

> *Cats here, cats there,*
> *Cats and kittens everywhere.*
> *Hundreds of cats,*
> *Thousands of cats,*
> *Millions and billions and trillions of cats.* *

Repetition of verses like these help to increase the child's auditory memory. Such strengthening of the auditory memory range aids in listening. Tape recorders are wonderful for retelling stories, and five-year-old children love to retell. Sometimes they need an audience and other times do not. Tape recorders provide a vehicle for spontaneous or unguided retellings (the children retell the story without questions or comments to serve as prompts). The tape recorder is the teacher's and child's best friend for rehearsing language and for determining strengths and needs. Tape recorders help children learn words. They listen to the tape and follow the story as they point to the words in a book. Children are further helped toward independent reading when the books they use help to build sound-symbol relationships. These books are full of spelling patterns such as those in the Dr. Seuss books mentioned. The following should be added to the classroom library for Ben and Sarah and their agemates.

Audiocassettes/Books That Build Sound-Symbol Relationships

Bemelmans, Ludwig. (1939). *Madeline.* Illustrated by author. New York: Viking Penguin. Book and audiocassette. Young children can follow the text and read along or can just listen. French and English songs included.

Brown, Margaret Wise. (1942). *The Runaway Bunny.* Illustrated by Clement Hurd. New York: Harper & Row. Book and audiocassette. Book and cassette allow children to discuss double-page pictures as they read along; listening and read-along sides are provided.

---

* From *Millions of Cats* by Wanda Gag, copyright 1928 by Coward-McCann, Inc. copyright renewed © 1956 by Robert Janssen. Reprinted by permission of Coward-McCann, Inc.

Burton, Virginia Lee. (1943). *Katy and the Big Snow*. Illustrated by author. Boston: Houghton Mifflin. Book and audiocassette. This is a word-for-word reading of the text; one side of the cassette is for straight listening; the other side includes signals for page turning. There is much to talk about in the illustrations when the book is shared.

Geisel, Theodor, (Dr. Seuss) (1957). *The Cat in the Hat*. New York: Random House. Book and audiocassette. Full of easy-to-recognize sound-letter patterns in the happy text of the cat who creates problems but solves them in the end. There is much to talk about and dramatize here and many comforting similar sounds and letters. This tale is longer and more involved than *Hop on Pop*.

Geisel, Theodor (Dr. Seuss) (1983). *Hop on Pop*. New York: Random House. Book and audiocassette. This text is full of sound-symbol patterns and is easy to follow. It includes a read-along side and a listening side.

Storytelling props provide a vehicle for drama. Hand puppets, role movies, chalk, scissors, and big books are a few of the props used by children and teachers to tell stories. Hand puppets may represent story characters. Telling stories with puppets attracts the listener to the character. Teachers use these to model the behavior, and the materials, once in the music and drama center, entice children to model the teacher's behavior and act the stories. Stuffed animals, wigs, and certain items of clothing also serve to enhance children's interest in books (Morrow 1981).

Living Alive Center

The living alive center in the kindergarten classroom may be inhabited by small mammals (gerbils or white mice) and reptiles (turtles, frogs, snakes, or lizards), insects, plants, birds—anything that can live in a classroom environment. It is the center for social studies and science ideas. The animals provide Ben and Sarah and the twenty other children in their classroom opportunities for observing and recording changes (print or drawings); story writing; research projects; incentives for reading about what animals and insects eat, how they eat, how they reproduce, how they grow, how they sleep, how they play, how they age, how they are born, and how they die.

Charts with questions about specific jobs (Did you water the plants?, Did you feed the turtles?, How tall is the flower today?) guide the children to focus, take responsibility, and complete tasks. Tape recorders are wonderful for recording observations. Some children may record by drawing pictures or by writing. The day Sarah's turtle died, she asked to dictate the following to her teacher:

My turtle died. I am sad. I will bury him. I will say a prayer. I will take care of my other turtle so it doesn't die.

Margaret Wise Brown's *The Dead Bird* and books with similar themes help five-year-old children understand that others have similar feelings when a loved one passes on. Learning to observe and care for living things helps them deal with feelings of tenderness, love, empathy, and even sympathy that only living things can provide. They learn to take responsibility for their actions.

The literacy-rich environment that facilitates natural learning—learning similar to the way language is learned in the home—is made up of centers and storage areas which include:

1. lots of reading and writing material (Morrow 1983).

2. a variety of reading materials including magazines, catalogues, *TV Guides*, telephone books, cookbooks, reference materials, and junk mail (Teale 1978).

3. a variety of writing materials that are accessible and are placed in appropriate places for writing, including low table tops and small chairs for the comfort of little ones (Hall, Moretz, and Stantom 1976).

4. books displayed for easy access and materials located where children spend much of their time (Taylor 1983). The classroom is a print laboratory (Searfoss and Readence 1989) where permission to use either reading or writing materials is unnecessary (Hall et al. 1976). Literacy routines, including storybook reading, are part of the day (Durkin 1966). Reading comics or reading a list of things to do each morning (Schickedanz and Sullivan 1984) encompasses early morning warmup activities. Writing notes or letters to children daily, which are placed in their personal mailbox, encourages writing in a functional meaningful way (Heath 1983; Taylor 1983). Asking questions about stories and written language creates language interactions, written and spoken (Gundlach et al. 1985). Five-year-old children begin to learn where they are and move slowly, but deliberately, into more sophisticated literacy activities (Baghban 1984). Classrooms must, therefore, have:

5. daily literacy routines, including reading aloud, writing notes, scheduled individual retelling sessions, and free-time for self-selected literacy activities.

6. cooperative activities between children and their teachers where reading and writing are used interactively.

7. knowledgeable, caring teachers, who are astute and sensitive to individual differences.

8. teachers who are aware of each student's knowledge, using that as a starting point to build literacy skills.

What Activities and Materials Foster Literacy?

Activities based on function and purpose, for example, making lists to remember what to get for the play-corner grocery, reading a picture book to dolls, and exchanging observations about the newborn gerbil, are the foci of the curriculum. Routines and daily schedules are essential. The following schedules illustrate daily routines for half- and full-day preschool or kindergarten programs. Structuring time is the key to naturalistic, literacy-rich, exciting school days.

Half-Day Kindergarten Program

8:30 to 8:55   Arrival activities

Children's Activities.   The children enter the classroom and store outdoor clothing in personally designated places. Individual activities during this time may include the following:

- caring for animals—feeding, cleaning living space, recording changes in size, food intake, and appearance, on appropriately displayed charts
- watering and feeding plants and insects and recording observations
- reading a letter found in one's mailbox
- writing a letter
- reading dialogue journal entries and responding (see p. 207)
- reviewing daily contract (see p. 211)—teacher-selected work and children's choices
- saying rhymes and singing songs right after the teacher says or sings them
- selecting of book for retelling
- signing up for individual conference times with the teacher
- signing up for free-time activities—dress-up corner, block play, easel painting, or viewing literature videos
- signing up for class maintenance activities (e.g., cleaning animal cages, keeping pencils sharpened)

Teacher's Activities.   The teacher greets and meets children, mentioning every name as each child proceeds and carries on activities. As the children begin to work, the teacher:

- observes and records children's behaviors that seem important for modifying environments to meet individual needs
- notes children's responses to his or her behaviors
- moves in and about classroom, responding to children's questions and comments
- encourages those who need it to stay on task
- notices and records interactions—peer with peer, adult with children
- notices ritualistic (routine) actions children carry out before, during, and after specific activities (i.e., sharpen pencil several times before writing)

- reads letters and notes in the teacher's mailbox
- guides small groups of children who have difficulty producing appropriate sounds
- reads and responds to children's dialogue journal entries
- reviews daily schedule and special need activities
- engages children in echoic reading/singing
- selects books for reading to children and for reading by the teacher
- plays alphabet identification games
- reviews the conference sign-up chart and encourages reluctant students to sign up

8:55 to 9:15   Get-Together Time

The teacher begins this activity time by using the same signal (e.g., ringing a bell, putting on a get-together hat, moving to the get-together spot, or displaying a large toy clock that is set at the daily get-together time). The teacher then:

- reviews morning routine, pointing to chart with pictures and words that represent activities
- notes any difficulties children have in recognizing activity signs
- discusses individually scheduled activities
- discusses special small group activities (for example, "Sarah will have a dictation session at the computer at 10:05")
- displays and names the books and authors for storytime that morning

Following the morning's special get-together activities, review can include:

- exercising to music
- reviewing with individual children observations of animals, plants, and insects
- singing along by the class of a special song for the week, upcoming event, or project
- reviewing, again, morning routine

A goal in literacy-rich classrooms is greater independent learners.

9:15 to 9:35   Individual Work Time: Reading and Writing Activities

Children's Activities.   Children continue their individual activities:

- writing in journals
- reading a self-selected book
- drawing or writing a story

- copying a song, language experience story, or poem posted at eye level
- drawing a picture or picture story

Teacher's Activities.   The teacher continues to circulate among the children:

- providing spellings of words on word cards when requested (see p. 188)
- guiding children in their identification of the regularities of sound-symbol relationships (i.e., helping children notice words that all begin with the same letters—spell, spin, spot, spur)
- staying alert to questions and puzzled faces
- using appropriate strategies to guide children who need it to stay on task
- making mental notes of behaviors

9:35 to 9:55   Whole Group Activity

This is the time for directed activities, which include social studies or science lessons, choral reading, and echoic reading activity. All should be presented so that children can follow the group lesson with individual actions that flow naturally into the next time period. (*Special Note:* Children involved in special projects should continue working on these if desired, joining the group when ready. Special events—visits by authors or by storytellers—should be attended by the group.)

9:55 to 10:50   Individual and Small Group Conference Times and Center Activities

Children's Activities.   During this time, the children:

- continue with contract activities
- have individual conferences with the teacher (about ten minutes)
- meet in special small groups
- work in centers on literacy activities
- engage in alphabet games
- work on special projects
- read and write independently
- place picture cards of a story in the proper order

Teacher's Activities.   The teacher's activities include:

- holding individual conferences with children and small groups
- moving around the classroom providing necessary guidance

- making mental and written notes about children's attention to task, or interactions with peers

10:50 to 11:15   Cleanup and Snack Time

11:15 to 11:35   Outdoor Play (weather permitting)

11:35 to 11:55   Storybook Reading Time
This time is used for prereading activities and storytime. Children who can and want to read to the group should select a book, rehearse reading it out loud, and be the story reader of the day.

11:55 to 12:10   Dressing and Farewells for Dismissal
Children receive direction to dress to go home. The teacher circulates, informally, saying to several children: "Tell me what you did today," "Tell me what you learned," and "Tell me what you need to continue to do tomorrow."

Whole-Day Kindergarten Program

The following schedule is appropriate for kindergarten and full-day preschools. The schedule illustrates the continuous nature of activities, the integration of the language arts, and the involvement of children in classroom decisions. Group lessons illustrated in this section will focus on teaching strategies to children. A class experience—here a class trip and special visitor—will be used to illustrate procedures.

8:30 to 9:00   Arrival Activities

Children's Activities.   Children enter the classroom and store their outer clothing. They carry on morning activities similar to those mentioned for half-day kindergartens and, also, move in and about centers and areas to:

- look at the displays of special books (i.e., there were three new books about dollhouses for Sarah in the library corner and two new books for Ben about dinosaurs in the same corner)
- look at and talk about the new baby frog in the living-alive center
- look at the "interesting word" of the day hanging in the writing corner, the library, and the private areas around the room, and write it on a word card (see p. 188)
- write the name of the new pet frog on a 4- by 7-inch labeling or word card paper

- look at their personal contract sheet and note assignments written in both print and picture formats
- look at the picture of the author, Bobbye Goldstein, who is coming to share her book *Bear in Mind* with the class. Take one of the three copies to read, look at, and copy words from
- write in his or her diary
- draw a picture
- continue to write or draw a story that was begun the day before
- look at the daily newspaper that is in its place in the classroom library corner
- tend to animals

Teacher's Activities.   Behaviors are similar to those in the half-day program schedule. The teacher moves from child to child, asking, "What are you beginning to do now? What will you do after that?" She is sure to be at eye level when speaking to the child in order to create a collegial environment. Notes are taken about children's curiosities and approaches to solving problems. Folders for specific children (not more than five at a time) are placed on the teacher's desk. She concentrates on observing those children with specific questions in mind. Sarah has not selected a book on her own for two weeks, and the teacher is observing her behaviors and asking herself, "What is Sarah doing instead of interacting with books? When (in what situations) does Sarah select books?" These were written on a piece of paper, and the teacher jots down notes in response to her questions. Ben sometimes remembers what he reads about, but other times does not. The teacher's observations of Ben's reading behaviors are based on her questions, "When does Ben recall most after reading? Is recall achieved when he reads out loud to himself? Does he remember best when he hears a story read to him, and then he reads it to himself?" The teacher moves about, encouraging independent work through direct questioning (What can you do now, to begin your day?). She notices Sarah staring at the ceiling with her journal open and a pencil in her hand. The teacher walks to her and smiles. Sarah asks, "How do you spell 'oxygen?' The teacher takes a 4- by 7-inch card from the stack that she always carries with her and writes the word on the card. She places it next to Sarah, who immediately copies it, and continues to write in her diary.

9:00 to 9:20   First Group Activity
This activity is required for all children at the beginning of a new week or after a vacation period. During the morning get-together the teacher greets the children and discusses routines and special events. To confirm knowledge of procedures, the teacher asks, "Ben, tell me what you are going to do first. Sarah?, Melissa?" etc. She continues to have three or four children retell

procedures immediately after she talks about them. As each child talks, the teacher writes the language on a wall chart. The chart is arranged to look like the children's individual contracts. A child or teacher can lead this group activity. Several examples are:

- show-and-tell activity
- story reader of the day—a child has previously selected a storybook and rehearsed reading it with the teacher or parent
- tongue twister of the day
- exercise or song time—Special exercise activities, e.g., "Simon Says" or "Follow the Leader", can be led by a child or teacher to music or a singing activity can also be used during this time
- model story writing—the teacher or a child who can write creates a short story for the group, which serves as a modeling activity for all children

After the activity, the teacher reviews routines and special small group activities. She also announces large group sessions. Both small and large group activities are posted, with scheduled times and children's names listed in appropriate places. Ben and Sarah know what to do.

9:20 to 10:00   Independent Work Time and Small or Large Group Activities

All children gather for the group activity. A story reading, with the purpose of guiding children to an oral or written (drawn) retelling, might be one large group lesson.

Small groups meet for approximately ten minutes. Several children might need guidance in print awareness skills. The teacher reminds each of the five children about the planned storybook activity. They know it will begin when their teacher sits in the library corner holding her copy of the book. That is her signal for starting an activity. As the children gather, the teacher tells each her purpose for the activity. As she hands each a copy of *Duck,* by David Lloyd and Charlotte Voake, she repeats, "This book will help you to learn the different parts of a book." The teacher knows that John has had difficulty predicting a book's content so she begins with this prereading skill. She has the children open the book to the title page. "This is the title—the name of the book, *Duck*. Now, you read it with me." The teacher repeats it chorally with the children. She continues this procedure with the author's name. "What is the other name?" asks Ryan spontaneously, pointing to the text. "Charlotte Voake is the illustrator of the book; she is the artist who drew the pictures," responds the teacher.

Other children need letter identification activities. On another day, the teacher will call these children together and provide the same alphabet books and chant with them or play the "I Spy" game in which children find something in the room that begins with either the same initial or ending sound as her keyword. These special skill groups are dissolved, reorganized, and changed regularly, to meet children's instructional needs.

Time is spent in individual instructional sessions:

- guiding oral retellings with picture books
- creating words using lists of spelling patterns
- discussing individual concerns or problems (for example, an aging grandparent or a pet)
- modeling diary writing
- reading object books to some children who need help understanding the relationship between speech and print
- encouraging a reluctant writer to create text
- listening to an excited new reader read a self-selected book
- listening to a child read his authored story
- helping a child with a sound-symbol pattern previously learned

10:00 to 10:40   Free Activity Time

Some children continue to work on projects (story writing; looking for more books about frogs; diary writing; reading picture, object, or story books) and others move to new activities. A workbench, large blocks, and cooking equipment can be used with adult supervision during free activity time. A parent volunteer monitors these centers. The teacher has set up special literacy activities in the living-alive center, the cooperative play area, the places-to-be-alone areas, the music area, and others. There is a chart with a photograph of the new classroom pet frog hanging next to the frog's aquarium. "Write what the frog looks like," is the picture's caption. The cooperative play area has some new props in it. There is a large cardboard carton painted like a train, a wooden wheel propped on top of half of a broomstick labeled turnstile, some coins in a box, and a box with a slot in the top with the sign, "Pay here." Train conductor's hats, money changers fastened onto belts, three-hole punchers, and a tape cassette recording of a moving train are ready for role-playing train people. The teacher has put special books in places-to-be-alone, with specific names of children posted at each. The music area is equipped with four cassette recorders and earphones. In each is a cassette tape recording of *Where the Wild Things Are*, narrated by the author, Maurice Sendak. A copy of the book is next to each player.

Self-monitoring tools are all around. There is a chart for each child where each writes the name and author of a book after reading (Figure 9–6). Contracts—individual work schedules—are prepared for each child. Some children are able to use these self-monitoring guides independently. Others need the teacher's guidance.

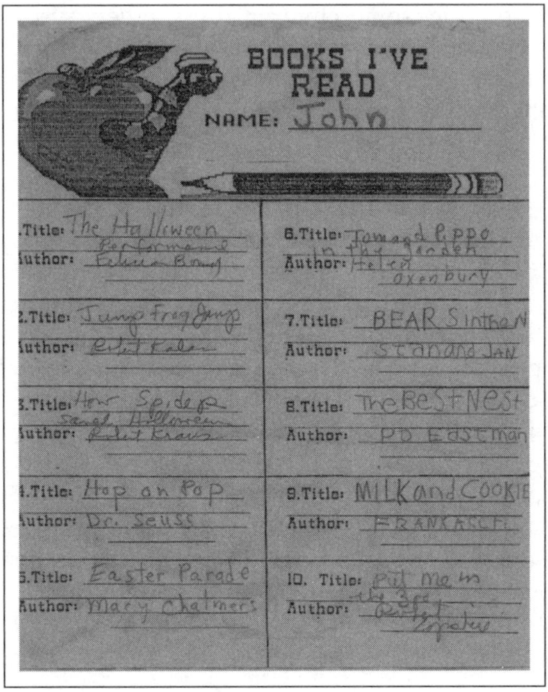

FIGURE 9–6 Books I've Read Chart

10:40 to 11:05 Cleanup and Snack Time

11:05 to 11:40 Whole Group Social Studies Activity
Modeling the Use of Literacy Skills
This is an instructional time. The purpose for this day's activity is to encourage children to increase vocabulary for writing as well as word recognition. The poetry anthology *Bear in Mind* by Bobbye Goldstein was selected for this lesson. The teacher posted a chart with "Bear Words" written at the top. When the group gathered, the teacher began a discussion to elicit "bear" words. As children spoke the words, the teacher wrote them, one under the other, on the chart. Each time a new word was added, the teacher reread the list from the beginning encouraging the children to read chorally with her.

Bear Words	
grizzly	*fuzzy*
brown	*polar*
big	*hugs*
strong	*scary*

After the together-time, some children drew, others scribbled, and some wrote strings of letters. All talked about their bear stories. Some children reproduced letters in sequences, wrote their names, and the names of other children and objects, inventing the spellings of words as they did so (Sulzby 1985).

11:40 to 12:10   Independent Reading and Writing Activities
The teacher puts lists of bear words on small pieces of paper and places them in the writing center, the library corner, the living-alive center—anywhere children might want to draw or write. Some children copy words, others illustrate each, and still others dictate a story to the teacher or onto the cassette tape recorder. The drama center now has several bear puppets that replicate characters in the poems in Goldstein's *Bear in Mind.* Other poems selected by Bobbye Goldstein (*What's on the Menu?*) were placed in private reading places and in the classroom library.

Alphabet puzzles are a new addition to the writing center. These help children recognize letters. Disks containing concentration and memory games are booted into two computers in the classroom library center, and Lotto, Spill-and-Spell and other word games are available. Some children ask for words to copy for their story. Others select the book *Duck* used earlier in the small group print-awareness lesson and copy the text.

12:15 to 1:15   Lunch and Outdoor Play (weather permitting)
Outdoor play follows lunch. In addition to the swings, slides, jungle gyms, and rubber tires for climbing, tricycles and bicycles are available for use in a special section of the playground. There is a sandbox and special outdoor living quarters for pets. Labels naming places are posted. The teacher reads these at the appropriate times during the course of the play period.

1:15 to 1:45   Whole (or Small) Group Lesson
Social studies or science is stressed during these literacy lessons. If, for example, several children are reading about prominent people, a biography might be read. This group lesson facilitates individual retellings for some. This time may also be used to model other strategies for developing literacy skills. Small groups would work together during this period for a purpose (finding books about the same topic, learning to bind a book, or reading a picture reference text).

1:45 to 2:30   Independent Reading and Writing,
Individual Projects, Center Activities, and Small
Group and Individual Conference Time
This is the time to complete independent lessons, encourage children to continue with work, or return books to the classroom library. Individual

conferences and ten-minute small group activities are scheduled. This is also the time when the teacher makes informal assessments based on observations and then uses these assessments in planning for instruction.

2:30   Cleanup and Get Together

Manipulative objects are put away, living things are attended to for the night and, finally, all come together and share the day's accomplishments and goals. A large easel is handy to write what children have learned today and what they still need to work on tomorrow. Each child has a personal copy of this chart in his or her basket of materials for recording ideas for himself or herself. The entire day's activities are reviewed. Then a musical activity is planned—one that includes actions to release tired muscles and minds. A closing favorite poem, song, or jingle is recited by all, chorally, as the teacher or a child points to the poster with the words printed on it. A book version of the poem, song, or jingle is displayed, and children know this is the final activity of the day. They move on their own to get their outer clothing.

2:55 to 3:05   Dressing and Farewells for Dismissal

Schedules and the environment are modified regularly to meet needs. The following guides shape that environment.

1. Think of yourself as a detective who continuously watches for clues about how children work. Ask yourself questions about needs ("Does Ben seem to need encouragement to start his project?").

2. Use consistent language to praise behaviors. Say, "I really like the way you wrote your story on story paper." The direct praise—mentioning the desired behavior—guides the child to identify and repeat that action.

3. Coax the reluctant learner into the activities by modeling desired behaviors. Hand Ben the pencil and a word card with his favorite friend's name written on it (or game or toy). Place a piece of writing paper in front of Ben, and one in front of yourself. Say, "I am copying Sarah's name on this paper. You try it." Stay with him until he continues independently. Move away, when it happens naturally.

4. Have children repeat directions and instructions orally after you offer them. This helps them to develop expectations.

5. Always tell children reasons for activities to make learning meaningful.

6. If a child is reading aloud and does not know a word, tell it to the child immediately so that the pace and comprehension of story are preserved.

7. If some children ask to spell words correctly, provide the spellings of words on a 4 by 7 inch word card. It is important to help children relax in order to compose freely, at this age, without concern for correct spellings. If spelling correctly, however, is an obsession for five-, six-, or seven-year-old children, eliminate that feeling by providing the word.

8. Be sure that materials and instruction facilitate success for children. Frustration discourages learning and promotes poor self-esteem.

Some of the strategies used for five-year-old children are also appropriate for six-, seven-, and eight-year-old children. Several of these will be described in this chapter and others in chapter 10.

Strategies

This section focuses on literacy activities for expanding language, comprehension, composition, and independence in the classroom setting. These activities are designed to coax children into monitoring their own growth. Strategies discussed in this chapter can be used throughout the primary, elementary, and upper elementary years in school. The activities are appropriate for large and small groups and individual instruction as described in the half- and full-day schedules. They are appropriate across curriculum areas.

Expanding Language

Talking—lots of talking—develops language. Children like Ben and Sarah have learned some of the rules of language before they came to school. They have lived in literacy-rich settings. They have also learned how to control language functions as described by Halliday (see chapter 3). They know that "please" and "thank you," as well as "excuse me" demonstrate concern and polite behavior. They also know other socially acceptable talk. They have learned instrumental language for getting what they want and for rejecting what they do not want. These children know that talking is central to their ever increasing transactions with caregivers and peers.

Ben and Sarah have begun to learn that talking in school can be similar to, but also different from, talk at home. Sometimes they give directions, and other times they discuss projects and family and school activities. Often children use language and costumes for creating roles. The dialogues they use resembles those of their parents, television characters, teachers, and children in the school building. There are small and large group discussions. These are times when talk can be free or directed. Directed talk is used to guide children to learn the rules that govern focused discussions and conversations in school. These rules include: answering questions that are asked; staying on the topic during discussions; self-questioning during listening to stay on task to help comprehend what someone else says; and talking about what others have said.

Answering Questions That Are Asked.   Questions asked by the teacher to guide expansion of language should help children to complete thoughts, be useful for clarifying ideas, and guide children to speak without exaggeration or overgeneralizations. Examples of questions that guide children to focus include: What else can you tell me about that? (clarification); Can you tell me a time that would not be true? (qualification); What other examples can you think of? (elaboration); and What might happen if you did that? (elaboration).

Staying on Topic during Discussions.   Sticking to the topic is difficult for many youngsters. Some of them are triggered by one idea and that takes them to the next. Something may happen in the classroom that helps a child remember a situation. A discussion about how doors lock to keep you safe triggered one youngster to blurt, "My dad locked himself out of his car and left the motor on." Though irrelevant to the group's focus, there might have been legitimate private associations made by the child. It is the teacher's role to keep children on task. A response by the teacher to bring the enthusiastic listener back to task might be, "That's really interesting. You might want to act that out for us next time using some dress-up clothes." The teacher can also suggest that "getting locked out" might be a good topic for tomorrow's discussion.

Topics children volunteer are never inappropriate. The personal meanings make them relevant to the group talk no matter how irrelevant they might be to the topic. Keeping the group on task is a necessary teaching goal. Informing children that there are other times to share personal ideas and providing this time are equally important. This is illustrated in the group discussion about Pilgrims and the Thanksgiving meal. This kindergarten group was led by five-year-old Ryan.

Ryan: Well, I think the Pilgrims had a lot of corn to eat because they had a lot of it.

Teacher: We have lots of corn too, and I think you're right.

Melissa: I think the Pilgrims had a big, b-i-g turkey.

Courtney: We have a big, big turkey, and my mom made it but it tastes like the one my grandma made.

Teacher: That's interesting, Courtney. I wonder how many people make turkey that tastes the same. That's a good topic for our discussion tomorrow morning. Now let me think (as she puts her finger to her temple, gesturing the thinking process). I think that the Pilgrims must have had bread made out of corn because they had lots of corn.

Ben: Yah! They probably use corn to make everything because they had a lot.

Ryan: Corn for everything? Did they make a house out of corn?

Teacher: I don't think it was strong enough. But I bet they made corn muffins.

Ben: Yah, and bread from corn, too.

Teacher: O.K., they made corn bread, too.

This discussion demonstrates the back-to-task strategy that works so effectively. No punitive remarks, no reprimands, and no directives ("Pay attention to the topic, Courtney.") were imposed.

Self-Questioning during Listening.   Children learn quickly that listening is important when sharing. Kindergarten children can learn to keep themselves on task by asking themselves questions about the discussion as someone talks. Ryan might have asked himself, for example, "What do I mean by everything? Do I mean building a house? Do I mean using corn to make a fire?" Self-questioning is a form of self-monitoring. Self-monitoring must be modeled by the teacher. This strategy is discussed in chapter 10.

Talking About What Others Have Said.   Talking about what others say increases oral language fluency. Playing roles to imagine other people's thoughts is one way to expand ideas. Comparing ideas also makes them relevant for others. Questions such as, "In what ways are your stories alike? How are they different?" invite the reluctant speaker to respond.

Several strategies, in addition to those discussed, guide children to engage in brainstorming sessions and show-and-tell activities.

Brainstorming.   Children seem to adore brainstorming. These are times when the teacher calls the group together to solve practical problems. The children "storm" their "brains" for ideas. Once, the class had decided to present a class play to their parents for Mother's Day. Many practical problems needed to be solved in order to begin to plan the event. A group gathering can result in a story map, which is used as a guide to help the children identify important issues (Cleland 1981) (Figure 9–7). The teacher writes the word *play* in the middle of the map. Then she asks, "What do we want our play to be about?" As children volunteer suggestions, she writes each. Her map guides the organization of ideas. It helps children realize that all of their ideas are part of a larger one that belongs to the entire class. This mapping strategy, also referred to as webbing, encourages children to talk about and organize ideas systematically (Bromley 1991). It can be used to solve classroom and individual problems which include ways to organize library books, topics for science projects, ways to keep the classroom clean, ways to help yourself pay attention, ways to retell stories, and directions for playing a game.

Show-and-tell.   This is a favorite time to talk. This group activity helps the kindergarten child move from talking during play to talking for an audience. It is wonderful not only for small children but for adults as well. Children know about show-and-tell, for they have seen adults show-and-tell about appliances, fast foods, and other products during television commercials. Ben and Sarah have also seen their teacher show-and-tell about their class pet frog. This marvelous practice is fun for the children only when they volunteer. Requiring each child to show-and-tell creates an unnatural environment for sharing. The most important aspect of show-and-tell for young children is the opportunity to talk. Talking in front of the group seems to help children move from short, egocentric, and undetailed language to elaborative oral text. The first time Melissa volunteered for show-and-tell,

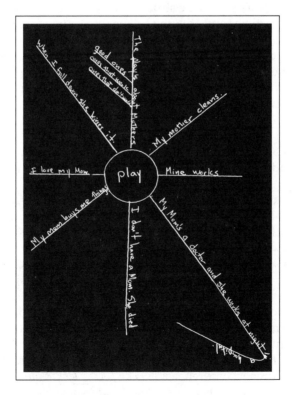

FIGURE 9–7 Brainstorming Map

she picked up her stuffed animal that she had brought from home and said, "This is my bear." Second and third show-and-tell sessions included phrases such as, "I like this book," and "This is my favorite toy." As time moved on, Melissa's language became more complex. The following illustrates a child's show-and-tell contribution after several months of voluntary sharing.

> *I went to the library with my Mom. She got a book and I got one, too. My book was in a different place than hers. Her book was with grown-up books and I couldn't read them so she took me to the place where there were only books for children, and I got three. This is my favorite one (as she shows the cover to the class) because it is about bears, and I like bears best of all.*

Melissa was able to "take off" using a familiar experience to share with her audience. She was prompted by her own experience and the knowledge that there would be a captive audience to share with.

The teacher shared part of herself during show-and-tell using interesting words and diverse syntactic structures. She used compound sentences, simple ones, adjectives, and adverbial clauses to share ideas.

Show-and-tell helped the teacher move into talks about specific topics. These developed from science and social studies activities, as well as stories. Topic talks were focused. There were rules during these times that children knew because they were modeled by their teacher and discussed by her. Sometimes, brainstorming maps helped these focused talks.

Comprehension
Five-year-old children benefit from comprehension instruction before, after, and during reading.

Before Reading Activities.   Before, or prereading, activities are important for helping children to predict (hypothesize) what the text is about. Caregivers guide children to predict story theme, story vocabulary, story genre, and personal ideas, early in life.

When Ben sat on his mother's lap and she read, she paced her language to guide Ben to predict "what comes next." When Sarah guided Melissa to read, she guided a peer to "take an educated guess" about what comes next in the story. The act of predicting guides children to attend to task during listening or reading and learn that it is important to know something about a book's content in order to enjoy it.

Predicting Story Theme.   Discussions about the story that precede reading expand children's comprehension. The terms *look, think,* and *predict* are the key words for guiding before children read (Russavage and Arick 1988). One teacher used the following guides with a group of children before reading Judi and Ron Barrett's *Cloudy with a Chance of Meatballs,* a story about food dropping like rain from the sky. It is especially good for noting story theme since the theme is so distinctly different.

> *"Hm'm,* Cloudy with a Chance of Meatballs. *What a funny name for a book (pointing her finger to her temple indicating that the words she is saying are hers, not the author's). I'm looking at the cover of the book and thinking, 'What is this book about?' There is a man holding a plate in his hand and an umbrella over his head. There are clouds in the sky. It looks like the meatball is bouncing off of the plate. Gee, where did the meatball come from?"* The teacher turns the back cover so that the children can see it, and says, *"Well, there's the meatball, and it looks like it is coming out of the clouds. There's a Mom and two kids sitting at a dinner table and their dog has his mouth open. I guess—I* predict *that the book is about people eating, and the food is falling down onto the plates. The name of the book, the title, says it's cloudy, so it must be a cloudy day when the people are eating. I'm thinking about the word* chance *in the title. What does that mean? Gee, first I* look *at the pictures on the cover, then I* think *about what I see, then* predict *what the book is about. It's about people eating meatballs that fall down from a cloud! Now I'll read it to see."*

Predicting Word Meanings as They Relate to the Story.   Some of the interrelationships between words may pose comprehension barriers for a few of the children. The teacher gathered those children before reading the story. She carried out the following prereading activity, in addition to the above, in order to guide comprehension of the story vocabulary (special words).

Teacher: I wonder what clouds have to do with meatballs? (word relationships)

Sarah: Probably nothing, except you can eat meatballs even when it's a cloudy day.

Teacher: But why the umbrella? (seeking perceptions of meaning)

Sarah: Well, the clouds will make it rain.

Teacher: But it doesn't look like it's raining in the picture. Maybe the word *chance* can help us. Maybe there's a chance that it is going to rain. Maybe he is not going to take any chances of getting wet, so he is carrying his umbrella. (relationship of content to word meanings)

Sarah: Yeah, it might rain, so the man isn't taking any chances of getting wet. He has his umbrella just in case there's a chance of rain.

Teacher: There must be other interesting words in this book. I think I'm going to find the word *storm* (as she says the word, the teacher writes it on a wall chart with the name of the book written at the top).

Sarah: I think *snow* and *ice* words are in the book (teacher writes these under her word).

After reading, the teacher and children individually and in small groups talked about surprising words, interesting words, and rhyming words. These informal conversations helped the children to use words from the storybook in other contexts.

Predicting Genre.   Ben was curious. "Teacher!" he exclaimed, quite out of turn, "This isn't a real story. It's made up." "I think you're right, Ben. It is probably fiction—a made-up story." By picking up Ben's interest, the teacher immediately guides him into the genre of the story. She observes an appropriate, purposeful opportunity to intervene in order to introduce the term *fiction* and does.

After Story Reading Activity.   Remembering what we hear and read illustrates recall. Small and large group story retelling sessions are wonderful for teacher modeling of such activities. The library corner has a soft chair with a story hat next to it. After reading, the teacher moves to the chair, puts on the story hat, and retells the story to Ivan who has signed up to be the listener for the day. Often he helped the teacher retell. The teacher would begin the story, and he would continue, following the story sequence, including episodes, and describing elements of illustrations. This sort of retelling encourages children to demonstrate comprehension. Retelling stories in a setting that resembles a family environment makes the activity feel natural for some and comfortable for most. Children, after listening to stories and reading at home, often ask to retell them to their caregiver. The activity is powerful for a wide range of language activities. Discussion concerning appropriate predictions, for example, spurred Ben to "blurt out" during a retelling session, "I was right. They did eat meatballs that fell down. And I was wrong. The meatballs didn't fall off a table, they fell down from the sky. And lots of other food, too. What a mess! And the cover didn't tell me that the book was messy." Spontaneous responses have enormous potential for both assessing and guiding instruction. The activity is powerful for it is easy to prepare for, suitable for a wide range of language activities in all content areas, flexible in its use, carried out with minimal teacher intervention, and is a risk-taking procedure, providing practice for reading, writing, and oral language skills (Brown and Cambourne 1987).

Retellings: Data for Assessment.   Transcripts of oral retellings and those written by children in later years provide concrete evidence (data) of growth in comprehension and also indications of children's needs. This activity is natural for literature-based reading and writing programs. The following skills and concept development occur in both oral and written retellings. Oral retelling demonstrates the ability to:

- clarify reading
- justify ideas in the book
- learn to share with an audience

Oral retellings illustrate:

- knowledge of story structure
- ability to sequence events
- knowledge of vocabulary from the story
- short-term memory for a story
- ability to personalize events in the story
- use of prior knowledge to make meaning of the story
- type of materials recalled (fact or inference)

Written retellings illustrate the above as well as:

- ability to edit ideas
- ability to edit the mechanics of writing (capitalization, spelling, or other punctuation)
- increased vocabulary for writing (spelling and meaning);
- ability to make judgments and confirm them;
- ability to summarize
- prior knowledge
- ability to distinguish facts from fiction and reality from fantasy
- genres in writing
- ability to learn decoding (spelling) rules.

Both oral and written retellings provide performance samples for assessing growth in comprehension over time.

The kindergarten year is the first time that formal, continuous records of retelling should occur. Table 7–5 (in chapter 7) helps adults record children's recall from story. This tool provides systematic information. The instructional and recording procedures that follow permit children, teachers, and caregivers to observe changes, over time. All of the above mentioned skills and the following can be monitored when children write their retellings:

- spelling development
- written language fluency (use of sentence patterns and syntactic elements)
- handwriting
- visual discrimination ability
- visual perception skills
- knowledge of the mechanics of writing (e.g., punctuation or capitalizations).

Unguided oral retellings are often spontaneous for kindergarten children. Sarah often says, "Teacher, teacher, listen to me tell the story." Retellings must be recorded on tape and transcribed for assessment and instructional purposes. The following oral retelling is Ben's spontaneous unguided retelling of H. A. and M. Rey's *Curious George Visits the Zoo*. After his teacher read it to him, Ben's retelling demonstrates that he was able to listen and attend to the story which is about:

Curious George, a monkey whose nature is described by his name George, visits a zoo and meets a character, referred to as "the man" who is obviously the zookeeper. George's introduction to the zoo is a walking tour where he sees an elephant, long necked giraffes, kangaroos with babies in their pockets, and several elephants with "floppy ears" and long tusks who were eating hay. Eating was an activity during George's visit that all were doing, for it was lunchtime. The zookeeper, who always wore a yellow hat, went to feed the lions. He had been carrying a pail of bananas for the monkeys, and set it down to get a drink of water. George, as most monkeys would, saw the bananas and grabbed them from the man. He made a mad dash carrying the pail with him through crowds of people who were watching the monkeys in the zoo. One of the monkeys grabbed a balloon from a small boy who was watching them from outside of their cage. The boy began to cry as the rest of the monkeys made loud noises. He wanted his balloon back. Curious George came to his rescue by snatching the balloon from the monkey while he was eating. He returned the balloon to the child and was cheered by the observers. And so the story ends happily ever after.

Ben's retelling:

The man with the yellow hat said to George, "Do you want to see a real elephant?" "Yes," said George. Then they went on to the zoo. Then they saw giraffes with their long necks. Then they saw some kangaroos with their special pockets carrying their babies. Then it was lunchtime and the man with the yellow hat said, "I'm going to see when they feed the lions." The man with the yellow hat said, "Stay here until I come back." And

George stayed until he, a zookeeper, came with some bananas in a bucket. Then he took the bucket and he ran until he saw a crowd around the monkey house. That was a place to hide for George. The monkey stole a balloon. And he went down. And he gave the balloon back to the boy. Then the zookeeper came. Then the zookeeper told George, "Next time do not take the banana."

These data, the transcript of Ben's retelling, which were recorded on tape, reveal that he has knowledge of, and can:

- identify the main character (George)
- identify six of nine other characters in the story (the man, giraffes, kangaroos, zookeeper, monkey, and lion)
- retell with some detail (man with the yellow hat, giraffes with long necks, kangaroos with special pockets)
- allude to the story's resolution
- recall a series of events
- end a story appropriately
- use dialogue when appropriate

After she and Ben review his strengths, the teacher concluded that Ben needs guidance in using appropriate story starters (Once upon a time . . .), understanding that stories have a goal or problem, understanding that episodes in stories lead to a resolution to the problem or goal, and following the story sequence.

Some children, like Ben, retell best orally. Others, like Courtney, role-play and those, like Ivan, draw. Still others love to use props to help them remember. A brown paper bag with a large yellow hat; a cuddly kangaroo, lion, or giraffe toy; a pail; and a toy monkey could spur some to retell by acting the story. Observing the children's behaviors and taking notes is another way to record children's comprehension. The retelling sheet (see Table 7–5) can be used to record all sorts of children's responses to literature during language arts time blocks.

Guided Retelling.   Some children need guidance to recall. Guides are referred to as prompts. Prompts are questions used to guide the direction of the retelling. The same questions used over and over again help children internalize the questions. They begin to use them to prompt themselves. Prompts (questions) are appropriate for oral retellings and also for written retellings when children write. Prompt questions for recalling stories can be found in Table 7–6.

Just as we guide children to hold the cup so juice will not spill, so must we guide comprehension of story. Prompts must be provided just in the nick of time. When children begin to retell hesitantly, prompts to encourage recall help them start. It should be pointed out that guiding children with prompts often limits the oral language they produce. Guidance, however, teaches children the story elements. The following transcript illustrates a prompted retelling between Melissa and her teacher. She selected the book *Through Grandpa's Eyes* by Patricia MacLachlan for her teacher to read. The story, about a blind grandfather and his grandson John, illustrates the bond between the old and young and also helps the sighted child understand how the blind "see" the world. Unguided retellings revealed that Melissa retold only episodes and often left out the main character, the story theme, problem, and resolution. The teacher placed the book on the table with the cover facing up.

Teacher: I am glad that you picked *Through Grandpa's Eyes*. It's one of my favorite books. Now let's see. Tell me about the story.

Melissa: Well, um, well, ah . . . well it's about this boy. and . . . ah . . . ah

Teacher: And who else?

Melissa: His grandfather. Yeah, and the grandfather can't see (Melissa pauses and looks at the teacher and smiles).

Teacher: And? (Melissa shrugs her shoulders). Where did the story happen, Melissa?

Melissa: In the grandfather's house.

Teacher: And where else did it happen?

Melissa: I don't know.

Teacher: Where else did it happen?

Melissa: In the kitchen, and in the bedroom, and outside the house, too.

Teacher: The story happened in lots of places. Now tell me when the story happened.

Melissa: In the morning.

Teacher: What happened first in the story.

Melissa: Well, the boy got up and his grandfather got up and then they knew it was breakfast so he did exercise and then they went down and had breakfast, and then . . . ah, and then

Teacher: And then what came next?

Melissa: And then they played the violin or something, and then they took a walk, and then they went to the pond, and then they watched TV.

Teacher: O.K. Now can you tell me what the problem is in the story?

Melissa: What?

Teacher: What was the boy's problem?

Melissa: Nothin.

Teacher: What was he doing?

Melissa: He was trying to think about what it would be like to be blind.

Teacher: What do you mean?

Melissa: Well, the grandfather was blind, and he wanted to play with him, but he couldn't because he couldn't see.

Teacher: So what did he do to play with his grandfather?

Melissa: Well, he closed his eyes and made believe that he was blind too.

Teacher: So his problem was that he wanted to play with his grandpa but his grandpa couldn't see, so the boy couldn't play.

Melissa: No, he could play, but the grandpa couldn't see, so the boy had to be like the grandfather so he could play with his grandpa.

Teacher: And how did he do that?

Melissa: He closed his eyes like this (closes her eyes).

Teacher: So he solved his problem by acting like his grandpa.

Melissa: Yep, and they did everything. And that's all I want to say.

The classroom library must include object books, books with predictable language—rhythm and rhyme—and stories with clearly delineated story structure to facilitate successful recall. This makes retelling a productively fun strategy.

Composition
For Ben, Sarah, and their classmates writing is an experimental activity. Children write stories and share personal communications using journals (drawings) and signs.

Writing Stories.   Ben uses writing to retell stories. He makes roll movies, creating one picture for each story episode. Each picture is taped together, as in a filmstrip, and rolled onto a paper tube (these taken from paper towel rolls). Writing has helped Ben to organize his ideas. He draws lines, letters, and words in several directions on a page. Like learning to talk, learning to write is a gradual process. Ivan and Melissa scribble, and Sarah and Nancy write sentences and even stories. Many of the children attempt to write even though words may not look correct. It is especially interesting to watch those who are not yet ready to write attempt to write stories. Several sit in the writing center and draw pictures, talking out loud to themselves about events that have occurred. For these children, oral language controls their attempts to write. These children may not have the ability to write words, but they are certainly print-aware and on their way to becoming readers and writers. They demonstrate that they understand the connection between reading and writing. The more children write, the more they move from imitating and reusing author's text to creating their own. Brown and Cambourne (1987) have noted that children learn to write as a result of retelling stories. Routman (1988) has observed that children go through stages in their writing development by interacting and retelling literature. The stages are as follows:

1. First retellings are almost word-for-word like the author's text.
2. Written retellings are partially the author's with some added details and changes.
3. Written retellings have the same title and characters but, in addition, some original elements are added to the author's structure. This creates an almost new story. This stage is also the time that a child retells the story, but completely in his or her own words.
4. The most satisfying influence retelling has for developing the ability to compose stories happens when children use the same characters as the author, but create a totally new story using similar story elements (sharing, humor, and dialogue).
5. Finally, after much composition, children write completely original, well-organized stories. They develop the ability to write using appropriate sentence structure and develop characterizations and succinct stories because of their interaction with literature. The abilities develop naturally as part of their interactions with literature. They all happened in language-rich home and school environments in the sixth, seventh, and eighth years of life.

Personal Communications.   Ashlee loves her journal. Each morning when she arrives, she takes it from her basket of materials. All of her work for language arts is in that basket. Ashlee pulls out the little book—a series of writing papers stapled together and a title page that says, "Ashlee's Journal." She turns to the page with the paper clip on it. Ashlee puts the clip in that page so that her teacher would respond to the message. The teacher responds to children's messages three times a week. With twenty-four children, that is just about all the time left for responses. She often tells the children to select the page for her response. Ashlee's journal entries are usually pictures of friends or favorite people. She labels her pictures with words that represent their names and special characteristics. Sometimes it is difficult to understand her writing so the teacher approaches her and says, "Ashlee, I need help reading your writing. Please tell me what you have written and I will put my writing next to yours so I am able to write back to you." This satisfies Ashlee. She feels that she is able to write, that her code is appropriate, and that her teacher's code is just another way to share similar ideas. The teacher has seen growth in Ashlee's ability to use written language to share ideas.

The teacher is able to assess growth in writing development using the journal entries (Figure 9–8). She assesses understanding of concepts of print (see Table 7–1), ability to write letters, word knowledge (how words look), awareness of syntax (how words are strung together to make sentences), and reasons for writing.

Sarah always selects a sign to designate that she wants to read alone. Objects are labeled with their names. The snake cage has "Snake" fastened on the table near it. Signs which guide children to carry out specific activities are posted all around the classroom. Signs with favorite songs fill the music and drama center. What a wonderful way to teach the art of communication

FIGURE 9–8 Journal Sample

using signs. Often, the teacher gathers the children together as a group to write signs with special words from favorite stories or field trips. Other times, she moves from child to child and suggests that they label their drawings. Ivan was drawing a picture of a ship with sails. When asked to tell about the boat, he began a monologue about the tall ships.

> *You see, these tall ships were the kind the Pilgrims and sailors used to cross the ocean. See this (as he pointed to what looked like a mast)? It's the mast. That means it's a sail and it sails the boat.*

As he spoke, the teacher took a 4 by 7 inch word card and wrote the word *mast* on it. She put the word card right under Ivan's picture of the mast. "You could label your mast with the word *mast* so all of us will know what it is." As she said label, she pointed to the word card. Her on-the-spot instruction worked. Ivan looked at the word, looked back at the teacher and said, "Mast?" "Yes," the teacher responded, "That word card says mast." The teacher used this technique in the nick of time. She provided Ivan with a tool for recognizing a word. Word cards were written in large letters as if they were signs. Children made signs for everything and hung them in appropriate places. The collection of signs, written with invented spellings tickled those who visited this kindergarten classroom.

A major concern for all teachers is to guide children to recognize letters and words when they see them and also to be able to read and write (spell) words correctly. It is well known that the best way to learn to read and write words is in meaningful contexts (Ashton-Warner 1963). Sylvia Ashton-Warner taught Maori children in New Zealand how to read and write words using the word card system mentioned above. Children's thirst for language was the powerful force that guided learning. Children learned words that were "organic"—words which had meanings in their lives. They were key words needed for living. Children selected the words to read and write, at will. This made sense to Ashton-Warner for, as she stated so well in her book *Teacher,*

> *What a dangerous activity reading is; teaching is. All this plastering on of foreign stuff. Why plaster on at all when there's so much inside already? So much locked in? If only I could get it out and use it as working materials. And not draw it out either. If I had a light enough touch it would come out under its own volcanic power. (p. 14)*

Words do come from children. At very early ages they become aware of the symbol system that is used for creating words. Youngsters in the print-rich environment of the home have played with written language. At an earlier age, Ben could not write letters but wrote lines, curves, and dots that resembled letters (see chapter 3). As he grew, these make-believe letters were mixed with real ones. As he wrote, he would identify the letters. The names of letters were learned from the story reading and alphabet books used by his caregiver before he came to school. They were learned from the signs hung in the nursery school classroom. They were learned as the family's car passed a fast food restaurant and his mom or dad pointed to the sign, read it, and named each letter in the words. Sarah, and Ben as well, knew the letters in their name probably before they knew any others. The alphabet song was part of their singing repertoire from birth but, now, at five, they have discovered that the song and the letters used to make words are related. Alphabet books and songs and attention to letters and words help Ben and Sarah learn the alphabet in functional ways. Some children, when they come to kindergarten, may need specialized approaches to learn letter names and their functions (see chapter 10). But, Ben and Sarah and most of their classmates have conceptualized the ideas that words are units of speech and written language. They listen and read and then write signs and journals, and draw pictures in response to literature.

Ben and Sarah, and their kindergarten classmates have discovered that writing is an important tool for sharing ideas, and requires effort (Sulzby 1985). Five-year-old children will put forth that effort. They will struggle and also ask for help in order to recognize words when they desperately want to read their favorite stories, signs, letters, and names of candy and spell words when they want to add a caption to a picture, write to a friend or relative, or write a word, sentence, or story.

Independence in the Classroom Setting

Willard Olson (1959) discussed the importance of naturalistic environments in classrooms. His work suggested that these environments embrace three concepts pertinent to independent learning: seeking behavior, self-selection, and pacing.

Olson's work illustrated that healthy children seek from environments experiences that are consistent with their maturity and needs. Although other aspects of activities may be present, the child ignores them until they are appropriate. Seeking behavior, what children search for, tells us much about what they are ready to learn. It seems natural that self-selection is a seeking-behavior that quenches the thirst for learning.

A lesson from nature illustrates that plants, animals, and human beings are sustained in life by self-selecting environments appropriate for meeting their needs. If appropriate environments do not exist or if no provisions are made to meet needs, plants may die. But animals and humans work creatively to establish conditions that advance their well-being (Olson 1959). We know that infants have a great ability to control the amount and timing of their food. We know that babies, too, accept and reject food based on taste preferences and needs.

If children are set free in environments with a variety of exciting books and objects, they will tend to appropriate time to respond to some of the materials. Each will react according to individual maturity. The sensitive teacher provides flexible blocks of time so that five-year-old children pace activities, some spending more time reading and writing and others less.

Goals for creating independent learners include strategies that encourage self-selection of materials for learning, while building self-esteem and confidence. Three strategies can be used in the early years to meet these goals. These are a daily or weekly contract, redirected questioning, and direct praise.

Contracts.   Contracts are study guides (Glazer 1980). They help children and teachers manage time and organize activities (Figure 9–9). Contracts can be divided into categories based on curriculum. We have included one divided into four parts. The first part includes reading activities—those assigned by the teacher and those selected by the child. The second part focuses on vocabulary. The third part includes composition (writing) activities, again with a section for teacher assigned and child assigned activities. The fourth is a review section which includes "What I learned today, and what I can work on tomorrow." Contract planning should be a collegial activity between the teacher and a child or a group of children.

The following guidelines should help develop contracts with children.

- Design a contract that can be used throughout the school year (The contract, itself, should be free of competitive activities and should not, for example, request that the child color the spaces when they complete tasks).
- Some of the materials should be teacher directed and others child directed
- Permanent activities appear weekly (Special and specific activities should be planned with children at the end of a day, every other day, or weekly, depending on the child's needs. Planning time must be scheduled as a regular activity.)

Contracts should be kept in each child's folder or basket of materials. Children will learn, by the end of the first week of school that the first thing each must do in the morning is get the contract, read it, and carry out activities. Kindergarten contracts, like those prepared for six- and seven-year-olds,

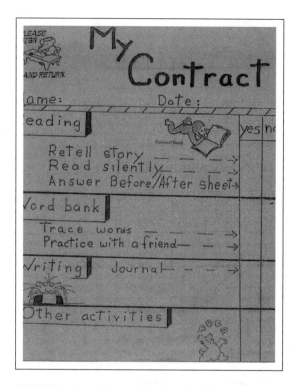

FIGURE 9–9 Example of a Child's Contract

should be appropriate for children who read words and for those who read pictures.

Redirected Questioning. Children ask questions all the time. Often they know the answers to their questions, but other times they do not. Some children need to hear ideas, especially if they include directions or instructions, again and again. Others need to hear themselves repeat information to remember the data. Redirecting children's questions helps them to hear their own answers. This strategy was best used with Allison, a child who had never been to preschool who always asked, "What do I do now?" Allison asked this immediately after she received directions or instructions. She also asked this between activities. Often the teacher was sure that Allison knew the answers to her own questions. The teacher redirected Allison's question back to her. "What do you think you should do now?" At the beginning of the school year, Allison usually shrugged her shoulders and said, "I don't know." The teacher persisted and repeated the question without response. After asking the question the same way three times, still without response, she asked, "What do you suppose you can do now?" This was also unsuccessful. The teacher, to avoid frustration, told Allison the answer. Immediately after telling it she said, "Now tell me what I just said." This helped the child hear for herself the expected behaviors and also remember the information.

Direct Praise.   Direct praise is just what the name implies. The praise directly tells the child what he or she did appropriately. This motivates the child to do it again. Terms like "very good" or "great," although encouraging for some, are vague. The description of the action, on the other hand, specifies what is good. Examples of direct praise such as those shown in Table 9–2 should serve as a model for teachers. We have found that when we use this technique, children model our behaviors and use direct praise with peers and adults.

Children need to feel in control of environments. Each child needs to know what he or she is able to accomplish independently and what he or she needs to learn. Each must feel confident enough to seek and select activities. The classroom environment, the materials, activities, and teacher

TABLE 9–2   Encouraging Self-Esteem

Activity	Direct Praise
A child makes the decision that a book she has self-selected is too difficult. She says, "I missed five words on that page, so it's too hard."	I really like the way you decided the book was too hard. Discovering that you have missed words is a good way to make that decision.
A child rejects a book using the fist-full-of-words rule. She puts it back on the shelf but exhibits an expression that could mean that she is dissatisfied with herself.	I really like the way you found out that the book is too hard for you to read. There are lots of hard words in that book. You know the fist-full-of-words rule, so all you need to do is pick another.
A child reads a book and retells it on her own. The retelling included the introduction, the story problem, and the main character. She says, "Uh, I forgot where the story happened."	It makes me feel happy that you know the story elements. I am really happy that you can tell yourself what you forgot.

behavior all serve to help children maintain the eagerness, zest, confidence, and pride that accompanies successful kindergarten experiences.

Summary

Five-year-old children are ready for school. Their social, emotional, intellectual, and physical development permits them to share and learn collegially in an environment prepared for their needs. The kindergarten room is that environment—one filled with activity. There are centers for storing things and for carrying out activities. Some children read words and others read pictures. Some children write words and others write squiggles that are meant to represent words. Some children role-play characters in stories and other characters in their lives. Kindergarten teachers who arrange flexible schedules, confer with children, provide materials and activities appropriate to meet their needs, and guide children to observe what they need to learn. When children and teachers share control, children will become independent, confident readers and writers.

10

The Seventh and Eighth Years of Life: Literacy and the School

This chapter addresses:

- What growth patterns characterize the seventh and eighth years of life?
- What is the role of the caregiver in nurturing the child's growth toward literacy?
- What activities and materials foster literacy?

What Growth Patterns Characterize the Seventh and Eighth Years of Life?

Six-year-old children find life hectic. This is the first formal year of school. High expectations for learning are often imposed by parents onto their children. For them, the desire to please the adult becomes a major factor in the desire to achieve. The important factor for six-year-old children is the establishment of an effective partnership between the teacher and themselves. The bond helps develop the desire to learn and the ability to take the risks necessary to do so.

At six children are inconsistent in behavior and are clumsy. One day they work well, stay on task, respond appropriately to most directions, and make decisions on their own. Other days they may be inattentive, achieve little, respond inappropriately to directions, and seem to be totally adult dependent (Ames and Ilg 1979b).

Seven-year-old children, because most have been through one year of formal school, have found their places in the classroom, playground, lunch room, gymnasium, and other locations in school. Children are in transition, at this age, from dependent to more independent school behavior. Their behaviors begin to resemble those of children ranging in age from seven to eleven years.

Physical Changes

Although growth is not as fast as the rapid increases in infant years, six- and seven-year-old children grow quickly. At six children can ride tricycles and, some, a bicycle. At seven they are confident with both. Six-year-old children find skipping, hopping, and jumping rope easy tasks. Saws, scissors, pencils, hammers, and sewing needles are among tools often selected at six. For seven-year-old children teachers still find it important to supervise the use of sharp tools even though they are well-coordinated and confident about their dexterity and physical strength.

With the beginning of the loss of baby fat and baby teeth, at six children begin to dress themselves, and some tie their shoelaces. At seven they tie their shoelaces, do jigsaw puzzles, and knit with large needles. Unlike six-year-olds, seven-year-old children have a healthy appetite and will probably grow two to three inches during the year. Many develop a taste for faddish foods. At seven they like to be with peers for that is where their main interests lie.

Emotional Changes

The marvelous self-concepts of six-year-old children help them to handle the strains of formal education. Sometimes the pressures to learn to read and write as well as other pressures cause children to engage in behaviors more typical of three-, four-, or five-year-olds. Temper tantrums are expected. But the big egos of children at six provide them with the ability to begin to control their emotions and reduce tantrums. Unlike six-year-olds who oppose their teacher, mother, or dad, at seven children like to take responsibility for grown-up things. They feel grown-up. They like to dust, wash, collect lunch money, walk dogs, and play with friends. Six-year-olds like to be children, following the rules of adults. Seven-year-olds, however, experience conflict between their desire to grow up and also to remain a child (Ames and Haber 1985). Six-year-old children will insist that rules be followed exactly. Seven-year-old children, partially because they like to be accepted by adults, consider modifications. They will laugh at adult jokes particularly ones told by parents and, like six-year-olds, enjoy crawling into their parents' bed and engaging in pillow fights. Seven-year-olds respond negatively to some characteristics of adults, referring to some as smelly because of perfume, alcohol, or tobacco and hairy because of beards. Some adults are "weird"—this attributed to double chins, facial lines and wrinkles, or enlarged pores resulting from age. Home is still the place where they feel most comfortable. Although academic achievement and social acceptance by peers is prominent, they can turn inward, with increased interest in themselves. The feeling of shame is experienced for the first time. At six children do not seem to experience this emotion and are interested in becoming the focus of attention much of the time. Seven-year-old children are often happy as part of a group. Both age groups are quite sensitive to important adults in their lives. They respond to sadness, joy, successes, and failures, seemingly experiencing the emotions of those significant people.

Social Changes

Six-year-old children are quite social. They like to visit friends without grown-ups. They like to play with two or three friends for short periods of time. Sometimes they are self-sufficient, assertive, and even bossy, demonstrating their desire to dominate situations and act "in charge." They are talkative and impulsive and interested in themselves. At seven children are more serious and seek others. Six-year-old children will do chores assigned by teachers and parents. At seven they will take more responsibility but complain about it.

Seven-year-old children are greatly influenced by unwritten traditions in our cultural heritage. Hopscotch, double dutch, blindman's bluff, and hide-and-seek are only a few games that are passed from one generation of seven-year-olds to another. Oral language traditions also influence their social activities. Jokes, riddles, and sayings ("sticks and stones will break my bones but words will never harm me") are favorites. Seven-year-old children everywhere repeat language like:

> *Rain, rain go away*
> *Come again another day.*

These language traditions provide the security children need for language to grow. This same tradition, however, often molds children into a rigidity noticeable in the behaviors of some seven-year-olds. At six children will wear clothing even if different from peers. At seven, on the other hand, they must wear shoes or jackets like the rest of the class. This need to be like others confirms their intolerance of differences—the obese, physically handicapped, or the academically different. Both age groups accept the adults in their lives as authorities, but at seven children seem to be more manageable, and self-control begins to become more evident.

Cognitive Changes

At six, children have a sense of the time of day and the day of the week. Time concepts are understood because the children usually connect them to personal events like, "On Tuesday, I get my new bike."

Six-year-old children have a great interest in print. They know that print has a function and a purpose. It can tell you how to cook or plant flowers and is a source of pleasure and news. They focus on letters and numbers and like to copy them. Seven-year-old children begin to see broader pictures. Their perceptions begin to modify. They focus less on details and more on whole units. While at six children require organization in a rigid way in order to function, at seven, they can find order even if things are in disarray. Seven-year-old children begin to see the world more like older children. Visual perception, the ability to see things in a personally specific way, is sharpening. It seems appropriate here to mention perceptual deficits in literacy activities. Problems with beginning to read, particularly with six-year-old children, have, at times, been attributed to these deficits. It is assumed that inadequate perceptual growth causes reading failure. We know, from experience, that many poor readers do have perceptual problems. They see things differently than most. But, we would be remiss if we did not admit that perceptual deficits are probably not the only reason for reading difficulties. Although we believe that perceptual processes are involved in reading activities, reading problems do not result from perceptual deficiencies alone. Many variables cause reading difficulties. Children's ability to perceive elements of oral and written language permits them to understand the relationship between print and speech.

What Is the Role of the Caregiver in Nurturing the Child's Growth toward Literacy?

These are the years that reading and writing are important. Books are great favorites with nearly all six-year-old children (Ames and Ilg 1979b). At seven children are in a transition period with reading (Ames and Harper 1985). They like to be read to but very much like to read themselves. Books for the classroom library include:

- wordless picture story and information books
- realistic fiction
- traditional literature, fables, and folktales
- children's magazines as well as local newspapers and popular national magazines
- books that build sound-symbol relationships

You can use the references cited earlier and select more books in the categories above to add to the classroom library. Magazines are now important for new readers. We recommend that subscriptions to the following magazines be part of the classroom library: *Chickadee,* The Young Nationalist Foundation, Toronto, Canada; *Cricket and Ladybug,* Open Court Publishing Company, Peru, Ill.; *Owl,* The Young Nationalist Foundation, Toronto, Canada; *Kid City,* Children's Television Workshop, New York, N.Y.; *Ranger Rick,* National Wildlife Federation, Washington, D.C.; *Sesame Street,* Children's Television Workshop, New York, N.Y.; and *Your Big Back Yard,* National Wildlife Federation, Washington, D.C.

Music and drama, as well as living-alive materials and equipment, should be altered to meet individual and group interests and needs. Daily schedules similar to the whole day described in chapter 9 are appropriate, but schedules should be flexible to allow for individual differences in time management and work choices. The following schedule is arranged in blocks in order to meet individual needs for collaborative projects and for independent work.

8:30 to 9:00
Children prepare themselves for the day using materials prepared by the teacher, self-select books, take care of classroom pets, or work with peers on small group endeavors. The teacher observes children's strengths and needs and records them.

9:00 to 9:20
Morning get-together times may include show-and-tell, a review of special or daily activities, news events, exercise or song time, brainstorming, or group story writing time.

9:20 to 10:40
This language arts time block is used for individual and small group language arts activities including retellings, story writing, writing related to content areas, creative writing, individual or small group skill-development activities, or self-monitoring activities related to reading and writing. The teacher may use this period to work with small groups of children who need help in predicting. She has recorded the behavior of the children in her classroom and sees a range of responses regarding the prediction of word meanings and theme. She gathers together some children who would benefit from some directed reading activity and works with them. (See chapter 9 for a discussion on predicting theme and word meanings.)

10:40 to 11:05
This time may be used for cleanup for some; others may prefer to continue to write, edit, or read their stories; it can be used for snack time with the storyteller of the day or a special events session if desired. The option to continue a project or be alone is possible during this time slot. Observing closely the children who continue to write and edit stories, the teacher continues to move from child to child helping with labels, looking at invented spelling, and helping the child to sound out the word he or she wishes to spell; she models the word when needed.

11:05 to 11:40
This time is used for a social studies activity in a large or small group, in which a literacy skill is modeled for children.

11:40 to 12:10
This time is used for independent reading and writing.

12:15 to 1:15
Physical activity is indoors Monday and Friday and outdoors Tuesday, Wednesday, and Thursday (weather permitting).

1:15 to 1:45
This time is used for math activities in a small or large group or individually. Children may also resume language arts activities from the morning session that relate to math, content, or literature study. Where needed, the teacher uses the redirected question technique to test comprehension of content (see chapter 9) and records student progress. Her observation, her notes, and brief informal and formal assessments that child and teacher review together guide the teacher in diagnosing weaknesses and strengths in order to plan her teaching. Since it is clear to the teacher that Ben and Sarah and children like them are very much individuals and learn in distinctly different ways, she relies on her observation and checks on comprehension to determine the most appropriate ways to arrange the environment and plan her instruction.

1:45 to 2:30
Collaborative peer work in language arts, content areas, or math with teacher guidance throughout continues. The option to work on a special project, continuing from earlier time should be available.

2:30 to 3:05
This is the time for cleanup, individual and get-together daily review, and dressing and farewells. The basket of materials is reviewed and set up for the next day.
Schedules need to be adjusted to respect the individual development of six- and seven-year-old children and to guide decisions concerning activities. These decisions should be made based on children's

- ability to attend to longer units of text
- awareness of the performance aspect of written products
- understanding that there is an audience who needs to understand what is said and written
- development of specific strategies for creating products that are shared
- planned, rather than experimental, reading and writing activities
- skills for making meaning of content and the written coding system
- ability and motivation to manage time
- ability and motivation to self-select materials
- ability to determine what they know and what they need to accomplish.

What Activities and Materials Foster Literacy?

Strategies for six- and seven-year-old children include those that expand language, improve comprehension, and prepare children to engage in private and public writing activities. Holdaway's model for learning—modeling expected behaviors, engaging children to partially participate with coaching, time for role-play (rehearsal) of behaviors without teacher intervention, and time to perform the accomplishment—should be followed in all activities.

Language Expansion Activities

Language expansion activities for reading have traditionally been subdivided into three categories: word identification, vocabulary knowledge, and comprehension skills. These divisions suggest that children need to process certain skills in a specific sequence in order to build vocabulary needed to read and write. Expanding language certainly includes these, but we now know that it also means the development of an awareness of how talking and writing can be controlled to share ideas and create words. Vocabulary building, both word identification skills and vocabulary knowledge, are important aspects of reading and writing. Understanding, identifying, and being able to write words is vital to comprehension. We know that there is a strong link between vocabulary knowledge and reading comprehension (Davis 1968; Thorndyke 1973). The exact nature of how words are learned, the definition of the word knowledge, and the exact effects of vocabulary on reading comprehension are, however, controversial issues (Glazer and Searfoss 1988). Children, when they learn to talk, extend their knowledge of words because there is a purposeful reason for doing so without formal instruction (Nagy and Herman 1987). Instruction in expanding language by teaching subskills is a common practice in many schools today. Word recognition skills have been taught to guide children to be able to say the word represented by orthographic (writing) symbols. Children are often taught to recognize these as whole units and, at times, by learning parts of words and the sounds they represent. Knowledge of sound parts is known as phonics. The issue of using phonics versus other approaches for beginning and troubled readers will continue to be controversial. There is research that supports this deliberate instructional process (Adams 1991), but there is also research that strongly suggests that phonics is unimportant for some beginning readers (Adams 1990). Understanding the relationship of sounds to symbols is vital. The controversial issue, therefore, seems to lie mainly with the emphasis on the instructional procedures and teacher expectations. Relevant questions are: Should phonics be taught in a deliberately planned lesson? or Should phonics be an integral part of other activities which enhance the development of reading and writing? We ask these questions, in part, because of our English language system. The English language has forty distinct sounds, but these are represented by only twenty-six letters. This means, therefore, that some letters represent more than one sound (or no sound, like the silent k in knowledge). There is no single speech sound that is represented by only one letter. "The problem is . . . that the correspondences are . . . complex. They are not one-to-one" (Smith 1985, 50). The sound for f can also be represented by the letters ph as in the word phone. Over the years, linguists have chosen to create alphabets that go beyond twenty-six letters as basic for spelling units to solve some of these problems. Special alphabets such as the Initial Teaching Alphabet (ITA), which represents all of the sounds, is an example of one of these. These artificial alphabets solve only the sound-symbol concerns. They do not address the major problem—mastery of traditional orthography. A summary of the assets and potential drawbacks for using phonics as a beginning strategy for recognizing words is shown in Table 10–1.

We believe that there is a place in some classrooms for instruction in sound-symbol relationships. The question is whether this is ever best done as an isolated activity. A knowledge of sound-symbol relationships is vital for spelling (writing) and reading. However, direct phonics instruction alone does not provide children with the experiences necessary for beginning reading and for expanding language.

The language in some literature seems to be particularly helpful in reinforcing certain sound-symbol patterns. Dr. Seuss, Colin Hawkins, and Jacqui Hawkins have created wonderful books using certain sound-symbol

TABLE 10–1 Drawbacks and Assets for Using Phonics

Drawbacks	Assets
Teaching letter sounds as an isolated activity distorts the sounds. Isolating consonant sounds requires an arbitrary vowel and the name of the consonant (e is needed to say the letter f).	Teaching sounds seems to be needed for some children.
Because a consonant is sounded with the help of a vowel, confusion occurs when words are written. Vowels usually disappear.	When children write naturally they use consonants first and write without vowels (they invent spellings). This is part of the development of the writing process
Phonics instruction often results in "word calling." Some children who have been overdosed on phonics will attempt to sound out every word. This results in a laboriously, de-emphasizing of the real meaning for reading. Sounding becomes reading. We refer to this as a case of "overphonics."	Some children, particularly those with language learning disabilities, do learn to read and write through a conscious manipulation of the sounds and symbols.

patterns. "Do you know Pat the cat? Pat the cat has a big hat," illustrates the repetitive use of the spelling pattern, at. Children enjoy hearing the rhyming pattern again and again and noting spelling similarities. The literature entices them to read and reread stories written with spelling patterns. The language in these books helps children understand the sound-symbol relationships when they hear the sounds of the language and see the printed page.

We will discuss word identification and vocabulary knowledge or comprehension of words in this section. Reading comprehension, or comprehension of text, is described separately. This seemed, for us, to be the best way to share the expansive amount of material included.

Word Identification Activities

Modified Key Word Approach. Words representing ideas that play key roles in children's lives are easy to learn. Beginning readers and writers enjoy learning new words when they own a strategy that helps them to remember words. The modified key word method (Glazer and Searfoss 1988) adapted from Ashton-Warner (1963) and Fernald (1971) is an effective hands-on strategy for recall.

This approach requires that each student have a mailing envelope, legal size if possible, with his or her name, for example, "Sarah's Word Bank," written on the front. Words can be elicited in informal ways or requested by children when they are involved in writing activities. Veatch and colleagues (1979) state that:

> The word a child gives must have an emotional impact for her; otherwise, it will probably not be retained. . . . The more powerful the word is (to the child) the better (p. 28).

Sarah learned to use this technique when she asked to spell words for her stories. She loved writing and often wrote without a care about correct spellings. Other times, she knew that she wanted to share her creations. These were the times when she would ask how to spell words. Sarah, in the spring of the year, wrote lots of stories about ice cream. Once she asked, "How do you write strawberry?" Her teacher pulled a 4 by 7 inch word card from her pocket and placed it in front of Sarah. She wrote the word, matching her voice to the flow of written language, holding onto the sound of the vowel until the next consonant was written. The first few times the teacher took Sarah's writing hand in hers and held onto her index finger. "Sarah," she'd say, "Say the word and trace it with me." She moved her hand and said the word guiding Sarah to move with her. "Do it again, yourself," the teacher would say. The word was traced at least three times. Then Sarah was told to turn the word card over so that she could not see it and write the word on a piece of paper. "Check your writing by looking at the word card, Sarah. If it's correct, put the card in your word bank envelope. If it's not, trace and say it again." Sarah needed guidance from the teacher for about three weeks before the teacher was sure that she could use the strategy on her own. Sarah was excited about her word bank envelope. Her goal was to be able to read the words and write them without looking. She wanted to have more than anyone else in her class. The teacher met with Sarah once a week, and Sarah would take out her word cards and read them. If she missed one, she had the option of discarding it or using the tracing strategy to learn it. The power to make the decisions about keeping or discarding words provided Sarah with feelings of confidence. Sarah liked to demonstrate her ability to write her words from memory. She created a special word book and during these individual sessions, she would read three words at a time and turn them over so she would not see them. Then, she would write each in her word book and excitedly say, "See, I can spell these without looking!" Other children in the classroom preferred to move away from their tables to test their recall. The teacher provided space on the chalkboard. There were as many spaces as there were children who needed wall space. Each space had a child's name at the top. Sarah and Ben sometimes worked together. Sarah would hold Ben's word cards, and he would read them as she flashed one and then the next. Ben would do the same with Sarah's. Sarah would write her words in her notebook, and Ben would check her cards to see if she wrote them correctly. Ben preferred to write his words on the chalkboard. This vocabulary building activity became a daily routine, one written into the daily contract by Sarah, herself.

Several important aspects of the procedure should be noted: the teacher must touch and say the word at the same time; words learned should be written from memory, never copied; words must always be written as a unit, not in syllable form; and children must rehearse words on their own, routinely, in order to increase their vocabulary for writing. It is important to remember that all words come from children. Words from all aspects of school and home create individual vocabulary growth. The truly integrated reading/language arts and content area classroom will be reflected in the variety of words in children's word banks.

This technique, modified from one used with children who have learning disabilities (Fernald 1971), is effective for all children, gifted as well as those in mainstream classrooms. It is also effective for adults when recalling symbols, math formulas, and new words.

Spelling to Expand Language. The discussion about phonics and the modified key approach to learning to read and write words leads us to a discussion on learning about spelling, for learning to spell is part of the language expansion process. Precursors to formal or correct writing (spelling) were discussed in chapter 3. Marie Clay's principles of the development of writing suggest that writing, including spelling, will occur naturally when rich language experiences suggested earlier occur in preschool years. Like talking, the more children write, the better they become at both composing and spelling. Temple et al. (1988), Gentry (1982), Morris (1981), Read (1971), and others have found that children spell words based on their knowledge of language. Young children (ages three to five) possess this knowledge without knowing that they do. The role of phonics for beginning writers and readers might, therefore, be making children aware of what some can already do—figuring out how their language works. The knowledge permits them to invent spellings of words. The inventive speller moves through stages that eventually result in traditional spelling (Gentry 1982; Morris 1981). Invented spelling might be compared to beginning speech. Often adults do not understand the words children attempt to pronounce for the articulatory muscles have not yet developed sufficiently to pronounce them conventionally. They say words their own way, and adults reward children for the attempts. As time moves on, mispronounced words are slowly, but surely pronounced correctly. Spelling moves from invented to traditional in much the same way. McGee and Richgels (1990) have divided this development into five stages, based on the work of Gentry (1982), Morris (1981), and Read (1975): nonspelling, early invented spelling, purely phonetic spelling, mixed spelling, and fully conventional spelling (p. 253).

Nonspelling Stage. This stage coincides with Clay's principles of writing discussed in chapter 3. The child demonstrates alphabet knowledge, writes letters, stringing them together, and is probably unaware of the concept of what words are (Figure 10–1).

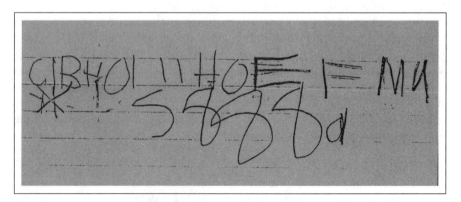

FIGURE 10–1   Nonspelling Stage

Early Invented Spelling Stage. In this stage the child knows almost all letters, knows that sounds and letters can be associated, invents spellings for words, often omitting vowels, demonstrates the development of his or her own strategy for spelling words (consistent use of letters or parts of words when writing), and begins to demonstrate an awareness of the concept of words (will write BK for book, hpe for happy).

Purely Phonetic Spelling Stage. In this stage the child bases words only on letter-sound relationships, represents all parts of words, has developed names for long vowels as a way of identifying these for spelling purposes, seems to articulate all short vowels the same way, omits silent vowels when writing words, and segments strings of letters at most word boundaries.

Mixed Spelling Stage. The child invents spellings based on sounds and symbols and writes letters for each sound in a word, writes words displaying knowledge of some conventions of spelling, which are not always correct, and displays awareness of basic English spelling conventions such as putting a vowel in every syllable (Figure 10–2).

Fully Conventional Spelling Stage. In this stage, the child displays knowledge of basic rules of the English spelling system, can detect his or her own misspellings, and can write lots of words correctly.

Adults must encourage children to write first without concern for spelling. Lots of free writing, teacher guidance, and directed teaching lead to traditional spelling.

Increasing Vocabulary Knowledge

Just talking, using new and interesting words, increases children's knowledge of language. Ben and Sarah's teacher used the interesting word approach daily. She would find a word that could be used in casual conversation. The word swung from the word mobile that she had hanging near the library center. The word was also written on the "Interesting Word Chart" hanging in the writing center. Ben and Sarah and their classmates heard the word used over and over again. Many of the children tried to guess what the word meant before the get-together time at the end of the school day when the word-of-the-day was usually discussed. Predicting the word's meaning became a game with the youngsters. They knew after the first week of school that their teacher would use a new word daily or at least three times during the week. One day, the teacher used what the children called "the best word of all."

Teacher: (as children come into the classroom in the morning) Melissa, the gerbil made a mess in his cage. He tore all of the paper and knocked the

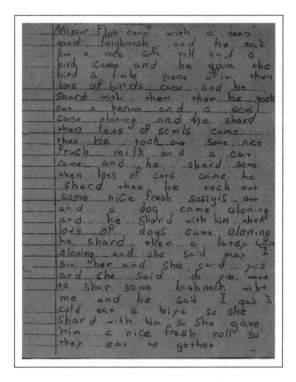

FIGURE 10–2   Mixed Spelling Stage

water bottle out of the holder. He's running all around the cage. I went over to him to try to calm him down, but he just wouldn't stop running and making that screechy noise he makes when he's mad. That gerbil is acting incorrigibly.

Melissa: (running to the animal, which is in her care) Oh my goodness, it's a mess! What's the matter, Rusty? Are you sick? Do you want some water?

Teacher: (follows Melissa to the living-alive center) He's still running. Maybe he's acting incorrigibly because he's hungry.

Melissa: I put a carrot in his cage, but he's not eating it. Maybe if I pick him up he'll act better.

Teacher: That's a great idea. Let's see if the incorrigible behavior stops.

Melissa: (Opens the cage and takes out Rusty) What's the matter, good boy? Are you okay? (pets Rusty on the head and back) You like that, don't you. Now you're not acting crazy.

Teacher: When you hold him, he's not incorrigible.

Melissa: You keep saying that word.

Teacher: Which word?

Melissa: The one that means Rusty was crazy.

Teacher: Oh, incorrigibly. What did you say it means?

Melissa: Crazy, cause Rusty just wouldn't act normal.

Teacher: He sure was crazy and wild. He acted like he wasn't tame.

Melissa: Yeah. Rusty was like a wild animal, but I tamed him by holding him, and now he's not acting

Teacher/Melissa: incorrigibly.

Using words and phrases in meaningful situations builds word knowledge. Using words again and again helps children remember. When children begin to use the words in their oral and written language, the words belong to them.

In addition, through alphabet books, games, and songs and through the use of many books that help develop sound-symbol relationships, Ben and Sarah can figure out many new words. They know the sounds of letters, groups of letters, and syllables because of games and rhymes they have used.

Comprehension for Reading

Our discussion will be concerned with children's responses for reading using storytelling, guided reading, unguided and guided retellings, self-monitoring activities, and "fix-up" strategies.

Storytelling

Storytelling experiences are powerful motivators for reading. The activity creates an intimacy that reading stories cannot (Morrow and Weinstein 1982). Telling also provides a model for children when they retell stories themselves. It is important when telling a story to remember the following:

- learn the story well, remembering special lines or phrases that are repeated again and again and repeat them when appropriate during the storytelling time
- look at the children, moving your eyes around the group in order to make personal contact with each listener
- make the story, not the drama, most important
- show the book before and after you tell the story and have several copies in the classroom library and on display in a book display rack

Devote a time period to storytelling. Children can take turns being a story-teller for the day. The story that the youngster selects to tell should be read and reread at least three times prior to the storytelling experience. Rereading builds word recognition as well as comprehension. Storytelling comple-ments Holdaway's model for learning. His common sense approach when applied to storytelling, functions in four steps.

Step 1: Observation.   The teacher, as the day's storyteller, holds up the book and asks children to predict from the words and pictures what the story is about. He provides time for the children to respond and then stands the book on a table and proceeds to tell the story. He makes eye contact with each child, emphasizing repeated language in the story.

Step 2: Partial Participation.   Some children sit near the teacher. As he makes eye contact and uses repeated language, he nods his head "yes" while looking at a child which encourages the youngster to repeat the phrase with him. Each time story language lends itself to group participation, encour-agement continues. The teacher/coach entices most of the boys and girls to use specific language-of-story as he tells.

Step 3: Role-Play.   Multiple copies of the book placed around the class-room are taken by several children. Some read the book; others attempt to find the repeated phrases and say them. Some point to the words; others look at the pictures to confirm their language. Several read together. Suffi-cient time blocks permit this independent role-play activity to continue for this is reading rehearsal time.

Step 4: Performance.   A child says, "Listen to me read," and the teacher does. Child may also ask to read or tell the story to a group of children. Some may read to a class pet or favorite doll.

Holdaway's model encourages the natural "burning" desire to perfect skills. Children are coerced to rehearse. Rehearsal results in ownership of the language in the text. The desire to share what has been accomplished creates a need to perform (Glazer 1992).

Guided Reading

Prediction Activities.   One of the most important guides for successful comprehension, discussed several times earlier in this text, is the ability to predict. According to the *Random House Dictionary*, "To predict is usually to foretell with . . . knowledge or . . . inference from fact or experience (p. 1523). When we predict, we are guessing. Readers may guess what books are about before they read. Educated guesses based on the cover illustra-tions, words, and children's prior knowledge about the book's topic help the child discover if he or she knows something about the book. The more familiar one is with the content, the closer the reader may be to the author's text. Prediction is based on the prior knowledge that each child brings to the book. We know that problems in comprehension often result from deficits in prior knowledge about content. Prior knowledge results from both semantic and episodic memory (Tulving 1972). Pearson and Johnson (1978) explain the comprehension process and the relationship between prior knowledge to this process as follows:

> *Comprehension is building bridges between the new and the known—Comprehension is active not passive; that is the reader cannot help but interpret and alter what he reads in accordance with prior knowledge about the topic under discussion. . . . Comprehension involves a great deal of inference making (p. 24).*

Story prediction activities were described earlier (see chapter 9). Additional activities can be carried out to alert children to the power that prior knowledge has when applied to reading.

Step 1. Use the word *predict* in several situations. Walk around the room and say, for example, "I think that the frog is hungry because he is croaking a lot and looking at his food bowl." Encourage children to make predictions as well. You might predict, then justify your prediction concerning what the weather will be like for the upcoming field trip. When a child predicts that it might be snowing, you need to ask why that prediction was made. A response like, "because it is very cold and the sky is gray," justifies the prediction.

Step 2. Place a chalkboard or easel with the surface divided in half by a vertical line near the lesson corner. Hold the book that you will read to the children so that all can see it. Say, "I am looking at the pictures and thinking. I am asking myself, what do I know about this story from the cover?" Answer your own question and write the response in the left column. Then say, "I made that prediction because . . . ," and write the justification to your response in the right column next to the prediction. Ask children to volunteer predictions and write under yours. After each response ask, "Why did you make that prediction?" Write each child's response exactly as the child says it. Show the back cover of the book and ask the same questions. Accept all predictions and justifications and write all down. Then say, "Listen to the story to see if your prediction was correct."

Carry out this activity several times weekly. Once the children understand the concept, they will be able to produce predictions before reading that guide them through the text.

Step 3. Once children understand the concept of prediction, recreate the chart into a guide sheet. Make sure that the sheet looks exactly like the chart used in the group modeling session. Keep multiple copies of these in the

My Name: _____ Date: _____	
Book: _____	
Author: _____	
My Prediction	Why Did I Make That Prediction?

FIGURE 10–3   **Prediction Sheet**

writing and library centers. Include prediction activities on children's contracts. Not all children will need to predict before reading, but it will be helpful for many and certainly fun for all (Figure 10–3 and Figure 10–3A).

Support Materials. Support materials act as confidence builders. Books with tapes provide support, building the self-esteem needed for new readers. A voice on the tape matches the words and pictures in the text. Earphones permit children to listen and look privately at books. Chapter 9 includes a starter library for early readers.

Big books provide wonderful "together" experiences. Oversized books with individual copies for each learner inspire children to read. We remem-

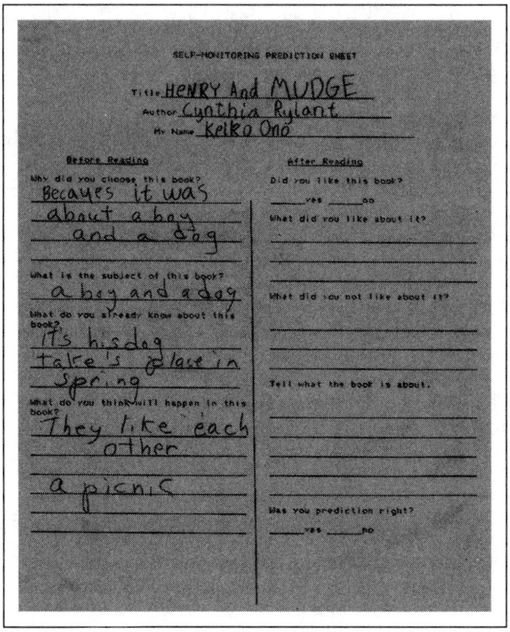

FIGURE 10–3A

ber when a retired college dean read the big book *Jump Frog Jump* by Robert Kalan to a group of six- and seven-year-old children. At the completion of the story, at least ten of these youngsters hurried to the classroom library to find a copy to read.

A slide projection of real-life activities that follow the plot of a special story is a wonderful sharing experience. One kindergarten teacher photographed her children acting out Ezra Jack Keat's *Peter's Chair,* a story concerned with feelings of rejection. The teacher read the book as the slides appeared on the screen. Each of the children was part of the story. This was exciting and enticing as well. *Peter's Chair* was a popular book in that classroom for weeks. The plot, the language, and the characters came alive with photos. The children became the characters in the book.

Unguided and Guided Retellings
The unguided and guided retelling strategies described in chapters 7 and 9 are appropriate for all elementary age children. Written retellings may be added to or may replace oral performance after reading when youngsters feel comfortable writing. Written retellings can be used to review comprehension. Prompts used for oral retelling can also be used for written retellings (see chapter 7).

Unguided written retellings are sometimes drawings of stories. Some six- and seven-year-old children find writing about what they have read easiest. Keiko, a mature six-year-old, loved to read. She read to herself most of the time. Keiko always seemed engrossed in her books but would never share information from reading orally. When the teacher modeled retelling by reading a story to the class and then retelling it, other children participated but not Keiko. The teacher thought that a story map might work to help Keiko record what she recalled. Keiko's responses, although sparse, indicated that she had read the book (Figure 10–4). A retelling guide sheet also resulted in sparse responses. Out of desperation, the teacher said, "Why don't you retell your story in writing." The teacher's last attempt to provoke story recall resulted in the retelling in Figure 10–5. Six-year-old Keiko just took off. She sat and wrote for almost forty-five minutes. Her retelling of Dr. Seuss' *Horton Hatches the Egg* clearly illustrates that she had read the story and remembered almost all of the elements. It was obvious that Keiko demonstrated comprehension best when she wrote freely. Prompts seemed to stop the natural flow of language that just came out when she wrote on her own.

FIGURE 10–4   Keiko's Prediction Sheet

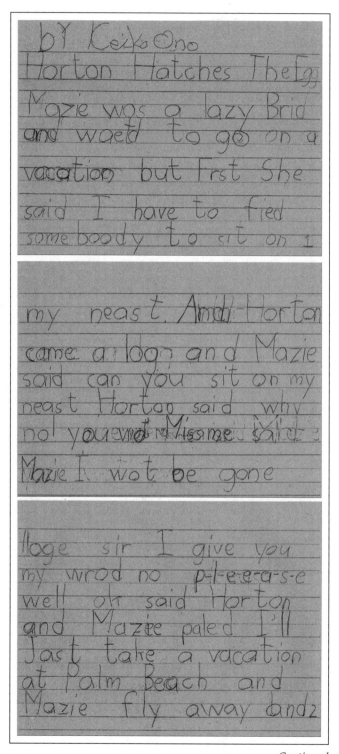

by Keiko Ono
Horton Hatches The Egg
Mazie was a lazy Brid
and waetd to go on a
vacation but Frst She
said I have to fied
some boody to sit on 1

my neast. And Horton
came along and Mazie
said can you sit on my
neast Horton said why
nol you evol Missme said
Mazie I wot be gone

loge sir I give you
my wrod no p-l-e-e-a-s-e
well ok said Horton
and Mazee paled I'll
Jast take a vacation
at Palm Beach and
Mazie fly away and 2

FIGURE 10–5 Keiko's Written Retelling *Continued*

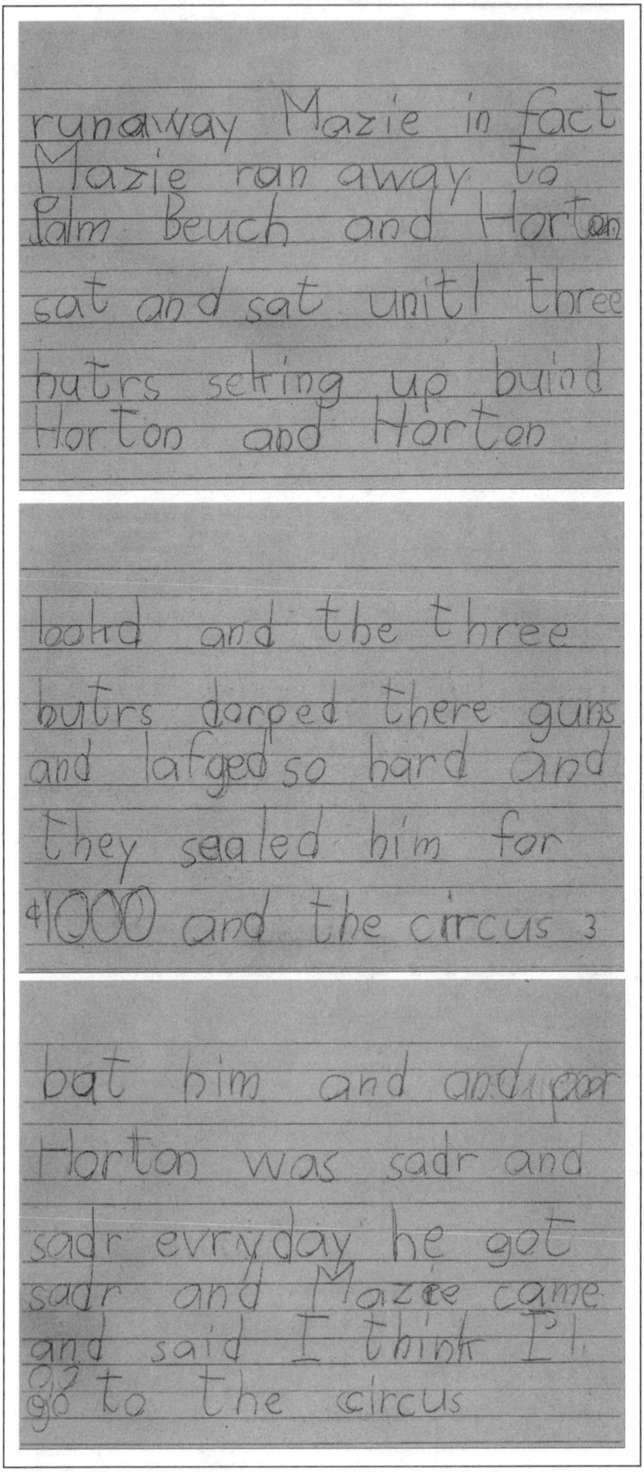

runaway Mazie in fact
Mazie ran away to
Palm Beuch and Horton
sat and sat unitl three
hutrs setring up buind
Horton and Horton

lootrd and the three
hutrs darped there guns
and lafged so hard and
they sealed him for
$1000 and the circus 3

bat him and and poor
Horton was sadr and
sadr evryday he got
sadr and Mazie came
and said I think I'l
go to the circus

FIGURE 10–5 *Continued*

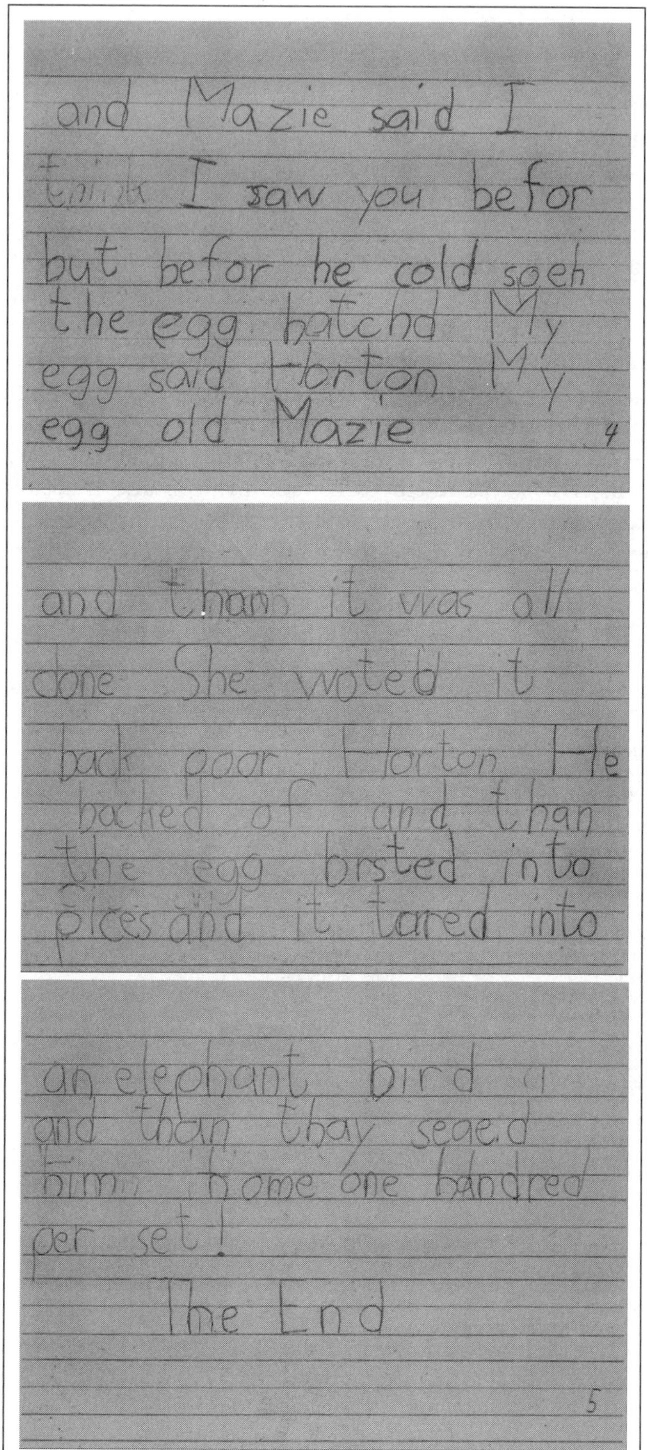

and Mazie said I
think I saw you befor
but befor he cold soeh
the egg hatchd My
egg said Horton My
egg old Mazie   4

and tham it was all
done She woted it
back poor Horton He
bached of and than
the egg brsted into
pices and it tared into

an elephant bird a
and than thay seaed
him home one hundred
per set!
          The End
                                      5

FIGURE 10–5   237

Self-Monitoring
Children need to take responsibility by learning how to describe what they know and what they need to learn (Glazer and Brown 1993). Oral transcriptions (see chapter 9) and written retellings like Keiko's provide the hard data for guiding children to look at what they know about a story and what they need to do to recall more next time. Teachers must provide children with tools for self-monitoring, integrating these into the instructional processes. Self-monitoring comprehension conferences, and guide sheets that replicate oral language prompt and facilitate self-assessment as well as recall of story elements. The best way to illustrate a self-monitoring session is to imagine that you and a child are sitting together at a conference table. Begin the conference with the child's retelling on the table, the book about which the retelling transcript is based, the self-monitoring guide sheet (Table 10–2), and several pencils with erasers. Both the self-monitoring guide sheet and the retelling should be in front of the child. Keiko's conference concerned

TABLE 10–2 Self-Monitoring Retelling Guide Sheet

Story Elements	Yes	No
I included an introduction.		

I included the setting.
  Where did the story take place?
  When did the story take place?		

I told the theme.
  The story is about (name the character).
  I included the other characters.		

I found the problem in the story.		
I included the story episodes. I remembered _____ (episodes). (number)		
I told how the problem was solved.		
I told the ending.		
I told how I feel about the story.		

Next time I need to remember _____

Name: _____ Story: _____

Author: _____Date: _____

her written retelling of *Horton Hatches the Egg* by Dr. Seuss. The following dialogue illustrates the instructional/assessment procedure desirable for guiding children to self-monitor comprehension of literature.

Teacher: Keiko, I really like the way you wrote your retelling May I read it? (With permission, the teacher reads the retelling out loud. Keiko joins in part way through.) I'd love to hear you read it.

Keiko: I don't want to.

Teacher: Okay, then let's see what you remembered after reading the story. This is a retelling check sheet. It includes all of the elements that make a good story. Let's read the first line together. (The teacher places a ruler under the first line, and reads chorally with Keiko "I included an introduction.")

Keiko: (Pauses, looks up at the teacher quizzically).

Teacher: An introduction is the beginning of the story. Let's see. What did you write first? Let's read it together (puts ruler under the first line).

Teacher/Keiko: Horton Hatches the Egg.

Teacher: That's the name of the story. Let's read more.

Teacher/Keiko: Mazie was a lazy bird.

Teacher: Tell me what you think that is.

Keiko: The beginning of the story.

Teacher: You're right! It's the beginning, and that is an introduction. Now read this with me again. (I included an introduction.) Did you include an introduction?

Keiko: Yes.

Teacher: Put your finger on the line in your retelling that is the introduction and read it.

Keiko: (with finger under the line) Mazie was a lazy bird and wanted to go on a vacation.

Teacher: Yes, you included an introduction. I really like the way you put your finger under the introduction and read it. Now, let's see. Did you include the setting. (The teacher puts the ruler under the next line.) Let's read it together.

Keiko: (begins to read alone) Where did the story take place?

Teacher: Did you write where the story took place?

Keiko: Yes.

Teacher: Show it to me in your story.

Keiko: Here it is.

Teacher: Read it.

Keiko: Mazie ran away to Palm Beach.

Teacher: Yes, that's one place in the story.

Keiko: And I have another one on this page.

Teacher: Where?

Keiko: (pointing to the place in her text) Then they sent him home one hundred percent.

Teacher: Yes. You included some places where the story happened.

Keiko: But I didn't tell where Horton sat on the egg.

Teacher: That's right you didn't. That's really great that you noticed that you did not include the place where Horton sat.

Children become familiar with story elements as they justify their responses. Keiko discovered that she wanted to include a real introduction next time she wrote her retelling, and she wrote at the bottom of her guide sheet, "I want to remember to say, Once upon a time, first." A secure, nurturing environment that fosters risk taking and trial and error encourages self-assessment.

When retellings are oral, they must be transcribed by the teacher for conferencing purposes. These transcripts should be typed or written so that the child is able to read the text. The same procedure is followed as with written retelling. The new reader may not be able to read her oral language for the oral text will probably include many words that she will not be able to recognize. It is recommended, therefore, that all transcripts be read by the child and the teacher together, as if a chorus, before self-monitoring takes place. The child may tell you, and then point, with your help, to the appropriate section of the retelling that includes each story element.

One fifteen-minute guided retelling conference weekly with some informal checks during the week is one way to manage these individual conference in a class of twenty-five. Some children will learn how to use the self-monitoring tool independently within the first several weeks of school. Others will take longer periods of time. Once children learn how to use the guide, they can carry out peer self-monitoring in pairs when the children are reading the same book. Checking each other's recall helps them learn story elements.

Self-monitoring facilitates natural role shifts between teachers and children. Children learn to identify and, therefore, perform or point out their behaviors. The following comments illustrate such actions:

- "Look, I can read this book."
- "See this Ms. Burke! My dad brought it for me from his trip."
- "Look at my self-monitoring sheet, teacher. It's all done. I can read it to you."
- "Watch Ms. Glazer. I know how to tie my sneaker all by myself."
- "Teacher, teacher, I read the whole book and it's about. . . ."
- "I wrote a whole page. See!"

Enthusiastic children and attentive teachers shift roles to show-and-tell each other about accomplishments. They pay attention to children when they have a need to display accomplishments. A good listener is a wonderful teacher.

Fix-up Strategies: Thinkalongs for Reading Alone

Often children find words easy to read, but content difficult. Sometimes content is familiar, but word meanings are new and often they are difficult to decode. Thinking and talking to oneself about the text helps readers, young and old, to better understand the materials. The reader, in an attempt to make meaning of the text, explains what he or she is doing while reading. In other words, the reader is involved in a dynamic process where construction and revisions of the meaning continuously occur during reading (Collins, Brown, and Larkin 1980; Rummelhart 1977). Good readers do this automatically and spontaneously (Brown and Lytle 1988). They fix-up the meaning-making process as they read. Educators have found that teaching specific strategies to children helps them guide themselves to understand a difficult text effectively (Bird 1980; Palincsar and Brown 1984; Brown and Lytle 1988). Farr (1990) refers to these as thinkalongs, for readers "think along" as they read, using prior experiences and individual perceptions of the ideas to create meaning. Several educators have created systems for guiding children to think about text independently (Eddy and Gould 1990; Wilson and Russavage 1989; Russavage and Arick 1988). These include prediction strategies discussed earlier and those that guide children to:

- make a picture in their minds about the text
- predict about the pictures, subtitles, words, and other information from text during reading

- ask themselves questions about the difficult information
- reread to clarify ideas
- reread to understand difficult words
- personalize the text

Imagine that you and the children have gathered in the library corner for a story reading time. You have selected Paul Galdone's version of Grimm's *Little Red Riding Hood* for modeling thinkalongs for the first time. Story reading times are perfect for such instruction. The following procedure adapted from the works of several educators has been used effectively for young children (Eddy and Gould 1990; Farr 1990; Wilson and Russavage 1989; Russavage and Arick 1988).

Procedure for Modeling Thinkalongs. Before reading, hold the book in front of the children. Put your finger to your forehead as if thinking. Say to the children, "I am going to read a story. I would like you to watch and listen to everything I do. I am going to try to let you know what I am thinking. When I am thinking about the story, not reading it, I will point to my brain to let you know I am thinking." The dialogue, which appears on the left side of Table 10–3 illustrates thinkalong modeling. The strategy used is indicated in the right column.

Thinkalong Strategies. Several thinkalong story reading sessions are necessary in order for children to become aware of these strategies. These sessions should be carried out on a regular basis at consistent times during the day. Children will talk about what you are doing as you carry out these thinkalongs. One child shouted during one session, "I know what you are doing, your brain is working and you are telling us what you are thinking." Follow-up modeling sessions should focus on one thinkalong at a time. That strategy ought to be modeled once a day for approximately two weeks for learning to occur (Glazer 1992). It is important to review each thinkalong by modeling all of the strategies regularly. Thinkalong activities interrupt the natural flow of language in books. It must, therefore, be a separate activity. Children must understand that, although unnatural, the strategy serves a function when reading alone.

Children should be encouraged to demonstrate thinkalongs in pairs. One might read as the other monitors the child's thinkalong using the thinkalong monitoring sheet (Figure 10–6), which should replicate the wall chart. This provides the rehearsal (role-play) necessary for learning the activity and also creates collaborative learning situations.

TABLE 10–3   Thinkalongs

Dialogue for Illustrating Thinkalongs	Thinkalong Strategy
Before Reading I wonder what this book is about?	Self-questioning
Read the title and then say, "I think it's about a little girl playing in the woods. And it must be cold because she's wearing a red cape and a hood. The picture helped me think it was cold. I know her name too, because the title says (takes finger away from temple as she reads) "Little Red Riding Hood."	Self-answer questions justifying response based on illustration Reread to justify own response
Puts finger back to temple and says, "I bet this book is about a girl who takes a walk in the woods and it is cold so she is wearing a heavy red coat. I also predict that she is going to get in trouble because there's a wolf behind a tree and he looks scary. I'm going to read the book to find out."	Predicts based on picture
During Reading At the point where Red Riding Hood is asked to take cookies to her Grandmother, you, the reader, stop reading, put your finger to your temple and say "I wonder if she will put on that Red Cape? I will read to find out."	Predicting during reading
At the point in the story where Red Riding Hood walks through the forest, stop reading, put your finger to your temple and say, "I remember when I came home one dark night. It was like a forest, and I felt scared." Continue to read.	Personalizing the text by making a picture in your mind about a real situation
After Reading Ask children to tell what they think you were doing. Responses should be written, as they are dictated, onto a large sheet of paper. This sheet should be reproduced so that children have individual thinkalongs as you read the next time.	

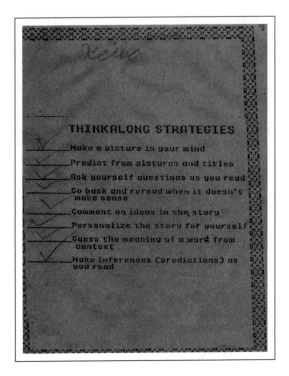

**FIGURE 10–6   Thinkalong
Monitoring Sheet**

Composition/Writing Activities for Six- and Seven-Year-Old Children

Donald Graves has said in his book, *Writing: Teachers and Children at Work,*

> *Children want to write. They want to write the first day they attend school. This is no accident. Before they went to school they marked up walls, pavements, newspapers with crayons, chalk, pens or pencils . . . anything that makes a mark. The child's marks say, "I am." (1983, p. 1)*

When children write, they are constructing information about the language of books. This helps them learn to read. As Marie Clay has written:

> *The child who engages in creative writing is manipulating the units of written language—letters, words, sentence types—and is likely to be gaining some awareness of how these can be combined to convey unspoken messages. The child is having to perform within the directional constraints that we use in written English. The child is probably learning to generate sentences in a deliberate way, word by word. He makes up sentences which*

fit both his range of ideas and his written language skills. Fluent oral language may permit the young reader to depend almost entirely on meaning and the eye may overlook the need for discriminating details of letters and words. Creative writing demands that the child pay attention to the details of print. To put his messages down in print he is forced to construct words, letter by letter, and so he becomes aware of letter features and letter sequences particularly for the vocabulary which he uses in writing again and again. These words become part of his writing vocabulary, the ones that he knows in every perceptual way. (1975, 2).**

Children learn about writing through the process of perceptual learning (Lavine 1972). They seem to identify distinct features of print by separating writing from other graphic displays. They do this by developing some internal rules about the graphic displays of the writing system. These have been discussed in several ways earlier in this text. Temple et al. (1988) categorize this development in stages. These include nonpictoriality—what is writing may not be a picture; linearity—figures must be arrayed horizontally in a straight line; variety—figures on a page are supposed to vary one from the other, and multiplicity—writing consists of many figures

What looks like writing to the child is writing (Morris 1980). Children have the opportunity, even at an early age, to develop these principles, which prepare them for writing. Most children's writing moves developmentally through stages, although these stages of development are not sequential or clearly defined (Clay 1975; Dyson 1985, 1986; Sulzby 1986b; Teale 1986). Children practice their way to formal composition. They form hypotheses about written language. They may, for example, believe that there is one-to-one visual relationship between objects and sounds. One mark or group of marks matches an object. This sort of comprehension eliminates the relationship between sounds and written symbols. Lack of attention to these relationships (sounds to symbols) probably prevails in the beginning stages of writing. As time moves on, development and experience result in the realization that sounds and figures are related in some way. When young children write, they believe that the length of the message is determined by the size of the object it represents (Temple et al. 1988). The word *hat* is small, because the hat, itself, is small. The word *elephant* is large because the animal is large. This hypothesis could be disrupted if, for example, a small child has the name Habiba-Lee. Here, the rule collapses.

Alvina Treut Burrows, often considered the pioneer in the writing movement, categorized children's writing into two kinds of experiences: practical writing and personal writing (Burrows, Jackson, and Saunders 1984). Practical writing serves children and adults in similar ways: it performs a service

---

* Reprinted with permission from Marie M. Clay: *What Did I Write?* (Heinemann Educational Books, Australia, 1975).

and usually requires an audience. Letters, memos, captions, lists, and reports are practical ways to share. Social studies or science reports are only a few of the real reasons to write. Sharing with an audience of peers, parents, grandparents, or pen pals far away is usually most important. The importance of sharing enhances the desire for teacher direction.

Personal writing is spontaneous. Children write for themselves. The audience is the writer. The purpose is to use writing as a vehicle for relaxation and as a way to communicate ideas, feelings, emotions, fears, joys, and hardships sincerely.

Practical Writing Activities

Practical writing activities for six- and seven-year-old children include writing in response to literature, list making activities, mailboxes and letter writing, and research projects.

Writing in Response to Literature. Research reviewed in chapter 1 strongly supports the notion that the kind of materials children are exposed to directly affects the writing they do. Beginning writers internalize story language and use it to meet their own purposes for writing. This was demonstrated when a two-year-old child looked out of a window on a snowy day and said, "Oh Mommy, look! Snow makes whiteness. It looks like popcorn." That child often heard her mother recite Marie Louise Allend's poem, "First Snow." The child saw the snow through Ms. Allend's poetry and used her words to create oral composition.

> *First Snow*
> *Snow makes whiteness where it falls,*
> *The bushes look like popcorn balls.*
> *And places where I always play,*
> *Look like somewhere else today.*

Literature with definitive story structure and repetitive language increases children's knowledge of language for writing. *Cloudy with a Chance of Meatballs* by Barrett influenced six-year-old Clara to write the story in Figure 10–7. Books included throughout this text add to children's knowledge of language for story writing.

List Making. This is a practical form of writing, wonderful for getting youngsters started. Grocery lists, things-to-do lists, shopping lists, places-to-go lists, and people-to-write-letters-to lists, remind us what to do. Listing

---

* From: *A Pocketful of Poems* by Marie Louise Allend. Text copyright © 1957 by Marie Allend Howarth. Selection reprinted with permission of HarperCollins Publishers.

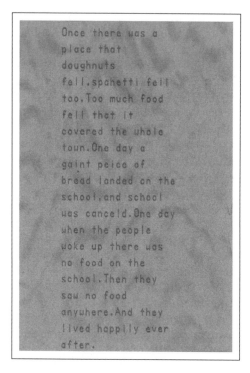

Once there was a
place that
doughnuts
fell.spahetti fell
too.Too much food
fell that it
covered the whole
town.One day a
gaint peice of
bread landed on the
school.and school
was canceld.One day
when the people
woke up there was
no food on the
school.Then they
saw no food
anywhere.And they
lived happily ever
after.

FIGURE 10–7   Clara's Story

information guides children to organize ideas in a systematic way. Lists are wonderful for sharing daily routines, interesting words, and story titles. List-format writing maps guide the reluctant writer to produce text. A wall chart that looks exactly like the listing map can hang in the classroom writing center. The list map in Figure 10–8 was created by a six-year-old.

Mailboxes and Letter Writing. Mailboxes for each child as discussed in chapter 9 lure six- and seven-year-old children to write letters. Routman (1988, 1991) sees these as support for children's early efforts to communicate. She believes that the relationship of reading to writing is exemplified through this activity. Everyone in the classroom building should have his or her own mailbox. Shoe boxes, 9 by 11½ inch envelopes, or manila folders may be used. It is important that plenty of paper be easily available for letter writing. Scrap paper is fine for daily messages. Letter writing is thrilling for youngsters and provides them with the rehearsal necessary for becoming a writer. Children's letters provide teachers with data necessary for assessing growth (Figure 10–9). These data include spelling trends, handwriting abil-

---

(blank ruled writing form)

Name: _____ Date _____

FIGURE 10–8 Listing Map

ity, knowledge of letter-writing format, use of punctuation, and format of writing: We ask, about children's writing, is it similar to stories, poems, or other materials used by the teacher as models for writing? What format does the child use? Does the child explain? Does the child describe? Does the child use narration? Does the child try to persuade someone to do something?

Research Projects. Writing reports is helpful for getting six- and seven-year-old youngsters to learn about animals, other people and their cultures, different sections of our country, and more. Research writing includes study skills. Steps for report writing include brainstorming, developing questions, note taking, and writing for an audience.

Brainstorming. Brainstorming, mentioned in chapter 9, results in maps which provide a visual guide for organizing ideas. Maps have been used with poor readers for instructional purposes in learning how to create stories (McGee and Richgels 1986; Pearson and Camperell 1985). They have

FIGURE 10–9 A Child's Letter

also been used for learning vocabulary (Earle 1970). We like to use the one shown in Figure 9–6 for collecting and organizing information, for creating a story and also for collecting ideas for research projects and demonstrating comprehension (Moore and Readence 1983; Alverman, Boothby, and Wolfe 1984). Maps (webs) should be kept in the writing center. Illustrate the function of the map by using it to collect information as part of a content discussion, not as a separate activity. A less-directed form of brainstorming is suggested by Calkins (1986). She recommends one-half hour to one hour of just writing at the beginning of projects for creating ideas. Brainstorming can also be used to write a collaborative group project. One teacher discussed fortunate and unfortunate experiences and created a group book written and illustrated by six-year-old children. Binding pages together with staples or by sewing the book provides books for the classroom library. How proud children feel when they select their own writing to read.

Developing Questions. Once topics are selected, questions need to be developed so that the searching process can take place. Two types of questions are important for guiding children of six and seven to read for reporting purposes. These include questions that can be answered by reading it "right-there" in the book, and questions that must be found "on my own" (Raphael 1982). These answers are not in the book but are implied by the content.

Right-there questions were easy for Sarah. At seven she felt very grown up when she could talk about famous people. Christopher Columbus, Benjamin Franklin, and Martin Luther King, Jr. were among her favorites. She always wrote questions that could be answered by looking right-there in the book, and copying the answer. When she decided that Martin Luther King, Jr. was her hero she wrote four questions: When was Martin Luther King born? Did he get married? What was his wife's name? When did he die?

Each question was written on a different piece of paper. Sarah selected David Adler's *A Picture Book of Martin Luther King, Jr.* She said, "This one probably has all of the answers in it." Sarah wrote the answers to her questions under each, one per page.

"On-my-own" questions were easiest for Sarah. She enjoyed reading and then related information in the book to ideas that were triggered by the text. Dr. King's famous quotation "I had a dream" made Sarah think of lots of things. She thought about her dreams, not those related to the book, but those dealing with sharing toys, candy, and her favorite Aunt Judy. In a sense, her dreams were as important to Sarah as Dr. King's were for him. Sarah wrote two "on-my-own" questions before reading the book and responding. These were: What can I do that is important like Dr. King did? I am thinking. Did Dr. King ever feel bad about some of the people who got killed? Sarah answered her questions by reading through the book. She had her papers on the table. As she read, she wrote information on her paper that seemed to answer her questions.

Note taking. Sarah wrote responses to her questions. The responses were her notes. She took them from the book. Like most new note takers, Sarah copied the information directly from the text. With more experience and confidence, the language of the text will be replaced with her own words. Writing questions and finding and recording answers prepares the youngsters for more sophisticated notes later on. Some youngsters may be able to expand their responses into narratives.

Writing for an Audience. Some students understand that sharing means "cleaning up errors" for others to read. Many may be ready to edit in order to share their compositions. We encourage youngsters to take responsibility for their own editing. We suggest modeling an editing session to the class. Begin by posting a narrative that you have written that includes names without capital letters and sentences that never end. Place a tape recorder close to your teaching area. Say, with the recorder in the <u>on</u> position, "I am going to read my story to see if I need to put any periods in it. I will know that I need a period when my voice stops." Read the story, and each time your voice drops, put a period after the word. When you complete this exercise say, "Gosh, I wonder if I am correct. I will play my tape, and listen to myself, and follow the story with my eyes."

It is important for the children to find their own errors and correct them. This builds confidence and eliminates the feelings that outside judgments are being made about their products. It is important to alert children to the idea of reading through their compositions several times, each time attending to one editing task. Posting a list of things to look for, as well as reproducing this list for children to use on their own, encourages independent editing. Children usually edit quickly and without much care during beginning stages. As time goes on, a quick review by the teacher or a peer, asking the child to review his story using the editing checklist as a guide will help some youngsters edit more thoroughly. The editing checklist shown in Table 10–4 can be used for all forms of writing.

Personal Writing

The first and second years of formal school should be filled with personal writing times in which children write just to write. They will write stories on their own. They will help each other with spelling, as well as illustrations.

TABLE 10–4   Did I Check My Writing?

Capital Letters
  Did I have to use a CAPITAL for the first letter at the beginning of a sentence?
  Did I use a CAPITAL for the first letter in a name?
  Did I use a CAPITAL for the first letter in each word in the title of a book or
    magazine?

Punctuation
  Did I reread to see if all sentences ended with
    a period (.)?
    a question mark (?)?
    an exclamation point (!)?

Spelling
  Did I check to see if there were misspelled words?
  Did I circle the misspelled word?
  Did I try to spell it right by listening to the sounds?
  Did I try to spell it right by asking someone?
  Did I try to spell it right by using a picture dictionary?
  Did I look to see if the word was in my word bank?

How Does My Writing Look?
  Did I ask someone to read my writing to be sure that it was neat?
  Did I ask a friend to read my writing to be sure that I stayed on the topic?
  Did I ask my friend to read my writing to be sure that I used good words?

FIGURE 10–10   Excerpt from Ashlee's Journal

Letters to friends are a favorite form of writing. The mailboxes provide a destination for their spontaneous communication.

Journals also provide an outlet for personal writing. They help to create the bonding between teacher and child so necessary for learning. Excerpts from the dialogue journals of a seven-year-old child are seen in Figure 10–10. This teacher responded to every entry. Two responses a week, however, are adequate. Children can mark the page in their journal for which they want the teacher's response.

Summary

Guiding children to become literate is an enormous responsibility. How children feel about themselves as readers and writers depends a great deal on how adults guide them. Healthy environments are necessary. Consider what you say to children. Think about your words and gestures. Think about how you would respond to your own comments. If your answers are positive, then proceed. If, however, your language, gestures, thoughts, or feelings tell you that discomfort, embarrassment, frustrations, anxiety, or fear might result, stop. Say nothing, and begin again. It is at the gentle hands and hearts of knowing and sensitive adults that children become successful readers and writers.

Six- and seven-year-old children grow quickly and are excited about school. These youngsters emerge as readers and writers during these years. Nurturing adults who provide a balance between structure and freedom, self-selected books and activities and directed lessons, and who engage in collegial decisions with children foster literacy development. Good feelings about books and reading and writing must permeate classrooms. These derive from respect for children's abilities and individual developmental trends. Children will grow quickly and become readers and writers when successful outcomes occur regularly. Adult perceptions of progress must be altered to meet the realities of children's ability to learn. Then, and only then, will we help children enjoy reading and writing.

Epilogue

Putting It All Together: Integrating the Language Arts in the Primary Classroom

Managing an integrated language arts classroom seems to be the biggest concern of teachers new to this system. Because the management aspects of holistic environments are intricate, we have created this appendix which describes the first three hours in such a classroom. Dialogue, descriptions, children's groupings, and individual and small group activities are detailed. Many of the incidents shared throughout the text are repeated in order to guide you to create a holistic view of reading, writing, listening, and speaking.

How do you put it all together? How do we manage a classroom of twenty-four so that children thrive as individuals, as well as members of a group? The best way for us to illustrate the integration of activities defined as language arts would be to take you to visit a classroom. Since that is impossible, we will try to create a picture of part of a day with words. We will describe an early morning get-together and the independent language arts time block designed for six- and seven-year-old children. Our goal is for you to understand the intricate nature of engaging twenty-five individuals in one-to-one and small and large group learning activities while observing their strengths and needs. This intricate task requires patience, management skills, and the knowledge of child growth and development discussed throughout the text. You are invited to spend a morning in Ms. Turner's class of ten girls and fourteen boys. It is October and most of the children have learned the daily routine. Many are able to manage their own time. Some are dependent upon their teacher or peers for guidance. The classroom is arranged much like the one pictured in Figure 9-3.

The Day Begins

(In an elementary school, somewhere in America)

7:30 A.M.
Ms. Turner's classroom was organized into four clusters of tables with places for six children at each. Six- and seven-year-old children were mixed. Changes were made when several children had to be together to work on a specific project or when new friendships were established.

Ms. Turner had arrived at 7:30 to put the new books on display in the library corner. The books *Duck* by David Lloyd, *Father Fox's Pennyrhymes* by Clyde Watson, *What's in the Cave?* by Peter Seymour, and *Wake Up, William!* by Anita Riggio had limited vocabularies and repeated sentence patterns that rhymed. Ms. Turner knows that Derick and Melissa remember words best when they are in contexts written with repeated sentence patterns and rhymes. Both children read and reread these books. This helped them build their sight vocabularies. Ms. Turner took out the contracts for the two children and wrote the day's assignment under the category "reading." It said:

> *There are new books in the book rack for you.*
> *Use the fist-full-of-words rule to pick one.*
> *Sign up for a conference.*

There were always several books available so each child was able to carry out the fist-full-of-words self-selection strategy. The risk of failing was minimized by Ms. Turner's careful planning. The conference sign up chart was posted on the wall near the classroom entrance. Next to it, hanging from a hook, was a pencil on a string. Each child's name was listed down the left side of the chart. The days of the week were written across the top. Children could check the day on which they would have a private conference with their teacher to retell stories they had read or heard. Ms. Turner looked over the names of the children who had signed up for conferences. She assigned the time each conference was to take place next to the child's name. Children checked this chart first thing in the morning and wrote the time on their contracts. Ms. Turner went to the library center. She had gotten books from the municipal library that had been requested by individual children. She put them in a basket labeled, "You asked for it." The appropriate child's name was attached to each book. She put prediction monitoring sheets in an envelope marked, "Predict About Your Book." She also put one inside the cover of each book. She put a new supply of lined and unlined writing paper in the library and writing centers. Sharpened pencils were placed into a canister, and erasers in an empty "eraser box" which had been full the day before. Winnie the Pooh, a toy bear that had fallen, was placed upright next to a book of the same name. Ms. Turner tidied the bed made from a bathtub, fluffed the several pillows on the floor, and placed some empty audio cassettes in a box near several tape recorders for children to use to record their story retellings. She stopped to read Tanya's written retelling of *Cloudy with a Chance of Meatballs,* which was fastened to the wall. Ms. Turner found that Tanya recalled one story episode out of more than ten. She needed a guided retelling session to help her recall more episodes. She read Eric's spontaneous story about his grandfather who was in the hospital. It included a vivid description of the hospital room. She noted a pattern in Eric's invented spellings and planned to make this part of his next conference with her. She was distracted by Charlie, the classroom gerbil, who was running around in his cage. Ms. Turner looked up at the clock. She realized that she had only thirty minutes to complete her preparations for her children. Charlie's food tray was empty. Ms. Turner wrote a note to Vincent, this week's caretaker, and tacked it onto the bulletin board in the living-alive center. It read:

> *Dear Vincent,*
> *Charlie's food tray is empty. I think he needs more food.*
> > > *Love,*
> > > *Ms. Turner*

The ant farm, which was observed daily by seven-year-old Alicia and Gail, seemed exceptionally busy. Several children wrote daily about the changes they observed using a story map. Ms. Turner discovered that the box of maps was empty. She dashed to the copy machine in the office to reproduce more for the children. Observational notes hung all around the ant farm. Alicia had not hung her notes. Ms. Turner thought that she might not have written them. Gail's notes hung on the wall. Ms. Turner wrote the following note to both girls and placed it next to the ant farm.

Dear Alicia and Gail,
Wow! What is going on in the ant farm? Alicia, I missed reading your ant
farm observations today. Please sign up for a conference to share them with
me.

Love,
Ms. Turner

Three books about plants were put next to the blooming cactus on the plant
table. They were about desert plant life and written with limited vocabularies. Ms. Turner was drawn to Crocky's cage. He seemed to be hopping
around more than usual. She opened the top of the can, labeled "Meal
Worms for Crocky," spooned out some, and placed them in the frog's feeding tray. Crocky, in his frog-like way, lapped up the worms with his long,
sticky tongue. Ms. Turner wrote on the chart posted next to his cage, "One
spoonful of meal worms, 8:21 A.M." Writing a note to Habbiba, Solomon,
Fred, and Anita—Crocky's caregivers—encouraged collaborative learning.
The note read:

Dear Habbiba, Solomon, Fred, and Anita,
Crocky was hopping around the cage. He looked hungry. So, I took one
spoonful of meal worms. I put it in his cage. Guess what! He gobbled it up!
The worms smell! Crocky eats them anyway.

Love,
Ms. Turner

A copy of the note was left in each child's mailbox. A second copy of the
letter was placed on top of an easy-to-read book about frogs.

Ms. Turner hurried to the writing center. She had had dialogues with ten
of the twenty-four children in their journals. It was important for her responses to be in the child's writing folders when they arrived. Several new
writing ideas on strips of paper were put into the "Writing Idea Box." These
included:

- retell your favorite story by writing it
- retell your favorite story by talking it onto a tape
- make a rhyme using these words:
  cat rat sat hat pat
  fat mat bat that vat

Ms. Turner put several blank story writing booklets on the shelf. Some were
cut in the shape of pumpkins. These were fastened with a staple, with
orange construction paper used to cover the blank writing paper inside. She

placed each child's daily contract in his or her work basket. It was almost 8:30. Ms. Turner had prepared more than nineteen different integrated reading/language arts activities for the children. That meant that each had choices. The children knew that the classroom was prepared for them to begin activities on their own. Books were always changing. Animals were added and some taken away. Story props and dress-up clothing were rearranged and changed regularly. But contracts, retelling monitoring sheets, prediction sheets, and other tools for recording and observing were always the same. So were the time blocks. Children knew the routines and expected changes. They were able, therefore, to take control of their learning in this risk-free classroom setting.

Ms. Turner had prepared for almost an hour, and there were still things to be done. She moved quickly to the door area, to greet each youngster as they "popped" into the classroom. Children moved to their tables, and Ms. Turner to hers. Some had begun to take a daily paper from the pile left on her desk. This morning she put an article about Michigan in Tommie's basket. Tommie had told Ms. Turner that he was going to visit his relatives in that state during vacation. She remembered that she had forgotten to put the reader's theater version of Dr. Seuss's *Horton Hatches the Egg* in the music and drama center. Ms. Turner felt that Alicia, Fred, Antonio, and Eshee needed to rehearse stories by reading them out loud. She knew that Eshee and Alicia would look for the script. They had been selecting dialogue plays, consistently, for three weeks. The readers' theater activity was perfect for these reluctant readers.

ATTENTION
New readers' theater play
Horton Hatches the Egg *by Dr. Seuss.*

The Children Arrive and Language Activities Begin

8:30 A.M. to approximately 9:50 A.M.
"Hi, Ms. Turner." "Morning Tommie. I left you an article from my paper about Michigan. It's in your basket. Since you're going to visit your Grandma in Lansing in two weeks, you might find it interesting." Ms. Turner peered beyond her newspaper to observe children's activity. She was torn, however, between reading the newspaper and observing youngsters to assess their strengths and needs. She put down the paper and pulled out her note pad and wrote some observations. She also made notes for herself, directing her observations.

Notes

8:40 A.M. *Fred walked to table. He "threw" down his book, sat in chair, and put chin on his hands. Took journal out of his work basket. Seemed to read my response. He took a pencil and began to write. Pressed hard on the point. Erased several times.*

Today—watch Fred's behavior in other situations. Read his journal. I wonder why Fred seems angry?

8:42 A.M. *Habbiba went directly to Crocky. Looked in cage and wrote on chart. Put worms in cage. Took paper and wrote.*

Today—read writing. Use direct praise to let Habbiba know that she's been an independent learner. Milestone—She went on her own and completed task.

8:45 A.M.

Ms. Turner went back to her table and to looking at the newspaper. She also listened to the activity in the room to assess children's self-direction. Sometimes she wished that she had eyes all around her head. She thought she heard Vincent talking to the gerbil. "Here's some food for you, Charlie. No wonder you're hungry. You're always running on your wheel." Several children, including Derick, signed up for a retelling conference. Derick noticed that all seven spaces, the total number of conferences in one day, were now taken. "It's a good thing I got here fast. I would have missed a time," said Derick to a classmate. Derick noticed the book *What's in the Cave.* He took it and proceeded to turn the pages reading and feeling the pop-up characters on each. Ms. Turner noticed that he did not use the fist-full-of-words rule. It seems, she thought, that he was sure that he could read it without checking. Derick and the four other children took their work baskets and went to their tables. Derick stood in the living alive corner beside Melissa.

Derick: I got a book already, so I can check one thing on my contract.

Melissa: What book did you get?

Derick: See. It's a pop-up book.

Melissa: What's it about?

Derick: (Shrugging his shoulders) I don't know. (As he turns the pages, he shares what is on the page.) It's about a, ah, a . . . What's this?

Melissa: A lazy lizard.

Derick: It's about a l-a-z-y lizard, and a fat bat, and a green snake.

Melissa: That says, "a sneaky snake."

Derick: And a sneaky snake and a . . . what's this word?

Melissa: Friendly.

Derick: A friendly frog. He's orange. I never saw an orange frog before (as he shrugs shoulders and turns the page). And a s-s-s-s

Melissa: Sly.

Derick: Sly spider and . . .

Derick and Melissa: A broody bird.

Melissa: (Derick looks on and holds book) A busy beetle. What else is in the cave?

Derick: A MONSTER.

Derick turned back to the beginning of the book and began to read again. Melissa took her work basket and walked to her table. Ms. Turner scribbled in her notebook:

> *Melissa—natural peer tutor for Derick. She used "echo reading." Derick completed the book. Began to read it a second time—natural rehearsal. Milestone—Derick accepted peer guidance. He selected a book he was able to read. Stayed with it to the end and then reread, independently.*

Ms. Turner was so absorbed in watching Derick, that she failed to note the activities of other children. It was such an active child-centered classroom.

Several children had gone to the library center, selected a book, and took a prediction sheet. Others took one of the several guided retelling sheets. Ms. Turner made note of the strategy sheets each child took. She would watch for the rest of the week to see if children selected the same worksheets daily. Matthew and Keiko found the plant books in the living alive corner.

Matthew: Is this for us?

Keiko: (Shrugging her shoulders) I don't know. But it's not our corner this week. So it's probably not. But I'm reading it anyway.

Matthew: Me too.

Ms. Turner had hoped that Derick and Brian would have taken them. The boys needed peer interaction to build confidence in their abilities to read.

By 8:50 the room was a hustle and bustle with language activities. Some children had begun to read self-selected books; others were reading the teacher's response in their dialogue journals while others wrote in the journal. Several were cleaning animal cages and recording their activities on charts and in notebooks. More seven- than six-year-old children were completing oral and written retellings that were begun the day before. Contracts were reviewed by most of the children within the first twenty minutes of the school day. Some children left them on the tables to use as a reference. Others seemed to review the contract and put it back into the work basket. Several appeared to be staring into space. Ms. Turner moved to the library center. This was where the morning get-together took place. It usually began at 9:00 and lasted for approximately fifteen minutes. The morning's activity included the usual "news and notes." Children who had special events in their lives shared them. It was also the time to review the day's events. Preplans for some of these get-togethers included story reading time. Gail was this morning's story reader. She clutched her James Stevenson's *That Terrible Halloween Night.* She would read it to the class this morning. She had taken the book home to rehearse reading it out loud. She looked up at the clock. Then she looked at Ms. Turner, who was already seated in the library center. A second chair was beside Ms. Turner. Gail sat in the chair. The children knew that it was time to come together, stopped what they were doing and came to the center. Ms. Turner smiled and bid the group, "Good morning." Ben told the class that he was going to get a new baby. Sarah confirmed the news by saying, "Yeah, it's coming in April." Derick reminded the class that there would be a book fair next month. He was the class messenger and had received a note from the principal's office asking him to remind everyone about the date. A sign "Today's story reader is Gail." was hanging on the chart next to the child. Ms. Turner smiled at her and she began:

Gail: Today, I am going to read *That Terrible Halloween Night* by James Stevenson. What do you think it's about (as she held the cover of the book toward the children)?

Gail began by asking children to predict. She had learned this from her teacher, who did it all the time. She read a page and then shared the picture. She did this until the book was completed. She announced that she would share the book and that she would write a retelling and make it into a book for the classroom library. After the morning get-together, Ms. Turner noticed that Jason seemed to be staring at the ant farm, and Kevin took his book out of his work basket.

Jason: Hey, what are ya doin with my book?

Kevin: I want to finish it. I only have a little left. You let me read it yesterday.

Jason: O.K. Finish it. But I want it soon!

Ms. Turner's thought about all of the things that occurred during the first forty-five minutes. She watched children:

- select a book
- read and respond to a journal entry
- care for a living thing and record some of the visible changes in the animals' behaviors
- read a book
- engage in collaborative learning
- sign up for conferences
- attend to other children's reading and writing
- respond to her modeling behaviors by reading her journal entry to them
- write a letter in response to hers
- make decisions about which activities to complete even though a group activity was occurring

Ms. Turner noticed individual strengths and needs during the forty-five-minute period and recorded them whenever she found time in order to plan for the next day's activities. She learned from the morning's observations and recorded the notes shown in Table E-1.

Discussion

Ms. Turner had, indeed, created an environment for observing children. She kept goals in her mind and took quick objective notes. She was careful not to be subjective and not use words like shy, lazy, lackadaisical, or day-dreamer. These were evaluative, relative terms and, therefore, inappropriate. Ms. Turner had data that helped her to provide the intervention necessary for further development.

9:20 to 11:30
Two hours were blocked for independent work, small group activities, and individual conferences. By this time of year, mid-October, most children could manage their own time using their contract as a guide. During this time, Ms. Turner acted as a model, exhibiting desired behaviors as a nur-

turing caregiver and as a consultant to the children. Walking to each of the four table areas while children were working let them know that she was available for consulting. She became their audience ready to listen to their creative stories, their retellings, and their experiences. Ms. Turner knew that the children believed that their work and even their attempts were valued. The classroom was a bustle of activity. Children seemed to know what to do and so did their teacher. A sketch of the activities follow.

Child	Behaviors	Teacher's Notes
Tommie	Took Michigan article. Adult input provides motivation. Did not see him read it.	Follow up to encourage reading. Say, "I'll talk to you about the article later. I am going to Michigan." or "Let me know when you've read the article. I have something to share about Michigan, with you."
Fred	Began journal writing independently. Seemed to respond to dialogue in journal—he wrote back.	Look for other settings where anger occurs. Find strategy to relieve anger. If a pattern, talk to school psychologist for suggestions.
Habbiba	Milestone day—she fed the frog without direction from peers or teacher. She also wrote her activities on her own. Hurrah!!!	Praise behavior. ("Habbiba, I really like the way you came to school, fed Crocky, and wrote what you did. That's very independent behavior.") Provide additional care-tending activities.
Derick	Demonstrated independence and enthusiasm about reading. Got involved with stories that have limited vocabularies and interesting formats (pop-up books yesterday, and *Rebus Bears* today). Solved problems—got help with word identification, spontaneously. Seemed to have need to read. Liked books with surprises in them.	Create success. Make books available daily. Be sure he knows how to get help. Will say, "Derick, I like the way you read with Melissa. Because you read with her, both of you knew all of the words." Provide books with surprises like, *Where's Spot,* and Bank Street "Ready-to-Read" Rebus Series. Needs prediction activities.

Child	Behaviors	Teacher's Notes
Melissa	As usual, independent. Fit in with most children. Took opportunity to interact with story, no matter who is involved. Seemed to have a natural way of guiding peers, and making herself and others feel good about it.	Continue as is. Be careful not to overuse as helper.
Cindy Allison John Shamir	All selected retelling guide sheet for first time.	Note if child completes the elements included, if each works alone or with another, and the effects of peer interaction on recall using guided retelling sheet.
Kevin	Loves to read anything. If interested, finds way to "skin the cat" and get the book. Stays by himself most of the time.	Share some of the reading.

Children's Activities

Ms. Turner's Activities

Table I: Derick , Melissa, Fred, Habbiba, Randy and Allison
Children each took their work baskets from the cubbies. Derick, Habbiba, and Randy found their journals and read and responded on their own. Melissa put the work basket on the table and went to the library. She was carrying one book. Fred, after completing journal writing, sat with hands in chin and looked around at others. He took paper out of the basket and fastened it onto a clipboard. He got up and left the classroom with the clipboard and pencil. He was collecting data about things on the bulletin board in the hall. The purpose was to become a better descriptive writer. His goal was to use at least two adjectives to describe each object. Allison went to get a retelling monitoring sheet. She took her

Ms. Turner took notes about as many children as she could. She wrote: "Derick, Habbiba, Randy—took journals first. Wrote for twenty minutes. Habbiba got up three times and sharpened pencil twice. Randy erased her first sentence three times. Fred wrote for three minutes. Read paper and also looked around. He said to Allison, "Want to do this with me?" Ms. Turner remembered that Allison scheduled a conference. She got her retelling evaluation sheet. She took a copy of the transcription of Allison's retelling and the guide sheet she had completed at home. She would guide Allison to monitor her own comprehension and then compare both evaluations. She noticed Melissa sitting and drawing. She went to her and said, "Melissa, I left your contract in your work

Children's Activities	Ms. Turner's Activities
book, her transcription which Ms. Turner had placed in her work basket, and her tape recorder to the table that said, "Conference! Do Not Disturb."	basket. Look at it. If you have questions, I will answer them before the retelling conference."
Table II: Keiko, Kevin, Shamir, Gail, John, and Anita Gail read *That Terrible Halloween Night* by Stevenson to these children on Halloween. They decided to retell it in writing. Every child has a copy of the book. Each read it at least once on their own. Keiko was rereading, and so were Kevin and Shamir. Gail had already taken out her pencil and Retelling Journal and placed the book at the top of the table. John took his Retelling Journal and began to write immediately. Anita took her contract and read and reread it. She looked about the table at peer activities. She seemed to be undecided about what to do. "Are you writing about the monster story?" "Yeah, I'm retelling it. Don't bother me!" grunted Kevin. Kevin wrote for fifteen minutes without stopping. During that time he stood up, sat down, took the paper under the table, sharpened his pencil twice, but continued to write for that period.	She continued note taking. Keiko, Kevin, and Shamir independently took the book and reread. They seem to like to reread stories, especially before a written retelling. Gail had taken the book and began to retell by looking at the pages. (Will review rules for unguided retellings at her next conference.) Keiko read the story and immediately began retelling. Shamir and Kevin read and then went to the library for a new book. Ms. Turner interacts: "Keiko, I like the way you reread, put away the book, and began to retell." Shamir and Kevin: "I'm glad you are picking a new book. Show me your retelling when it's done." To Anita, who seems to need to confirm what is to be done by talking about it, "I'm glad you use your contract to find out what to do. It's good to see what your friends are doing, too." Ms. Turner provided direct praise and told each child that he or she was engaging in appropriate behavior. Inappropriate behaviors, because they did not interfere with others, were ignored. Note: Story reading to group seemed to build Gail's confidence. She read easily, began written retelling, and smiled.
Table III: Matthew, Solomon, Eshee, Cindy, Tanya, and Alicia Newspaper "copy," as the children referred to it, was placed on the table. The group newspaper project was on its way. Copies of children's work were on the table. Each child was responsible for a topic. "Chinatown" was Eshee's topic. This would	Ms. Turner noticed that Matthew took books after Solomon did. He watched Solomon pick up a book about crabs. Matthew picked up a science book too. Solomon noticed, and said, "Your topic is sports. Here are three books on that." Matthew took the *Pete Rose* book. He looked at the cover, then opened

Children's Activities	Ms. Turner's Activities
be the social studies column. Science was Solomon's favorite. He was not specific about his topic. Tanya could not decide. She choose *My Doctor* from the selection Ms. Turner presented. Alicia and Cindy decided they liked TV, and Matthew would write about sports. Ms. Turner put several books in the middle of the table. She had not marked each with a child's name. She hoped that each would seek one pertinent to the topic. Some of the books were: *Tales from Gold Mountain* and *Mei Li* both for Eshee; *My Doctor* for Tanya; *Is This a House for a Hermit Crab?, Nessa's Fish, Under Your Feet,* and *The Story of The Seashore* were earmarked for Solomon. He could read these and a variety of science topics were represented by the titles. For Matthew Ms. Turner included, *How to Be a Good Basketball Player, I Can Read about Racing Cars, Pete Rose,* and the poetry book *Sports Pages.* She also left a *New York Times, USA Today, Newsweek,* and *Time Magazine.* Several copies of *Chickadee* were put with the newspapers. Children got their work baskets. Paper and pencils were put on the table by Ms. Turner. Some had their own project notebooks and pencil. Others took paper from the pile on the table.	the book and held up his hand to use the fist-full-of-words rule. Solomon opened his notebook. He read the book and began to do a written retelling. Eshee found both books about China. "These are stories," he said to himself. As he got up he opened *Tales from Gold Mountain.* He stood at his table and read. A minute of reading went by and he sat down and continued. Tanya sat in her chair. She looked about, played with a toy bear, and scratched her eye. Alicia took *Newsweek,* and said, "Cindy, there's TV stuff in here." Cindy took *USA Today* after Alicia selected it, and said, "Stuff is in here too." Alicia seemed to use the index. She turned to a page and looked at pictures. Cindy turned each page of the paper, talking about the photos. Her talk did not seem to relate to TV. Solomon read and wrote. Tanya sat. Cindy seemed to read pictures in the newspaper. Alicia seemed to read the magazine. Matthew needed direction and then found a book. He demonstrated his knowledge of the self-selection strategy.
Table IV: Antonio, Vincent, Eric, Brian, Tommie, Jason, and Michael	Ms. Turner knew that she could not observe and record the behaviors of this group today. She had only two eyes, one hand for writing, and one brain for thinking about the children. She watched in-between the note taking for the other three groups. She remembered that:
Michael, Tommie, and Brian, upon entering the room, went for their work baskets. Antonio, Vincent, and Jason went to see Charlie, the gerbil. Antonio opened a notebook and began to talk and write. "Today, Charlie is still running on the wheel. He is running 10 times." The other two boys watched and talked about the gerbil. Jason moved to his work table. Vincent	• Jason, for the first time, directed his behavior.

Children's Activities	Ms. Turner's Activities
followed within two minutes. Antonio stayed for ten minutes and watched. He wrote and watched and wrote and watched for the entire time. Tommie and Brian took out their "Word Envelope." "I'll hold your word cards first, Brian," said Tommie. "Okay, but do them slow. Yesterday you went so fast I could hardly read them." Tommie put Brian's words on the table. He took one and "flashed" it toward him. "Spaghetti. Next one, please. Tuesday, Holy Communion, suit, splashed, dirty," etc. "Now it's my turn, Brian. You hold my cards." Tommie read words, and upon seeing one said, "I don't know that. Do you?" "Cracker Jacks." "Oh," said Tommie. "I don't like them even though I wrote it. I'm gonna throw it away." "I'll take it," said Brian. "I love them," he said, as he began to trace the letters and say the word simultaneously. The boys put the word cards down and found their section of the board, labeled with each of their names, to write their words. They wrote as many as they could before returning to their stacks to reread to recall the rest for writing. Vincent took his contract and wrote under "reading"—"Two chapters today." He picked up his *Encyclopedia Brown* book, took a pillow, propped it up against the corner wall, and began to read.	• Tommie began working without teacher motivation as previously noted. • Antonio's notes should be checked. Did he really look and write about it? • Vincent needed prompts to begin to retell independently.

Ms. Turner had walked through the room, talking—nurturing her children into literacy. Some were immersed; others were not. Some stayed on task for long periods of time; others did not. Some children sat at their tables and wrote; others sat on the floor. Some sharpened pencils three times before beginning their written retelling; others wrote immediately. Children worked individually; others worked in pairs. There was a low, even humming of children's voices throughout the two-hour period. Shamir told Habbiba about his birthday party as he wrote his retelling. Gail showed Anita the "big girl" book that she could read. Anita continued to draw her picture, almost ignoring Gail's show-and-tell. Kevin skipped over to Derick's table three times to ask him how to spell the word *frog*. Derick finally took a 4 by 7 inch word card and wrote it for him. Keiko and Melissa read the words in their word bank envelope to each other. Keika wrote hers on the chalkboard and Melissa checked to see if they were written correctly. Matthew and Solomon took a prop bag and the *Berenstain Bears* book that was inside. Both put on the bear hat and mittens. Matthew read one page while Solomon read the other. Both boys check the box on their contract that indicated that they had engaged in reading that morning. Ms. Turner began individual conferences. She carried out three oral retelling sessions. Children told, and she recorded their retellings on tape. She would transcribe them that evening and carry out a self-monitoring conference before the end of the week. Ms. Turner gathered five of the children together who needed guidance in understanding how to create words using a spelling pattern. A seven-minute spelling game helped these youngsters add words to their word banks. Each wrote at least five new words that rhymed. Shamir called them "it" words. He wrote four. They were "fit," "sit," "kit" and "bit." Randy read a story to her doll in the drama center. It was one she had written herself. Solomon used the fist-full-of-words rule, selected a book, and, for the first time, attempted to use the prediction sheet. Ms. Turner saw this and, when she was free, went over to him and said, "Solomon, how wonderful! You selected your book using the rule and wrote a prediction sheet." Allison disagreed with Sarah about which Halloween costume would be the best. Twenty-four six- and seven-year-old children knew how to proceed at the beginning of the school day. They learned from modeled behavior and direct instruction. Ms. Turner understood the characteristics of six- and seven-year-olds. She knew six-year-olds were more fun but went to opposite extremes. They loved one moment and hated the next. They would cooperate at times, but hated to be wrong. Her seven-year-olds were a bit more reserved. They had quieted down after their first year. While six-year-olds were the focus of their world and active—sometimes aggressive, her seven-year-olds tended to be thoughtful, sensitive to the needs of others, and even withdrawn. More seven-year-olds used the "places to be alone with books" than six-year-olds. Sometimes the teacher was concerned but remembered that next year would bring more expansive behaviors. Six-year-olds were eager for all of the new experiences provided in this wonderful classroom. Their warm expressions of affection demonstrated their delight. Seven-year-olds were more serious in their approach to activities.

And growth continues. . . .

If now you feel the warmth of Ms. Turner's classroom, you may better understand the joy of learning that is created only when collegiality and appreciation for differences exists. All children learn. All youngsters, whatever their behavior, must be welcomed into the wonderful world of language learning. Every child and every adult, who interact in literacy-rich environments, have their own nature and rhythm for living and learning. It is these differences that make teaching and learning exciting experiences.

References

Abravanel, E. (1968). The development of intersensory patterning with regard to selected spatial dimensions. *Monograph of the Society for Research in Child Development, 3* (2, Serial No. 118).

Adams, M. J. (1990). *Beginning to read: Thinking and learning about print.* Urbana-Champaign, IL: Center for the Study of Reading, University of Illinois.

Adams, M. J. (1991). *Beginning to read: Thinking and learning about print.* Cambridge, MA: MIT Press.

Ainsworth, M. D. S. (1973). The development of infant-mother attachment. In B. M. Caldwell & N. N. Ricciuti (Eds.), *Review of Child Development Research* (Vol. 3). Chicago: University of Chicago Press.

Alverman, D. W., Boothby, P. R., & Wolfe, J. (1984). The effect of graphic organizer instruction on fourth graders' comprehension of social studies texts. *Journal of Social Studies Research, 8,* 13–21.

Ames, L. B., & Haber, O. D. (1985). *Your seven year old: Life in minor key.* New York: Dell.

Ames, L. B., & Ilg, F. L. (1979a). *Your five year old: Sunny and serene.* New York: Dell.

Ames, L. B., & Ilg, F. L. (1979b). *Your six year old: Loving and defiant.* New York: Dell.

Ashton-Warner, S. (1963). *Teacher.* New York: Simon & Schuster.

Baghban, M. (1984). *Our daughter learns to read and write.* Newark, DE: International Reading Association.

Bates, E. (Ed.). (1979). *The emergence of symbolic cognition and communication in infancy.* New York: Academic Press.

Beers, J. (1980). Developmental strategies of spelling competence in primary school children. In E. H. Henderson & J. W. Beers (Eds.)., *Developmental and cognitive aspects of learning to spell.* Newark, DE: International Reading Association.

Bender, A. E., & Bender, D. A. (1982). *Nutrition for medical students.* New York: Wiley.

Bird, M. (1980). Reading comprehension strategies: A direct teaching approach. *Dissertation Abstracts International, 41*(6), 2506-A.

Bissex, G. L. (1980). *Gyns at wrk: A child learns to read and write.* Cambridge, MA: Harvard University Press.

Blank, M., & Bridges, W. H. (1964). Cross-model transfer in nursery-school children. *Journal of Comparative and Physiological Psychology, 58,* 277–282.

Bleich, D. (1975). *Readings and feelings.* Urbana, IL: National Council of the Teachers of English.

Bloom, L. (1970). *Language development: Form and function in emerging grammars.* Cambridge, MA: MIT Press.

Bloom, L. (1975). Language development review. In F. D. Horowitz (Ed.), *Review of child development research* (Vol. 4). Chicago: University of Chicago Press.

Bowlby, J. (1969). *Attachment.* New York: Basic Books.

Braun, S. J., & Edwards, E. P. (1972). *History and theory of early childhood education.* Worthington, OH: Charles A. Jones.

Briggs, C., & Elkind, D. (1973). Cognitive development in early readers. *Developmental Psychology, 9,* 279–280.

Bromley, K. (1991). *Webbing.* Boston: Allyn and Bacon.

Brown, C. S., & Lytle, S. L. (1988). Merging assessment and instruction: Protocols in the classroom. In S. M. Glazer, L. W. Searfoss, & L. M. Gentile (Eds.). *Reexamining reading diagnosis: New trends and procedures* (pp. 94–102). Newark, DE: International Reading Association.

Brown, H., & Cambourne, B. (1987). *Read and retell.* Portmouth, NH: Heinemann.

Brown, R. (1973). *A first language: The early stages.* Cambridge, MA: Harvard University Press.

Brunner, J. S., & Feldman, C. F. (1982). Where does language come from? *The New York Times Review of Books, 29(11), 34–36.*

Burke, E. (1986). *Early childhood literature: For love of child and book.* Boston, MA: Allyn & Bacon.

Burke, E. (1990). *Literature for the young child* (2nd ed.). Boston, MA: Allyn & Bacon.

Burns, J., & Richgels, D. S. (1989). An investigation of abilities associated with the "invented spelling" ability of four-year-olds of above average intelligence. *Journal of Reading Behavior, 21,* 1–14.

Burroughs, M. (1972). *The stimulation of verbal behavior in culturally disadvantaged three-year-olds.* Unpublished doctoral dissertation, Michigan State University, E. Lansing.

Burrows, A. T., Jackson, D. C., & Saunders, D. O. (1984). *They all want to write* (4th ed.). Hamden, CT: Library of Professional Publications.

Butler, D. (1979). *Cushla and her books.* London: Hodder and Stoughton.

Calfee, R. C., & Calfee, K. H. (1981). *Interactive reading assessment (IRAS).* Unpublished manuscript. Stanford University, Stanford.

Calkins, L. M. (1986). *The art of teaching writing.* Portsmouth, NH: Heinemann.

Campos, J. J., Barrett, K. C., Lamb, M. E., Goldsmith, H. H., & Stenberg, C. (1983). Socioemotional development. In P. H. Mussen (Eds.). *Handbook of Child Psychology* (4th ed.). (pp. 856–858). New York: Wiley.

Cattell, J. (1960). *The measurement of intelligence of infants and young children* (rev. ed.) New York: Psychological Corporation.

Chomsky, N. (1965). *Aspects of a theory of syntax.* Cambridge, MA: MIT Press.

Chomsky, C. (1971). Invented spelling in the open classroom. *Words, 27,* 499–518.

Chomsky, C. (1976). *Approaching reading through invented spelling.* Paper presented at the meeting of the Theory and Practice of Beginning Reading Instruction, Learning Research and Development Center, University of Pittsburgh.

Clark, M. (1976). *Young fluent readers: What can they teach us.* London: Heinemann.

Clay, M. (1975). *What did I write?* Auckland, New Zealand: Heinemann Educational.

Cleland, C. (1981). Highlighting issues in children's literature through semantic webbing. *The Reading Teacher, 34(6),* 642–646.

Collins, A., Brown, J. S., & Larkin, K. M. (1980). Inference in text understanding. In R. J. Spiro, B. Bruce, & W. Brewer (Eds.), *Theoretical issues in reading comprehension.* (pp. 385–407). Hillsdale, NJ: Erlbaum.

Condon, W., & Sander, L. (1974). Neonate movement is synchronized with adult speech: Interactional participation and language acquisition. *Science, 183,* 99–101.

Coody, B. (1982). *Using literature with young children* (3rd ed.). Dubuque, IA: Brown.

Crago, M. (1975). One child and her books: A case study 11–24 months. *Children's Libraries Newsletter, 11,* 41–47.

Dale, P. S. (1976). *Language development: Structure and function* (2nd ed.). Seattle: Holt Rinehart and Winston.

Davis, J. B. (1968). Research in comprehension of reading. *Reading Research Quarterly, 3,* 499–545.

deVilliers, P. A., & deVilliers, J. G. (1979). *Early language.* Cambridge, MA: Harvard University Press.

Dewey, J. (1966). *Democracy and education.* New York: Free Press.

Durkin, D. (1966). *Children who read early.* New York: Teachers College Press.

Durkin, D. (1974–75). A six year study of children who learn to read in school at the age of four. *Reading Research Quarterly, 10,* 9–61.

Durkin, D. (1989). *Children who read early* (5th ed.). New York: Teachers College Press.

Dyson, A. H. (1985). Individual differences in emerging writing. In M. Farr (Ed.). *Advances in writing research: Children's early writing development* (Vol. 1). Norwood, NJ: Ablex.

Dyson, A. H. (1986). Children's early interpretations of writing: Expanding research perspectives. In D. Yoden & S. Templeton (Eds.), *Metalinguistic awareness and beginning literacy.* Exeter, NH: Heinemann.

Earle, R. A. (1970). *The use of vocabulary as a structured overview in seventh grade mathematics.* Unpublished doctoral dissertation. Syracuse University, Syracuse, NY.

Eddy, B. L., & Gould, K. A. (1990). Comprehension system 8: A teacher's perspective. *Literacy: Issues and Practices, 7,* 70–75.

Egeland, B., & Farber, E. (1984). Infant-mother attachments: Factors related to its development and changes over time. *Child Development, 55,* 753–771.

Egner, K. (1989). Symbolic expression in the lives of children. *The Educational Forum, 53*(3), 241–254.

Farr, R. (1990). *Thinkalong strategies.* Paper presented at the meeting of International Reading Association, Atlanta.

Fein, G. G. (1983). Pretend Play: New Perspectives. *Curriculum Planning for Young Children* (pp. 22–27). Washington DC: National Association for the Education of Young Children.

Fein, G. G., & Schwartz, S. S. (1986). The social coordination of pretense in preschool children. *The young child at play: Reviews of research* (Vol. 4). Washington, DC: National Association for the Education of Young Children.

Fernald, G. M. (1971). *Remedial techniques in basic school subjects.* New York: McGraw-Hill.

Finocchiaro, N. (1964). *English as a second language: From theory to practice.* New York: Simon & Schuster.

Fodor, M. (1966). *The effect of systematic reading of stories on the language development of culturally deprived children.* Unpublished doctoral dissertation, Cornell University, Ithaca, NY.

Freiberg, S. (1977). *Every child's birthright: In defense of mothering.* New York: Basic Books.

Frodi, A., Bridges, L., & Grolnick, W. (1985). Correlates of mastery-related behavior: A short-term longitudinal study of infants in second year. *Child Development, 56,* 1291–1298.

Furth, H. (1970). *Piaget for teachers.* Englewood Cliffs, NJ: Prentice-Hall.

Garvey, C. (1977). *Play.* Cambridge, MA: Harvard University Press.

Garvey, C. (1984). *Children's talk: The developing child.* Cambridge, MA: Harvard University Press.

Genishi, C. (1988). Children's language: Learning words from experience. *Young Children, 44,* 10–23.

Gentry, J. R. (1982). An analysis of developmental spelling in Gyns at Wrk. *The Reading Teacher, 36,* 192–200.

Gentry, R. (1978). Early spelling strategies. *Elementary School Journal, 79,* 88–92.

Gibson, E. J. (1969). *Principles of perceptual learning and development.* New York: Appleton-Century-Crofts.

Gibson, E. J., & Levin, H. (1975). *The psychology of reading.* Cambridge, MA: MIT Press.

Glazer, S. M. (1980). *Getting ready to read: Creating readers from birth through six.* Englewood Cliffs, NJ: Prentice-Hall.

Glazer, S. M. (1992). *Reading comprehension: Self-monitoring strategies that create independent readers.* New York: Scholastic.

Glazer, S. M., & Brown, C. S. (1993). *Portfolios and beyond: Alternative assessment in reading and writing.* Norwood, CT: Christopher Gordon Publishers.

Glazer, S. M., & Searfoss, L. W. (1988). *Reading diagnosis and instruction: A C-A-L-M approach.* Englewood Cliffs, NJ: Prentice-Hall.

Golinkoff, R. M., & Gordon, L. (1983). In the beginning was the word: A history of the study of language acquisition. In R. M. Golinkoff (Eds.), *The transition from prolinguistic to linguistic communication* (pp. 1–25). Hillsdale, NJ: Erlbaum Associates.

Goncu, A., & Kessel, F. (1984). Children's play: A contextual-functioning perspective. *Analyzing children's dialogues: New directions for child development.* San Francisco: Jossey-Bass.

Goodman, K., & Goodman, Y. M. (1979). Learning to read is natural. In L. B. Resnick & D. Weaver (Eds.), *Theory and practice of early reading* (pp. 37–154). Hillsdale, NJ: Erlbaum Associates.

Goodman, Y. (1967). *A psycholinguistic description of observed oral reading phenomena in selected young beginning readers.* Unpublished doctoral dissertation. Wayne State University, Detroit.

Graves, D. (1983). *Writing: Teachers and children at work.* Portsmouth, NH: Heinemann.

Gundlach, R., Mclane, J., Scott, F., & McNamee, G. (1985). The social foundations of early writing development. In M. Farr (Ed.), *Advances in Writing Research* (Vol. 1). Norwood, NJ: Ablex.

Hall, E. (1959). *The silent language.* New York: Doubleday.

Hall, M., Moretz, S. H., & Stantom. (1976). Writing before grade one: A study of early writers. *Language Arts, 53,* 582–585.

Hall, N. (1987). *The emergence of literacy.* Portsmouth, NH: Heinemann.

Halliday, M. A. K. (1975). *Learning how to mean: Exploration in the development of language.* London: Edward Arnold.

Hansen, H. S. (1969). The impact of the home literacy environment on reading. *Elementary English, 46,* 17–24.

Harste, J. C., Burke, C. L., & Woodward, V. A. (1982). Children's languages and world: Initial encounters with print. In J. A. Langer & M. Smith-Burke (Eds.), *Reader meets author: Bridging the gap* (pp. 105–131). Newark, DE: International Reading Associates.

Harste, J. C., Burke, C. L., & Woodward, V. A. (1983). *The young child as writer and informant* (Final Report of NIE G-80-0121). Bloomington, IN: Language Education Department, Indiana University.

Heath, S. B. (1983). *Ways with words: Language, life and work in communities and classrooms.* Cambridge, England: Cambridge University Press.

Herron, R., & Sutton-Smith, B. (Ed.). (1971). *Child's play.* New York: Wiley.

Hiebert, E. H. (1981). Developmental patterns and interrelationships of preschool children's print awareness. *Reading Research Quarterly, 16,* 236–260.

Holdaway, D. (1979). *The foundations of literacy.* New York: Ashton Scholastic.

Holdaway, D. (1986). The structure of natural learning as a basis for literacy instruction. In M. R. Sampson (Ed.), *The pursuit of literacy* (pp. 56–72). Dubuque, IA: Kendall/Hunt.

Holmberg, M. C. (1980). The development of social interchange patterns from 12 to 42 months. *Child Development, 51,* 448–456.

Ilg, F., Ames, L., & Bates, L. (1955). *Child behavior.* New York: Harper & Brothers.

International Reading Association. (1986). IRA position statement on reading and writing in early childhood. *Reading Teacher, 8,* 822–824.

Izard, C. (1979). Emotions as motivations: An evolutionary developmental perspective. In H. E. Howe & R. A. Dienstbier (Eds.). *Symposium on Motivation 1978* (Vol. 27). Lincoln: University of Nebraska Press.

Jewell, M. H., & Zintz, M. V. (1986). *Learning to read naturally* Dubuque, IA: Kendall/Hunt.

Jorde-Bloom, P. (1986). Organizational norms: Our blueprint for behavior. *Child Care Information Exchange* (pp. 38–42).

Kagan, J. (1981). *The second year: The emergence of self-awareness.* Cambridge, MA: Harvard University Press.

Kellogg, R. (1970). *Analyzing children's art.* Palo Alto, CA: Mayfield.

Kogan, N. (1983). Stylistic variation in childhood and adolescence: Creativity, metaphor and cognitive styles. In P. H. Mussen (Ed.), *Handbook of child psychology* (5th ed., Vol. 3). New York: Wiley.

Kolata, G. (April 4, 1989). Infant I.Q. tests found to predict scores in school. *The New York Times.*

Krippner, S. (1963). The boy who read at eighteen-months. *Exceptional Child, 30,* 105–109.

Lavine, L. (1972). *The development of perception of writing in prereading children: A cross-cultural study.* Unpublished doctoral dissertation, Cornell University, Ithaca, NY.

Leichter, H. J. (1964). Some perspectives on the family as educator. In H. J. Leichter (Ed.), *The family as educator* (pp. 1–43). New York: Teachers College Press.

Lenneberg, E. (1967). *Biological foundations of language.* New York: Wiley.

Lieberman, J. H. (1977). *Playfulness: Its relationship to imagination and creativity.* New York: Academic Press.

Lieven, E. V. M. (1978). Turn-taking and pragmatics: Two issues in early child language. In Campbell and Smith (Eds.), *Recent advances in the psychology of language: Language development and mother-child interactions.* New York: Plenum.

Lilley, I. M. (1967). *Friedrich Froebel.* Cambridge, England: Cambridge University Press.

Lindfors, J. (1987). *Children's language and learning* (2nd ed.). Englewood Cliffs, NJ: Prentice-Hall.

Mandler, J. M., & Johnson, N. S. (1977). Remembrance of things passed: Story structure and recall. *Cognitive Psychology, 9,* 111–151.

Mason, J. (1977). *Reading readiness: A definition and skills hierarchy from preschoolers' developing conceptions of print* (Tech. Rep. No. 59). Urbana: University of Illinois, Center for the Study of Reading.

McCarthy, P. (1954). Language development in children. In L. Carmichael (Ed.). *Manual of child psychology* (pp. 492–631). New York: Wiley.

McGee, L. M., & Richgels, D. J. (1986). Attending to text structure: A comprehension strategy. In E. K. Dishner, T. W. Bean, J. E. Readence, & D. W. Mouse (Eds.). *Reading in content areas: Improving classroom instruction* (2nd ed.). Dubuque, IA: Kendall/Hunt.

McGee, L. M., & Richgels, D. J. (1990). *Literacy's beginnings: Supporting young readers and writers.* Boston, MA: Allyn & Bacon.

McLoyd, V. C. (1983). The effects of the structure of play objects on the pretend play of low-income preschool children. *Child Development, 54,* 626–635.

McLoyd, V. C. (1985). Social class and pretend play. In C. C. Brown & A. W. Gottfried. (Ed.), *Play interactions: The role of toys and parental involvement in children's development* (pp. 96–104). Skillman, NJ: Johnson & Johnson.

McNeill, D. (1966). Developmental psycholinguistics. In F. Smith & G. A. Miller (Eds.), *The genesis of language: A psycholinguistic approach* (pp. 15–84). Cambridge, MA: MIT Press.

McNeill, D. (1970). *The acquisition of language: The study of developmental psycholinguistics.* New York: Harper & Row.

Mead, M. (1946, September 23). Trends in personal life. *New Republic, 115,* 346–348.

Mead, M. (1977). Grandparents as educators. In H. J. Leichter (Ed.), *The family educator* (pp. 66–75). New York: Teachers College Press.

Menyuk, P. (1963). Syntactic structures in the language of children. *Child Development, 34,* 407–422.

Miller, P. J. (1982). *Amy, Wendy and Beth: Learning language in South Baltimore.* Austin: The University of Texas.

Montessori, M. (1965). *Spontaneous activity in education.* New York: Schocken Books.

Moore, D. W., & Readence, J. E. (1983). *A quantitative review of graphic organizer research.* Paper presented at the annual meeting of the American Educational Research Association, Montreal, Canada.

Morris, D. (1980). Beginning reader's concept of words. In E. H. Henderson & J. W. Beers (Eds.), *Developmental and cognitive aspects of learning to spell.* Newark, DE: International Reading Association.

Morris, D. (1981). Concept of word: A developmental phenomenon in the beginning reading and writing process. *Language Arts, 58,* 659–668.

Morrow, L. M. (1981). *Supertips for storytelling.* New York: Harcourt, Brace, Jovanovich.

Morrow, L. M. (1982). Relationships between literature programs, library corner designs and children's use of literature. *Journal of Educational Research, 75,* 339–344.

Morrow, L. M. (1983). Home and school correlates of early interest in literature. *Journal of Educational Research, 76,* 221–230.

Morrow, L. M. (1989). *Literacy development in the early years.* Englewood Cliffs, NJ: Prentice-Hall.

Morrow, L. M. (1993). *Literacy development in the early years: Helping children read and write* (2nd ed.). Englewood Cliffs, NJ: Prentice-Hall.

Morrow, L. M., & Weinstein, C. S. (1982). Increasing children's use of literature through program and physical design changes. *Elementary School Journal, 83,* 131–137.

Nagy, W., & Herman, P. (1987). Breadth and depth of vocabulary knowledge: Implications for acquisition and instruction. In M. McKeown & M. Curtis (Eds.), *The nature of vocabulary acquisition* (pp. 19–35). Hillsdale, NJ: Erlbaum.

Nelson, K. (1973). Structure and strategy in learning to talk. *Monograph for the Society for Research in Child Development, 38* (149, Serial Nos. 1 and 2). *New York Times.* (April 4, 1989).

Nodine, C. F., & Simmons, F. G. (1974). Processing distinctive features in the differentiation of letter-like symbols. *Journal of Experimental Psychology, 103,* 21–28.

Olson, W. C. (1959). Seeking, self-selection, and pacing in the use of books by children. In J. Veatch (Ed.), *Individualizing your reading program.* New York: Putnum.

Pace, R. W. (1983). *Organizational communication.* Englewood Cliffs, NJ.: Prentice-Hall.

Palincsar, A. S., & Brown, A. (1984). Reciprocal teaching of comprehension fostering and comprehension monitoring activities. *Cognition and Instruction, 1,* 117–175.

Paris, S. G. (1975). Integration and influence in children's comprehension and memory. In F. Restle (Ed.), *Cognitive theory* (Vol. 1). Hillsdale, NJ: Erlbaum.

Parten, M. B. (1932). Social participating among pre-school children. *Journal of Abnormal and Social Psychology, 27,* 243–269.

Pearson, P. D., & Camperell, I. (1985). Comprehension of text structure. In H. Singer & R. B. Ruddell (Eds.), *Theoretical models and processes of reading* (3rd ed., pp. 323–342). Newark, DE: International Reading Association.

Pearson, P. S., & Johnson, D. D. (1978). *Teaching reading comprehension.* New York: Holt, Rinehart & Winston.

Pei, M. (1966). *Glossary of linguistic terminology.* New York: Anchor.

Pflaum, S. W. (1986). *The development of language and literacy in young children.* Columbus, OH: Merrill.

Piaget, J. (1951). *Play, dreams, and imitations in childhood.* New York: Norton.

Piaget, J. (1952). *The origins of intelligence in children.* New York: International University Press.

Piaget, J. (1955). *The language and thought of the child.* New York: Meridian.

Pinnell, G. S. (1985). Ways to look at the functions of children's language. In A. Jaggar and M. T. Smith-Burke (Eds.), *Observing the language learner* (pp. 57–72). Newark, DE: International Reading Association.

Random House Dictionary of the English language. (1966). New York: Random House.

Raphael, T. E. (1982). Question-answering strategies of children. *The Reading Teacher, 36,* 1816–1890.

Rasmussen, M. (Ed.) (1979). *Listen! The children speak.* Washington, DC: World Organization for Early Childhood Education.

Read, C. (1971). Preschool children's knowledge of English phonology. *Harvard Educational Review, 4,* 1–34.

Read, C. (1975). *Children's categorization of speech sounds in English* (Report No. 17). Urbana, IL: National Council of Teachers of English.

Read, K. (1976). *The Nursery School.* (6th ed.). Philadelphia: Saunders.

Reger, R. (1966). The child who could "read" before he could talk. *Journal of School Psychology, 4,* 50–55.

Rheingold, H. L. (1982). Little children's participation in the work of adults: A nascent prosocial behavior, *Child Development, 53,* 114–125.

Rogers, C. S., & Sawyers, J. K. (1988). How play relates to other behaviors. In Rogers, C. S., & Sawyers, J. K. (Eds.), *Play in the Lives of Children.* Washington, DC: National Association for the Education of Young Children.

Rousseau, J. (1962). *Emile* (W. Boyd, Ed. and Trans.). New York: Teachers College Press.

Routman, R. (1988). *Transitions: From literature to literacy.* Portsmouth, NH: Heinemann.

Routman, R. (1991). *Invitations: Changing as teachers and learners K–12.* Portsmouth, NH: Heinemann.

Rubin, Z. (1980). *Children's friendships.* Cambridge, MA: Harvard University Press.

Rumelhart, D. E. (1975). Notes in a schema for stories. In D. Bobrow & A. Collins (Eds.), *Representation and understanding: Studies in cognitive science.* New York: Academic Press.

Rumelhart, D. E. (1977). Toward an interactive model of reading. In S. Dornic (Ed.), *Attention and performance. VI.* Hillsdale, NJ: Laurence Erlbaum.

Russavage, P. M., & Arick, K. L. (1988). Thinkalong: A strategy approach to improving comprehension. *Reading: Issues and Practices, 5,* 32–41.

Sanders, J. M. (1976). Exploring books with a preschooler. *Children's Library Newsletter, 6, (1),* 5–12.

Sarafino, E., & Armstrong, J. W. (1986). *Child and Adolescent Development* (2nd ed.). St. Paul, MN: West.

Sartre, Jean-Paul (1964). *The words.* (B. Frechtman, Trans.). New York: Braziller.

Schickedanz, J. A., & Sullivan, M. (1984). Mom, what does U-F-F spell? *Language Arts, 61,* 7–17.

Searfoss, L., & Readence, J. E. (1989). *Helping children learn to read* (2nd ed.). Englewood Cliffs, NJ: Prentice-Hall.

Sigel, I. E. (1982). The relationship between parent's distancing strategies and child's cognitive behavior. In L. M. Laosa & I. E. Sigel (Eds.), *Families' learning environments for children* (pp. 47–86). New York: Plenum.

Skinner, B. F. (1957). *Verbal behavior.* Boston, MA: Appleton-Century-Crofts.

Slobin, D. (1979). *Psycholinguistics* (2nd ed.). Glenview, IL: Scott, Foresman, & Company.

Smith, F. (1978). *Reading without nonsense.* New York: Teachers College Press.

Smith, F. (1985). *Reading without nonsense* (2nd ed.). New York: Teachers College, Columbia University.

Snow, C. E. (1983). Literacy and language: Relationship during the preschool years. *Harvard Educational Review, 53,* 165–189.

Sowers, S. (1988). Six questions teachers ask about invented spelling. In T. Newkirk & N. Atwell (Eds.), *Understanding writing: Ways of observing, learning, and teaching* (2nd ed., pp. 130–141). Portsmouth, NH: Heinemann Educational.

Staub, E. (1975). To rear a prosocial child: Reasoning, learning by doing and learning by teaching others. In D. J. DePalma & J. M. Foley (Eds.), *Moral development: Current theory and research.* Hillsdale, NJ: Erlbaum.

Stauffer, R. G. (1970). *The language-experience approach to the teaching of reading* (2nd ed.). New York: Harper & Row.

Steele, F., & Jenks, S. (1977). *The feel of the work place.* Reading, MA: Addison-Wesley.

Stein, N. L., & Glenn, C. G. (1975). *A developmental study of children's recall of story material.* Paper presented at ASCD, Denver.

Stein, N. L., & Glenn, C. G. (1977). An analysis of story comprehension in elementary school children. In I. R. O. Freedle (Eds.), *Discourse processing: Multi-disciplinary perspectives* (pp. 00–00). Norwood, NJ: Ablex, 1977.

Stewig, J. W. (1989). Book illustration: Key to visual and oral literacy. In *Using literature in the elementary classroom.* Urbana, IL: National Council of Teachers of English.

Sulzby, E. (1985). Children's emergent reading of favorite storybooks. *Reading Research Quarterly, 20,* 458–481.

Sulzby, E. (1986). Children's elicitation and use of metalinguistic knowledge about "word" during literacy actions. In P. Yaden & S. Templeton, *Metalinguistic awareness and beginning literacy.* Exeter, NH: Heinemann.

Sulzby, E. (1986b). Writing and reading: Signs of oral and written language organization in the young child. In W. Teale & E. Sulzby (Eds.), *Emergent literacy: Writing and reading.* Norwood, NJ: Ablex.

Taylor, D. (1983). *Family literacy: Young children learning to read and write.* Exeter, NH: Heinemann.

Teale, W. (1978). Positive environments for learning to read: What studies of early readers tell us. *Language Arts, 55,* 922–932.

Teale, W. H. (1986). The beginnings of reading and written language development during the preschool and kindergarten years. In M. R. Sampson (Ed.), *The pursuit of literacy: Early reading and writing* (pp. 1–29). Dubuque, IA: Kendall/Hunt.

Teale, W. H. (1988). Emergent literacy. Reading and writing development in early childhood. In P. Shannon (Ed.), *Assessment in emergent literacy* (pp. 99–153). Rochester, NY: National Reading Conference.

Teale, W. H. (1990). The promise and challenge of informal assessment in early literacy. In L. Morrow & J. Smith (Eds.), *Assessment for instruction in early literacy* (pp. 45–61). Englewood Cliffs, NJ: Prentice-Hall.

Teale, W. H., & Sulzby, E. (Eds.), (1986). *Emergent literacy writing and reading.* Norwood, NJ: Ablex.

Temple, C., Nathan, R., Burris, N., & Temple, F. (1988). *The beginnings of writing* (2nd ed.). Boston, MA: Allyn & Bacon.

Thorndyke, R. L. (1973). *Reading comprehension in fifteen countries.* New York: Wiley.

Tierney, R., & Pearson, P. D. (1983). Toward a composing model of reading. *Language Arts, 60,* 568–580.

Tulving, E. (1972). Episodic and semantic memory. In E. Tulving & W. Donaldson (Eds.), *Organization of memory* (pp. 185–191). New York: Academic Press.

Tunmer, W. E., Herrinan, M. L., & Nesdale, A. R. (1988). Metalinguistic abilities and beginning reading. *Reading Research Quarterly, 23*(2), pp. 134–158.

Veatch, J., Sawicki, F., Elliott, G., Flake, E., & Blakey, J. (1979). *Key words to reading: The language experience approach begins* (2nd ed.). Columbus, OH: Merrill.

Vygotsky, L. S. (1962). *Thought and language* (Ed. and Trans. by E. Haufman & G. Vakas). Cambridge, MA: The MIT Press.

Walker, G. H., & Keurbitz, I. E. (1979). Reading to preschoolers as an aid to successful beginning reading. *Reading Improvement, 16*, 149–154.

Wardhaugh, R. (1972). *Introduction to linguistics.* New York: McGraw-Hill.

Watson, R. (1987). Learning words from linguistic expressions: Definition and narrative. *Research in the Teaching of English, 21*, 298–317.

Weinstein, C. S. (1977). Modifying student behavior in an open classroom through changes in the physical design. *American Educational Research Journal, 14*, 249–262.

Wells, G. (1986). *The meaning makers: Children learning language and using language to learn.* Exeter, NH: Heinemann.

White, B. L. (1975). *The first three years of life.* Englewood Cliffs, NJ: Prentice Hall.

White, D. N. (1954). *Books before five.* New York: Oxford University Press.

Wilson, R., & Russavage, P. (1989). School wide application of comprehension strategies. In J. D. Coley & S. S. Clewell (Eds.), *Reading issues and practices.* Maryland: State of Maryland Reading Association.

Children's Literature References

Adler, D. A. (1982) *A picture book of Hanukkah.* Illus. by Linda Hiller. New York: Holiday House.

Adler, D. A. (1989). *A picture of Martin Luther King, Jr.* New York: Holliday House.

Ahlberg, J., & Ahlberg, A. (1979). *Each peach pear plum.* New York: Viking.

Ahlberg, J., & Ahlberg, A. (1982). *The baby's catalogue.* Boston: Little, Brown.

Ahlberg, J., & Ahlberg, A. (1986). *The Jolly Postman or Other People's Letters.* Boston: Little, Brown.

Ahlberg, J., & Ahlberg, A. (1988). *Starting school.* New York: Viking Kestrel.

Alexander M. (1968). *Out, out, out!* New York: Dial.

Aliki (1968). *Hush little baby.* Englewood Cliffs, NJ: Prentice-Hall.

Aliki (1974). *Go tell aunt Rhody.* Illus. by Steven Kellogg. New York: Macmillan.

Aliki (1984). *Feelings.* New York: Greenwillow.

Allend, M. L. (1957). *A pocket full of poems.* New York: HarperCollins.

Arnosky, J. (1987). *Racoons and ripe corn.* New York: Lothrop, Lee & Shepard.

Aruego, J. (1971). *Look what I can do!* New York: Scribner.

Asseng, M. (1981). *Pete Rose: Baseball's Charlie Hustle.*

Bang, M. (1983). *Ten, nine, eight.* New York: Greenwillow.

Barrett, J. (1978). *Cloudy with a chance of meatballs.* New York: Macmillan.

Barton, B. (1986). *Airplanes.* New York: Crowell.

Barton, B. (1986). *Boats.* New York: Crowell.

Barton, B. (1986). *Trains.* New York: Crowell.

Barton, B. (1986). *Trucks.* New York: Crowell.

Barton, B. (1990). *Bones, bones, dinosaur bones.* New York: Harper Collins.

Bemelmans, L. (1939). *Madeline.* New York: Viking Penguin.

Blume, J. (1985). *The pain and the great one.* New York: Dell.

Bridwell, N. (1969). *Clifford takes a trip.* New York: Scholastic.

Bridwell, N. (1969). *Clifford, the big red dog.* New York: Scholastic.

Bridwell, N. (1971). *Clifford's tricks.* New York: Scholastic.

Bridwell, N. (1976). *Clifford's good deeds.* New York: Scholastic.

Briggs, R. (1978). *The snowman.* New York: Random House.

Brooks, L. L. (1977). *Ring o'roses.* New edition. New York: Frederick Warne.

Brown, M. (Ed.). (1985). *Hand rhymes.* New York: Dutton.

Brown, M. (Ed.). (1985). *Party rhymes.* New York: Dutton.

Brown, M. (Ed.). (1985). *Play rhymes.* New York: Dutton.

Brown, Marcia. (1961). *Once a mouse.* New York: Scribner.

Brown, M. W. (1942). *The runaway bunny.* Illus. by Clement Hurd. New York: Harper & Row.

Brown, M. W. (1946). *Little fur family.* Illus. by Garth Williams. New York: HarperCollins.

Brown, M. W. (1947). *Goodnight, moon.* Illus. by Clement Hurd. New York: Harper & Row.

Brown, M. W. (1958). *The dead bird.* Illus. by Remy Charlip. Reading, MA: Addison Wesley.

Bruna, D. (1968). *I can count.* New York: Methuen.

Bruna, D. (1972). *b is for bear.* New York: Methuen.

Bruna, D. (1980). *My toys!* New York: Methuen.

Burton, V. L. (1943). *Katy and the big snow.* Boston: Houghton Mifflin.

Carle, E. (1969). *The very hungry caterpillar.* New York: Philomel.

Carle, E. (1971). *Do you want to be my friend?* New York: Crowell.

Carle, E. (1989). *Animals, animals.* New York: Philomel.

Chorao, K. (1984). *The baby's bedtime book.* New York: Dutton.

Cohen, M. (1986). *Will I have a friend?* Illus. by Lillian Hoban. New York: Macmillan.

Conover, C. (1987). *The adventures of simple Simon.* New York: Farrar, Straus, Giroux.

Cooney, B., reteller. (1982). *Chanticleer and the fox.* New York: Harper & Row.

Crews, D. (1978). *Freight train.* New York: Greenwillow.

Crews, D. (1980). *Truck.* New York: Greenwillow.

Degen, B. (1983). *Jamberry.* New York: Harper & Row.

Demi. (1987). *Fluffy bunny.* New York: Grosset & Dunlap.

Denslow, S. P. (1990). *At Taylor's place.* Illus. by Nancy Carpenter. New York: Bradbury.

dePaola, T. (1978). *Pancakes for breakfast.* New York: Harcourt Brace Jovanovich.

dePaola, T. (1985). *Tomie dePaola's Mother Goose.* New York: Putnam.

de Regniers, B. S. (1988). *Sing a song of popcorn.* Illus. by Caldecott Medal Artists. New York: Scholastic.

DiFiori, L., illus. (1983). *The farm.* New York: Macmillan.

Dijs, C. (1987). *Who sees you: On the farm.* New York: Grosset & Dunlap.

Dreamer, S. (1986). *Animal walk.* Boston: Little, Brown.

Dunn, J. (1984). *The little puppy.* Photographs by Phoebe Dunn. New York: Random House.

Eastman, P. D. (1960). *Are you my mother?* New York: Random House.

Ehlert, L. (1988). *Planting a rainbow.* San Diego: Harcourt Brace Jovanovich.

Ehlert, L. (1990). *Feathers for lunch.* San Diego: Harcourt Brace Jovanovich.

Eichenberg, F. (1952). *Ape in a cape: An alphabet of odd animals.* New York: Harcourt Brace Jovanovich.

Emberley, B. (1967). *Drummer Hoff.* Illus. by Ed Emberely. Englewood Cliffs, NJ: Prentice-Hall.

Ets, M. H. (1955). *Play with me.* New York: Viking Penguin.

Fisher, A. (1986). *When it comes to bugs.* Illus. by Chris and Bruce Degen. New York: Harper & Row.

Flack, M. (1931). *Angus and the cat.* New York: Doubleday.

Flack, M. (1932). *Ask Mr. Bear.* New York: Macmillan.

Flack, M. (1939). *Angus and the ducks.* New York: Doubleday.

Flack, M. (1941). *Angus lost.* New York: Doubleday.

Freeman, D. (1968). *Corduroy.* New York: Viking.

Fox, D. (Ed.). (1987). *Go in and out the window.* New York: The Metropolitan Museum of Art & Henry Holt and Co.

Francine. *Francine sings a keepsake of favorite animal songs.* (1985). Berkeley, CA: Lancaster Productions (audiocassette).

Gackenbach, R. (1975). *Do you love me?* Boston: Houghton Mifflin.

Gag, W. (1928). *Millions of cats.* New York: Coward, McCann & Geoghegan.

Galdone, P. (1979). *The three little pigs.* New York: Clarion.

Galdone, P. (1984). *The teeny-tiny woman.* New York: Clarion.

Galdone, P. (1985). *The three bears.* New York: Clarion.

Galdone, P. (1988). *Three little kittens.* New York: Clarion.

Galdone, P., reteller (1979). *The monkey and the crocodile.* New York: Clarion.

Galdone, P., reteller and illus. (1968). *Henny penny.* Boston: Houghton Mifflin.

Galdone, P., reteller and illus. (1974). *The little red hen.* New York: Clarion.

Galdone, P., reteller and illus. (1981). *The three billy goats gruff.* New York: Clarion.

Geisel, T. (Dr. Seuss) (1968). *The foot book.* New York: Random House.

Geisel, T. (Dr. Seuss) (1957). *The cat in the hat.* New York: Random House.

Geisel, T. (Dr. Seuss) (1983). *Hop on pop.* New York: Random House.

Gibbons, G. (1984). *Halloween.* New York: Holiday House.

Gibbons, G. (1987). *Farming.* New York: Holiday House.

Gibbons, G. (1987). *The pottery place.* San Diego: Harcourt Brace Jovanovich.

Ginsburg, M. (1980). *Good morning chick.* Illus. by Byron Barton. New York: Greenwillow.

Ginsburg, M. (1982). *Across the stream.* Illus. by Nancy Tafuri. New York: Greenwillow.

Glazer, T. (Ed.). *Children's greatest hits* (Vols. 1 and 2). Mount Vernon, NY: CMS Records (audiocassettes).

Goldstein, B. S. (1989). *Bear in mind.* New York: Viking Penguin.

Goldstein, B. S. (1992). *What's on the menu?* New York: Viking Penguin.

Grimm, J., & Grimm, W. (1975). *Hans in luck.* Illus. by Felix Hoffman. New York: Atheneum.

Hague, K. (1981). *The man who kept house.* Illus. by Michael Hague. New York: Harcourt Brace Jovanovich.

Hague, K. (1984). *Alphabears: An ABC book.* Illus. by Michael Hague. New York: Holt, Rinehart & Winston.

Hart, J. (1982). *Singing bee!* Pictures by Anita Lobel. New York: Lothrop, Lee & Shepard.

Hayes, S. (1990). *Nine ducks nine.* New York: Lothrop, Lee & Shepard.

Hayes, S. (Ed.). (1988). *Clap your hands: Finger rhymes.* Illus. by Toni Goffe. New York: Lothrop, Lee & Shepard.

Hennessy, B. G. (1989). *A, B, C, D, tummy, toes, hands, knees.* Illus. by Wendy Watson. New York: Viking Kestrel.

Hill, E. (1967). *Evan's corner.* Illus. by Nancy Grossman. New York: Holt.

Hill, E. (1984). *Spot's toys.* New York: Putman.

Hoban, R. (1960). *Bedtime for Frances.* Illus. by Garth Williams. New York: Harper & Row.

Hoban, R. (1964). *Baby sister for Frances.* Illus. by Garth Williams. New York: Harper & Row.

Hoban, R. (1964). *Bread and jam for Frances.* Illus. by Garth Williams. New York: Harper & Row.

Hoban, R. (1968). *Birthday for Frances.* Illus. by Garth Williams. New York: Harper & Row.

Hoban, R. (1970). *Bargain for Frances.* Illus. by Garth Williams. New York: Harper & Row.

Hoban, T. (1978). *Is it red? Is it yellow? Is it blue?* New York: Greenwillow.

Hoban, T. (1985). *A children's zoo.* New York: Greenwillow.

Hoban, T. (1985). *What is it?* New York: Greenwillow.

Hoban, T. (1986). *Red, blue, yellow shoe.* New York: Greenwillow.

Hoban, T. (1986). *Shapes, shapes, shapes.* New York: Greenwillow.

Hopkins, L. B. (1979). *Go to bed! A book of bedtime poems.* Illus. by Rosekrans Hoffman. New York: Knopf.

Hopkins, L. B., collector. (1988). *Side by side, poems to read together.* Illus. by Hilary Knight. New York: Simon & Schuster.

Hutchins, P. (1982). *I hunter.* New York: Greenwillow.

Hutchins, P. (1986). *The doorbell rang.* New York: Greenwillow.

Hutchins, P. (1990). *What game shall we play?* New York: Greenwillow.

Johnson, C. (1955). *Harold and the purple crayon.* New York: Harper & Row.

Jorgensen, G. (1989). *Crocodile beat.* Illus. by Patricia Mullins. New York: Bradbury.

Kalan, R. (1981). *Jump, frog, jump.* New York: Scholastic.

Keats, E. J. (1964). *Whistle for Willie.* New York: Viking.

Keats, E. J. (1967). *Peter's chair.* New York: Harper & Row.

Kellogg, S. (1979). *Pinkerton, behave!* New York: Dial.

Kovalski, M. (1987). *The wheels on the bus.* Boston: Little, Brown.

Kraus, R. (1979). *Owliver*. Illus. by Jose Aruego & Ariane Dewey. New York: Windmill.

Krauss, R. (1945). *The carrot seed*. Illus. by Crockett Johnson. New York: Harper & Row.

Kunhardt, D. (1942). *Pat the bunny*. New York: Western.

Kunhardt, E. (1984). *Pat the cat*. New York: Western.

Kuskin, K. (1956). *Roar and more*. New York: Harper & Row.

Kuskin, K. (1975). *Near the window tree*. New York: Harper & Row.

Langstaff, J. (1974). *Oh, a'hunting we will go*. Illus. by Nancy Winslow Parker. New York: Atheneum.

Lear, E. (1987). *The owl and the pussy cat*. Illus. by Paul Galdone. New York: Clarion.

Lewis, R. (1988). *Friska: The sheep that was too small*. New York: Farrar, Straus & Giroux.

Lindbergh, R. (1990). *The day the goose got loose*. Illus. by Steven Kellogg. New York: Dial.

Lionni, L. (1985). *Frederick's fables*. New York: Pantheon.

Lionni, L. (1987). *Swimmy*. New York: Knopf.

Lloyd, D. (1988). *Duck*. Illus. by Charlotte Voake. New York: Lippincott.

Lobel, A. (1972). *Frog and toad together*. New York: Harper & Row.

Lobel, A. (1976). *Frog and toad all year*. New York: Harper & Row.

Lobel, A. (1978). *Gregory Griggs and other nursery rhyme people*. New York: Greenwillow.

Lobel, A. (1979). *A treeful of pigs*. Illus. by Anita Lobel. New York: Greenwillow.

Lobel, A. (1979). *Days with frog and toad*. New York: Harper & Row.

Lobel, A. (1979). *Frog and toad are friends*. New York: Harper & Row.

Lobel, A. (1981). *On market street*. Illus. by Anita Lobel. New York: Greenwillow.

Lobel, A. (1987). *Owl at home*. New York: Harper & Row.

Lynn, S. (1986). *Clothes*. New York: Macmillan.

Lynn, S. (1986). *Food*. New York: Macmillan.

Lynn, S. (1986). *Home*. New York: Macmillan.

Lynn, S. (1986). *Toys*. New York: Macmillan.

Macdonald, M. (1980). *Rosie runs away*. Illus. by Melissa Sweet. New York: Atheneum.

MacLachlan, P. (1979). *Through Grandpa's eyes*. New York: Harper & Row.

Magorian, M. (1990). *Who's going to take care of me?* Illus. by James Graham Hale. New York: HarperCollins.

Mahy, M. (1987). *17 kings and 42 elephants*. Illus. by Patricia MacCarthy. New York: Dial.

Marshall, J. (1972). *George and Martha*. Boston: Houghton Mifflin.

Marshall, J. (1988). *Fox on the job*. New York: Dial.

Martin, W., Jr. (1983). *Brown bear, brown bear, what do you see?* Illus. by Eric Carle. New York: Henry Holt.

Martin, W., Jr., & Archambault, J. (1989). *Chicka Chicka Boom Boom*. Illus. by L. Ehlert. New York: Simon & Schuster.

Matthiesen, T. (1981). *A child's book of everyday things*. New York: Putnam.

Mayer, M. (1969). *Frog, Where Are You?* New York: Dial.

Mayer, M. (1971). *A boy, a dog, a frog and a friend*. New York: Dial.

Mayer, M. (1974). *Frog Goes to Dinner*. New York: Dial.

Mayer, M. (1975). *One frog too many*. New York: Dial.

Mayer, M. (1976). *Hiccup*. New York: Dial.

McDonald, M. (1990). *Is this a house for hermit crab?* Illus. by S. D. Schindler. New York: Orchard.

McCully, E. A. (1984). *Picnic*. New York: Harper & Row.

McPhail, D. (1984). *Fix it*. New York: Dutton.

McPhail, D. (1987). *First flight*. Boston: Little, Brown.

Merriam, E. (1988). *You be good and I'll be night*. Illus. by K. & L. Schmitt. New York: Morrow.

Miller, M. (1989). *At My House*. New York: Crowell.

Miller, M. (1989). *In my room.* New York: Crowell.

Miller, M. (1989). *Me and my clothes.* New York: Crowell.

Miller, M. (1989). *More first words.* New York: Crowell.

Miller, M. (1989). *My first words.* New York: Crowell.

Miller, M. (1989). *Time to eat.* New York: Crowell.

Miller, M. (1991). *Every day.* New York: Crowell.

Mitchell, C. (1978). *Playtime.* Pictures by Satomi Ichikawa. New York: Collins-World.

Mott, E. C. (1991). *Steam train ride.* New York: Walker.

Murphy, R. C., foreword. (1967). *Larousse encyclopedia of animal life.* New York: McGraw-Hill.

Oppenheim, J. (1986). *Have you seen birds?* Illus. by Barbara Reid. New York: Scholastic.

Ormerod, J. (1981). *Sunshine.* New York: Lothrop, Lee, & Shepard.

Ormerod, J. (1986). *Moonlight.* New York: Lothrop, Lee, & Shepard.

Oxenbury, H. (1981). *Dressing.* New York: Simon & Schuster.

Oxenbury, H. (1981). *Family.* New York: Simon & Schuster.

Oxenbury, H. (1981). *Friends.* New York: Simon & Schuster.

Oxenbury, H. (1981). *Playing.* New York: Simon & Schuster.

Oxenbury, H. (1981). *Working.* New York: Simon & Schuster.

Oxenbury, H. (1985). *The Helen Oxenbury nursery storybook.* New York: Knopf.

Pearson, T. C. (1984). *Old MacDonald had a farm.* New York: Dial.

Pearson, T. C. (1986). *A apple pie.* New York: Dial.

Piper, W. (1954). *The little engine that could.* New York: Platt & Munk.

Pomerantz, C. (1984). *All asleep.* Illus. by Nancy Tafuri. New York: Greenwillow.

Pomerantz, C. (1984). *The half-birthday party.* Illus. by DyAnne DiSalvo-Ryan. New York: Clarion.

Pomerantz, C. (1984). *Where's the bear.* Illus. by Byron Barton. New York: Greenwillow.

Potter, B. (1902). *Tale of Peter Rabbit.* New York: Frederick Warne.

Prelutsky, J. (1983). *Zoo doings.* Illus. by P. O. Zelinsky. New York: Greenwillow.

Prelutsky, J. (1986). *Read-aloud rhymes for the very young.* Illus. by Marc Brown. New York: Knopf.

Provensen, A., & Provensen, M. (1978). *The year at Maple Hill farm.* New York: Atheneum.

Quackenbush, R. (1975). *Skip to my lou.* Philadelphia: Lippincott.

Rae, M. M. (1988). *The farmer in the dell: A singing game.* New York: Viking Penguin.

Rathmann, P. (1991). *Ruby the copycat.* New York: Scholastic.

Rey, H. A., & Rey, M. (1985). *Curious George visits the zoo.* New York: Scholastic.

Rice, E. (1980). *Goodnight, goodnight.* New York: Greenwillow.

Riggio, A. (1987). *Wake up, William!* New York: Atheneum.

Rockwell, H. (1973). *My doctor.* New York: Macmillan.

Rockwell, H. (1975). *My dentist.* New York: Greenwillow.

Rose, P. (1979). *My life in baseball.* New York: Doubleday.

Rossetti, C. (1986). Mix a pancake. In Jack Prelutsky's *Read-aloud rhymes for the very young.* New York: Knopf.

Rossini, G. (1965). *Cinderella.* Illus. by Beni Montresor. New York: Knopf.

Rylant, C. (1982). *When I was young in the mountains.* Illus. by Diane Goode. New York: Dutton.

Sattler, H. (1984). *Baby dinosaurs.* Illus. by Jean D. Zallinger. New York: Lothrop, Lee & Shepard.

Selsam, M. (1973). *A first look at . . . . . series.* New York: Walker.

Sendak, M. (1962). *Alligators all around.* New York: Harper & Row.

Sendak, M. (1962). *Chicken Soup with Rice.* Nutshell Library. New York: Harper & Row.

Sendak, M. (1962). *One was Johnny.* New York: Harper & Row.

Sendak, M. (1963). *Where the wild things are.* New York: Harper & Row.

Seuss, Dr. see Geisel, T.

Seymour, P. (1985). *What's in the cave?* UK edition: Child's Play.

Slier, D. (1985). Photographer, selector. *What do babies do?* New York: Random House.

Smith, M. (1991). *There's a witch under the stairs.* New York: Lothrop, Lee & Shepard.

Smith, J. W. (1986). *The Jessie Willcox Smith Mother Goose.* New York: Derrydale.

Spier, P. (1967). *To market, to market.* New York: Doubleday.

Spier, P. (1972). *Crash! bang! boom!* New York: Doubleday.

Spier, P. (1977). *Noah's ark.* New York: Doubleday.

Spier, P. (1985). *London Bridge is falling down.* New York: Doubleday.

Steig, W. (1988). *Spinky sulks.* New York: Farrar, Straus, Giroux.

Stevens, J. (1984). *The tortoise and the hare: An Aesop fable.* New York: Holiday House.

Stevens, J. (1987). *The town mouse and the country mouse.* New York: Scholastic.

Stevenson, J. (1980). *That terrible Halloween night.* New York: Greenwillow.

Tafuri, N. (1983). *Early morning in the barn.* New York: Greenwillow.

Tafuri, N. (1984). *All year long.* New York: Greenwillow.

Tafuri, N. (1984). *Have you seen my duckling?* New York: Greenwillow.

Tripp, W. (1976). *Granfa Grig had a pig and other rhymes without reason from Mother Goose.* Boston: Little, Brown.

Tudor, T. (1954). *As is for Annabelle.* New York: Macmillan.

Turkle, B. (1976). *Deep in the forest.* New York: Dutton.

Udry, J. (1961). *Let's be enemies.* Illus. by Maurice Sendak. New York: Harper & Row.

Viorst, J. (1970). *Try it again Sam.* Illus. by Paul Galdone. New York: Lothrop, Lee & Shepard.

Watson, C. (1971). *Father Fox's Pennyrhymes.* New York: Harper & Row.

Weiss, N. (1989). *Where does the brown bear go?* New York: Viking.

Wells, R. (1973). *Noisy Nora.* New York: Dial.

Wells, R. (1981). *Timothy goes to school.* New York: Dial.

Wildsmith, B. (1982). *Cat on the mat.* New York: Oxford.

Wildsmith, B. (1983). *The Nest.* New York: Oxford.

Williams, S. (1990). *I went walking.* Illus. by Julie Vivas. San Diego: Harcourt Brace Jovanovich.

Williams, V. B. (1982). *A chair for my mother.* New York: Greenwillow.

Wright, B. F. (1916). *The real Mother Goose.* New York: Macmillan.

Yektai, N. (1987). *Bears in pairs.* Illus. by Diane deGroat. New York: Bradbury Press.

Yolen, J. (Ed.). (1986). *Lullaby songbook.* Illus. by Charles Mikolaycak. New York: Harcourt Brace Jovanovich.

Zelinsky, P. O. (1990). *The wheels on the bus.* New York: Dutton.

Zelinsky, P. O., reteller. (1986). *Rumpelstiltskin.* New York: Dutton.

Zemach, M. (1965). *Teeny tiny woman.* New York: Scholastic.

Zemach, M. (1983). *The Little Red Hen.* New York: Ferrar, Straus and Giroux.

Ziefert, H. (1987). *Where's the cat?* Illus. by Arnold Lobel. New York: Harper & Row.

Ziefert, H. (1987). *Where's the dog?* Illus. by Arnold Lobel. New York: Harper & Row.

Ziefert, H. (1987). *Where's the guinea pig?* Illus. by Arnold Lobel. New York: Harper & Row.

Ziefert, H. (1987). *Where's the turtle?* Illus. by Arnold Lobel. New York: Harper & Row.

Zolotow, C. (1985). *My grandson Lew.* Illus. by William Pene du Bois. New York: Harper & Row.

Zuromskis, D. S. (1978). *The farmer in the dell.* Boston: Little, Brown.

Index